Across the Edge

Ice cliff on Rogers Peak, Antarctica

Across the Edge

Pushing the Limits across Oceans and Continents

PETER CLUTTERBUCK

Whittles Publishing

Published by
Whittles Publishing Ltd.,
Dunbeath,
Caithness, KW6 6EG
Scotland, UK

ISBN 978-184995-577-5

Printed and bound by CPI Group (UK) Ltd, Croydon, CR0 4YY

This book is dedicated to my parents, Richard and Angela, who supported me in my endeavours, and who taught me how to learn from my many mistakes; to my late wife, Bonnie, who shared some of these adventures and always welcomed me home from the others; and to my sons, Michael and Richard, who have shared many recent adventures with me.

Peter R. Clutterbuck

AUTHOR'S NOTE

Most of the source material in this book was derived from original diaries, logbooks and magazine articles. The remainder relied on my memory, so the details of events and conversations may not be precise. Although the author and publisher have made every effort to ensure that the information in this book was correct at press time, the author and publisher do not assume and hereby disclaim any liability to any party for any loss, damage or disruption caused by errors or omissions, whether such errors or omissions result from negligence, accident or any other cause.

   If you have a hard time understanding some of the specialist language used in sailing and mountaineering you will probably appreciate the explanations in the Glossary.

   Measurements such as distances and mountain heights, dimensions of yachts etc are given in the units used at the time, and in some places you will find the imperial or metric equivalents given in parentheses.

CONTENTS

Journeys to remote and unexplored places

Across the edge. The edge of what? In this book the edge is the boundary that encloses the civilised world in which we live: the world of air conditioning, central heating, traffic jams, 24/7 news, fake news, elections and other facets of our comfortable and yet stressed civilisation.

Beyond this edge is a fascinating and often untouched world where nature rules, with dust storms, blizzards, ice caps, breaking ocean waves. A world of staggering beauty, and crystal clear, starry nights. This is a world of high-risk adventures, where meticulous planning is needed to anticipate and defuse the risks involved. Hardly anybody lives in most of these desolate regions – the conditions are too tough.

There are still plenty of areas never visited or explored, and where satellite imagery is too coarse to be much use. I have been lucky to visit some of these places, partly in connection with my work, and the adventure of getting there is described in this book.

Along the way I had plenty of crises: stranded in central Australia without water, smashed up in a high-speed motorbike accident in Turkey, rolled upside down in a Land Rover in the Arabian desert, stranded in Arctic Alaska, rammed in the North Pacific, dismasted in the North Atlantic, being hit by an earthquake while climbing an erupting volcano at night, hiding in a tree root next to an angry buffalo in Africa. And my favourite place? Antarctica.

We are led to believe that the world is ruined: over-populated and polluted. But most of it is not, mainly because nobody goes there – it's either too hot, too cold, too dry, too wet, too stormy, too mountainous or just plain too dangerous. When I look out of an aeroplane window I'm constantly amazed at how much of our land is completely undeveloped, and how empty of features the oceans are.

Only 11 per cent of the world's land is cultivable, and that 11 per cent is where most of us live. Most built-up areas are along the coasts, and the inland continental areas are often very sparsely inhabited. Sailing across oceans, you can go for weeks without seeing another vessel.

However, some areas are becoming heavily polluted as a result of carelessness, and increasing population expanding the built-up regions. These areas need more protection.

Nearly 90 per cent of the world's population live in the northern hemisphere. The air in the southern hemisphere is noticeably clearer than in the northern. This is partly due to less pollution, but also less desert dust, and less smoke from wildfires – the unsurprising results of both the hemisphere's significantly lower land area and its lower population density.

Some of the regions I visited are now much the same as they have always been, although much easier to access and very much easier to get out of in an emergency. Also, technology has now allowed us to live and travel in hostile climates in safety and comfort. But as the inhabited areas expand some places have changed adversely. More of the world has been developed at the expense of the natural environment.

Can these pristine regions be preserved?

Action needs to be taken to preserve some of these pristine wildernesses, including the creation of more national parks, preferably linked together. Pollution needs to be reduced, especially in the air, the waterways and the sea, where it has global impact. Then there is the issue of climate change, which is not easy to forecast accurately. Global warming has been inexorable for most of the last 18,000 years. The climate has changed many times in history, and we are now in another natural warming phase, probably being accelerated by human impact. It is not known, however, how much this human contribution could be, as it is very hard to gauge. There are some beginnings of change to a more diversified energy mix: more renewable power, more electric vehicles, fewer carbon emissions, more carbon capture projects. Nuclear power is one of the safest and cleanest, but the public are concerned about safety, especially from war or terrorism. The best solution is to use less energy, as all types currently in use or proposed have their unwanted side effects.

Wind turbines approaching the height of the Eiffel Tower and solar panels over a wide area change the surface from its pristine state, and they need much larger areas than oil or gas. Also, the power they produce is intermittent. Oil and gas developments are more compact and can be located in waste lands that no one is interested in, or offshore. But they cause greenhouse gas emissions, which can be collected in carbon capture projects, storing the gas underground. A mix of energy sources is therefore, in my opinion, optimal.

On many of the journeys I made in earlier times, no one knew where I was, or whether I had been in an accident. Often, *I* did not know where I was. This made the adventure that much more exciting, not knowing what was ahead and being always aware that I had to be very careful.

I read a book recently on the history of *Homo sapiens*, whose author, Yuval Noah Harari, concluded that the hunter-gatherer living in the wild, hunting and exploring, was probably much happier than the average human today. If that is correct, it could explain why we like to go back to nature – camping, barbecuing, stargazing – and for the lucky ones mountaineering, sailing and adventure tourism (a recent development). Much of the allure of my travels was to try to capture the excitement and adventure of the explorers of a century or more ago. My dream job would have been to command a clipper in the Roaring Forties.

The call of adventure

Since I was a young boy, I have been intrigued by what is out there beyond the edge. What is it like? What are the dangers? Has anyone been there before? Could I survive there? I read hundreds of books on polar exploration, ocean crossings, desert crossings and adventures in far-off places. I promised myself that if I were lucky enough to visit some amazing places I would write a book too, so that others could share my experiences. I've had the good fortune to go to 105 countries and to meet some wonderful people along the way. I've faced many extremes, including temperatures ranging from −40ºC/F[1] to 59ºC (138ºF) in the shade.

Some of the more remote places explored in this book include central Australia, the Empty Quarter of the Arabian peninsula, Oman, Iran, the Himalayas, Arctic Alaska, Iceland, Patagonia, central Africa, Namibia, Ethiopia, Greenland and Antarctica; and at sea in the Pacific, Atlantic and Indian Oceans. Many of my journeys took place in the 1960s and 1970s, before the jet age of mass tourism, before mobile phones and before satellite navigation. In past decades it was easy to get lost, and then, especially if injured, there was no way of calling for help. Sometimes I got into trouble, as I did not have the right experience or equipment. The sense of adventure, of the unknown, and the need for self-reliance was heightened. For me, central Australia in 1967 was a more remote and dangerous place than an unexplored Antarctic mountain range in 2007.

Many of the wonderful places I had the good fortune to visit came as a result of my postings overseas as an engineer in the oil and gas industry. Nature usually places oil and gas fields in remote areas: deserts, swamps, jungles, polar regions and offshore, under seas and oceans. Most of these areas were not appealing but they were still remote. In these places I was always especially careful to minimise the environmental impact of my

---

1 Fahrenheit and Celsius meet at −40º.

company's activities, and more recently to minimise their carbon emissions. There is still, of course, much more to be done to make energy cleaner yet still affordable.

While much of my travel was connected to my work, some I did just for the excitement. I justified it on the basis that it made me a better person, more self-reliant, able to withstand hardships, with a better understanding of the environment and therefore more useful to society. I have always been careful to leave the minimum possible trace of my travels; most of these journeys involved sailing or mountaineering and were 'green', with a comparatively low carbon footprint.

I wanted to share these adventures, and to this end much of the material in this book has been published in magazines and videos. I have tried to capture the beauty of these places with the photographs presented here, so that you too can experience something of the thrill of seeing such wonderful places.

A VIOLENT NIGHT AT SEA

In June 1995 I was racing my 43-foot Grand Prix trimaran, *Spirit of England*, across the Atlantic from the Azores to England. Brian Thompson had raced with me on the outward leg, which we had won, and in doing so we had broken the record by two days, rocketing along at over 20 knots down the grey Atlantic swells.

John Chaundy had been racing against us in his trimaran, which had pitchpoled. Fortunately, he was rescued, and he joined me for the return leg of this Azores and Back race, doublehanded.

Soon after the start we were comfortably in the lead. Then at sundown the wind came up on the nose and we put a reef in. An hour later we were doing 12 knots, and we decided to put in a second reef, furl the genoa and hoist the staysail. I then collapsed in the doghouse, exhausted from all the deck work. It was 11 p.m., pitch-black, and raining as the wind rose. There was a deafening crash in the bow cabin. We must have hit something. 'Mast's gone!' John yelled.

I clipped on my harness and underwater headlight to slide down the forward cross beam and inspect the damage on the starboard hull, which was rising up 6 feet with every wave and crashing down again. The mast was broken just outside the starboard hull, the top 40 feet pointing straight down. One of the bottom spreaders was broken off and the other was busy grinding holes in the hull.

The seas were now beam on and rising. There were two holes in the starboard hull, three in the main hull: one where the mast base had ripped out, one big one where the mast rotation spanner bracket had broken through, and one where the forestay had ripped through the foredeck and torn off the pulpit. All appeared to be taking water. The broken mast was grinding pieces off the outer hull with big booming noises, hanging off a mass of halyards, reef lines, wire and so on. John had narrowly escaped being guillotined by the port shroud, which had knifed across the cockpit as the mast came down, but he had been leaning forward at the time, checking the instruments.

We started cutting loose what we could with bolt cutters and an emergency saw knife, but there were some 60 points of attachment between mast and boat. We both got seasick and weakened rapidly, unable to hold any food down, grinding down to an exhausted stalemate. We could not pull the masthead up to the deck, as it would have been 20 feet aft of the transoms. The gear over the side weighed half a ton, and would need daylight and a calm to retrieve. But daylight was five hours away.

We slashed most of the running rigging with the saw knife, and the smaller wires with the bolt cutters. The bar-tight headstay with its furled genoa was what was causing the broken mast sections to grind away at the hull, and it needed releasing immediately.

Although the wind was strengthening and the seas were getting bigger all the time, we gave up, exhausted, and collapsed below in our oilskins. The bow cabin was soaked with all the water pouring in through the leaks all over the bunks, but we slept through the crashes and bangs of the mast grinding the hull. I was lacerated and bruised, and had damaged my right elbow. John had put his back out. He was lucky not to have been killed when the mast rotator had punched through the deck, as it was just above where his head would have been on the bunk, but he had been on watch at the time.

What more could we do? We would have to chop away the mast and rigging before it broke the boat up, but we could not do any more in our exhausted state in the dark. We could only pray that the boat would hold together until dawn. We were in the lap of the gods. I prayed like never before. Even if we were still intact by dawn, we still had to cut the mast loose and make a jury rig, then sail hundreds of miles to land. What chance did we have?

1 Early adventures

I was on a school expedition to Scotland in the winter of 1966, inside a tent with two classmates as a storm raged outside in the darkness. We anchored the tent to large rocks, which we built around us in a wall, and huddled in our sleeping bags as the storm built. We were on our own in an uninhabited region. Suddenly, a huge gust ripped the tent away and we were in the full force of a howling gale and driving rain as the canvas disappeared into the darkness. We were left in our bags on the groundsheet, drenched and terrified. What were we to do?

1950s influences

Since many of these adventures occurred many decades ago, I have included this section to help put everything into perspective. The world was a very different place 'back in the day', in the 1950s and 1960s. This section of the book describes many of the factors that influenced me during my travels, with 21 homes in various countries while I was growing up.

What gave me the curiosity to cross the edge into wide-open spaces, across ice caps, oceans, mountain ranges and deserts? My family comes from generations of military service, and this instilled a sense of adventure in me. Our ancestors were Vikings who settled in the Outer Hebrides, maybe putting some salt into the family's blood. My uncle, Lad, served on the *Ark Royal* aircraft carrier, which was responsible for the sinking of the giant German battleship *Bismarck* in May 1941. Another uncle, Bobby, commanded submarines, escorting convoys to northern Russia hundreds of miles north of the Arctic Circle in the chilly, grey wastes of the North Atlantic. These maritime adventures filled me with a desire to experience the sea and to cross oceans.

My father, Richard, spent his early years at 157 Cromwell Road, London. The house was destroyed by a bomb during the Second World War. He spent several years in East Africa and the North African desert in Montgomery's Eighth Army, fighting General Rommel's Afrika Corps. He lived in tents for four years during the war. He travelled by motorbike across the desert. It was four years before he got back to England. His stories gave me a fascination with deserts and their wide horizons.

One evening, he returned to his grass hut, and found a crocodile in it. Another time, a group of soldiers carried out a daring ambush at night, only to find that they had captured a handful of baboons.

In 1953 there were wild celebrations when Hillary and Tenzing reached the top of Mount Everest. The leader of this British team was Sir John Hunt, who lived opposite us in the military Staff College Bungalows in Camberley, and one evening, Sir Edmund Hillary came to visit. Inspired by these legendary men, I started wondering if I could ever give mountaineering a try.

By troopship to Malaya

In 1956 we were posted to Malaya, which had been a British colony since 1826. I wrote in my schoolbook, aged six, that an officer had told my father to move house 'in five mins' time', and to go to Malaya. He was to fight the Communist Terrorists in the jungle.

In those days troops and families were posted by ship. We left on 4 January 1956 on a troopship called the RMS *Carthage*, which had been fitted with eight 6-inch and two 3-inch guns for the war. It was a great adventure, and I longed to see a storm for myself.

My prayers were answered – and then as we sailed south I wished I hadn't prayed for the storm. A terrible westerly Atlantic gale hit us, so I soon prayed for calm instead. Our cabin was above the waterline and the porthole was constantly battered. Everyone was seasick. We had friends in lower deck levels, who had to bolt down steel storm covers over their portholes.

But one of the ladies on board was not sick and agreed to take me up to the top deck to see the waves. I was not disappointed. They were the height of the ship, rising up above the top deck some 50 feet above the water, dark green with spray blowing everywhere. The ship heaved, rolled and shuddered from end to end as it fought the storm. The waves broke the windows in the restaurant on the top deck, filled the large room and destroyed much of the furniture, smashed up as it surfed back and forth.

After that, the next six weeks were magical. The ship headed on south, stopping three times to refuel in Africa: at Dakar, Cape Town and Durban. We rolled badly in the swells from the Roaring Forties in the Southern Ocean, and I was taught how to hold a soup bowl on the side away from me, to counter the roll in such a way that if a really bad wave came the soup would land in my own lap rather than in someone else's across the table. There was a small salt-water pool on deck, but because of the rolling it couldn't be filled more than quarter full; when you were swimming it was like being on a beach with the surf coming from one end then the other. I was shown the massive engines and I steered the ship sometimes.

We crossed the Equator twice, with much celebration by King Neptune. We went through the Trade Winds four times, memorable for the flying fish. Soon, tropical islands appeared, and after we had refuelled at Ceylon

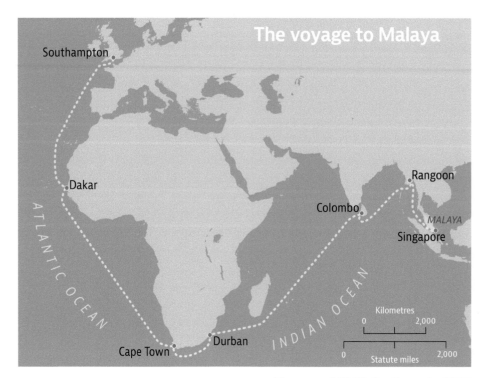

Voyage of RMS *Carthage* in 1956

RMS *Carthage*

PC looking at Cape Town 1956

and Rangoon we docked at Singapore to board the train to Kuala Lumpur. Most of these stops were in former British colonies that still retained a good relationship with Britain.

Adventures in Malaya

Malaya was fascinating. We started out living in a hostel surrounded by monkeys, which aggressively charged at us. Geckos patrolled the walls of our rooms, chasing insects. We moved to a bungalow called 16 Malaya Command, and later a bungalow on the edge of the jungle, where wildlife cruised around. One day a long black snake crossed our lawn, eating a frog on the way, and headed for the steps up to the house. My father donned his battledress: army boots, gaiters and a huge knife. He and the snake eyed each other up and lunged back and forth, both threatening to go for the kill. My father won. One time it rained so hard we went swimming on that lawn.

The jungle was enthralling. Everything was dying, rotting and being reborn in a damp, mysterious place full of sudden noises and rhythmic screeches. Above the dense undergrowth, close to the ground, were wide-open spaces with just a few solid tree trunks and encircling creepers towering upwards in the perpetual shade to a high canopy of leaves almost impenetrable to light. I had two close shaves with snakes, both brightly coloured and deadly poisonous. We always expected to come across a tiger, but in fact the only wildlife to bother me were leeches, black worms that dug under my skin. The way to get them out was with a lighted cigarette, but often the head would break off, and my mother would have to dig the rest out with a knife.

We went to school in 3-ton Bedford Army lorries, with wire netting strung between the sides and a canvas roof to keep the schoolchildren

PC and Robin in Malayan jungle

British Army school bus in Kuala Lumpur

My father in Malaya

British Army patrol Malaya 1958

enclosed; we used to crawl up the wire, looking like monkeys trying to escape from a zoo. It was a great status symbol to be in the first bus to arrive, so I sat behind the driver's cab and learned a few words in Malay – 'left', 'right', 'straight', 'go faster'. We were able to consistently arrive first until it was discovered that our bus kept arriving only partly full; a lot of irate mothers were complaining that it never turned up. Fortunately no one leaked who had been responsible, or I would have got to know the cane. I had seen a caning done on stage in front of us 200 boys, and it seemed very harsh.

In 1958, when I was eight, it was time for me to go to boarding school. The British Army paid most of the fees – no army officer could have afforded them on his own. During this time my father was posted to Christmas Island in the Pacific, to manage the engineering works connected with four nuclear bombs; while he was there they were exploded in the air only a few miles from where the soldiers were lined up, facing away from the blast to avoid being blinded. They all had to take showers for weeks afterwards to wash off the radioactive dust. Recreation included fishing for sharks in the surf, using telegraph wire.

Adventures in the 1960s

My father used to take me on canoeing and camping expeditions in wild places, usually in a howling gale with driving rain, to toughen me up. By the time I was 12 or so we'd climbed the highest mountains in England and Scotland. I'd also been on a church camp in Wales, where my mother and aunt were cooks, and climbed Snowdon when I was 10 or so, with a group of older teenagers. We got lost in fog and ended up on the top of a cliff. I hitched my stick onto my pack, but it got dislodged and fell off the cliff; I'll never forget the sight of it disappearing into the fog and clouds below, and I knew that's what would happen to me if I slipped.

My father took me on a Scottish holiday, going by ferry across the Firth of Forth next to the famous railway bridge; my home was the back of the car in a sleeping bag. Then he took me on a hike up Ben Nevis; we strode up in thick cloud and driving rain, encountering snow on top. It was a gruelling slog and, as I wrote in my diary, 'too cloudy to take any photographs, and too cold to hold a camera'.

After that, we went to Mallaig on the west coast, where my father's regiment was planning to build a road along a sea cliff to connect an isolated farm to the rest of Britain; a narrow path cut into the cliffs was to be widened by blasting the rocks. As we were on the way out, the farmer's three dogs came rushing out, barking and snapping at us. We both had walking sticks and my father chose to smash the dogs in the teeth, driving forwards inch by inch as if it was the battle of Waterloo. This angered them even more. They gave ground inch by inch, snarling and growling. They tried to break through our sticks and around to the side of us, as if they were Hannibal's troops and we were the Romans, surrounded at the battle of Cannae. Fortunately, the cliff was too steep for them to go round us, but my job was to act as a rearguard and smash any that attempted to do that. We made it, and I learned a lot about courage in the process. I now saw my father as a military man; in close combat situations he was fearless.

We also went on two family sailing holidays, renting old wooden sailing yachts on the Norfolk Broads. We went in March, as when the temperatures dropped below freezing, it was cheaper and less crowded. I fell in love with sailing, and used to go out on my own in the tiny clinker-built dinghy with its single lugsail. I would get up before dawn, sometimes with frost still about, and sail ahead of the others on the bigger boat, which would overhaul me around noon. Then in the evening I'd catch up, after they'd moored on the riverbank.

For my father, though, sailing was a hazard rather than a joy: breakages when things got carried away in squalls; lots of tacking back and forth to get up the rivers against the wind; and lowering the mast every time we got to a bridge. The boats weren't that seaworthy, and the gear, made of bronze, kept breaking. We had our fair share of this, with sudden gybes smashing blocks, and squalls heeling the boat until the portholes were underwater. Once, I saw a yacht that had failed to get its mast lowered before a closed railway swing bridge. The mast was sheared off amid much yelling and shouting.

Other adventures took place on land. We went on a super family holiday in 1962, driving across the Kansas dustbowl to the Rockies. My father and I climbed Homestake Peak; there was no path and I got severe altitude sickness. At the top, we straddled the Continental Divide, one leg aiming west for the Pacific, one east for the Atlantic.

The next big event in my life was starting public school in England. The school had a predominately military tradition; over 1,000 former pupils had been killed in both world wars, 14 of them awarded the Victoria Cross.

Dr Edward Wilson, an Old Boy, was my personal hero. There was a beautiful painting of him at the school, standing by his sledge and dogs, sketching an ice cliff. He had been Sir Robert Falcon Scott's second-in-command on both of his Antarctic expeditions, and a brilliant scientist. His first expedition had been the first to venture into the interior. His second included a winter journey in −59°C (−75°F) temperatures and 24-hour darkness to collect emperor penguin eggs in order to determine whether or not birds were descended from dinosaurs, a theory that remained unaccepted until 80 years later. It was, however, that expedition which, having reached the South Pole, was to end in tragedy. Nevertheless the rock samples Wilson had collected would prove the existence of continental drift and plate tectonics, 60 years later. He was decades ahead of his time.

Boarding school expeditions

The winter of 1962–63 was particularly cold, sub-freezing for several weeks – the coldest, we learnt, since 1740. For some inexplicable reason global warming was not having an obvious effect, even though carbon dioxide levels had been rising for over 100 years and were increasing sharply during that decade. In fact, in our part of the world it was actually getting colder. Snow drifted 3 feet deep. The school heating was unable to cope and often froze up. Ice formed on the toilets and icicles hung from the taps. Our bedside glasses of water froze over. We all wore outdoor clothing, including overcoats, hats and gloves, indoors.

Yet it was that year when I did the Duke of Edinburgh's bronze medal award and expedition, which a group of us completed on an overnight backpack trip. Food was abominable, everything in heavy tins. Our packs were uncomfortable, being more like stepladders with tents lashed on. Boots seemed designed to make blisters. How anyone could be expected to win a war in this kit was beyond me.

I then did the silver expedition in March. This involved going by train to Scotland, then ferry to the Isle of Arran. We camped in Glen Rosa by a swollen river, and climbed the nearby mountains in winter blizzards in our antiquated army gear. We did hair-raising night exercises under the light of a winter moon on the Scottish hillsides. A big storm came down and washed our camp away, with the river overflowing. We all piled into the one tent left standing – the big mess tent – then next day moved into the Territorial Army huts in Brodick village and strung up 300 feet of rope to dry out our clothes.

Next morning, I started on the expedition itself with two other boys: Hare and Lloyd. We had to cross some mountains and return along the coast, spending two nights out. Our packs weighed 40 lb each – a lot for 15-year-old boys. The first night was a disaster. We camped on a peat bog, which had very little strength for holding tent pegs in, so we piled a half-ton of boulders around the tent in case of another storm. But as the tent didn't have a fitted groundsheet water flowed in and over our floor. Sure enough, another storm came down in the middle of the night and blew the tent away; we were left in our bags on the groundsheet, drenched and terrified. We wrestled the tent back in pitch darkness and, soaked and freezing cold, hung on to the sides of it all night to stop it blowing away again.

In the morning we climbed a pass and were hit by a snowstorm. We pitched camp for a second night, then walked back along the beach and completed the expedition, still soaked through, and with many blisters. We were amazed how much harder it had been than expected, on account of the extreme weather. We were not equipped for such conditions.

By now, it was time for me to take the first steps on my own career path. The Royal Engineers were mainly civil engineers, building roads, airstrips, harbours, fuel supply systems and so on. I decided to study to become a civil engineer, doing the same sorts of things around the world. My studies would eventually lead me to the oil and gas industry, which gave me everything I wanted: adventures, travel, engineering projects, sailing, climbing, some great people to work with, many good friends, and most of all, my new family.

2 Dirt tracks across deserts and continents

I was in a Land Rover in the Arabian desert in 1973, trying to get to a drilling rig across untracked sand dunes. We were on the top edge of a big sand dune slip face when suddenly the vehicle tipped over and threatened to roll all the way to the bottom, resulting in certain death. Battery acid and petrol were dripping onto the roof inside, bubbling and fizzing. What were we to do? No one knew where we were. We could not right the vehicle. We had no radio. Walking would be suicidal. We were low on water. How could we get out of this?

To Australia

Australia: a wide-open land with tough, hard-drinking men in the hot, dusty outback. It seemed a magical place, and one that would test me to the limit after my years of private education. What would the Aussies think of me as a privileged POHM (Prisoner of Her Majesty)? Would I be tough enough to cut it Down Under? How would I make a living? Could I cross this huge continent? I was just 18 years old, and very naïve about street realities.

I got my chance in my gap year, before going up to Cambridge University. For ten shillings,[2] I could get on a Royal Air Force troop carrier provided that it had an unoccupied seat. So on 16 January 1967 I was on a Comet jet from the Air Force base at Changi, in Singapore, to Darwin and over the red continent to Canberra, then a six-hour bus ride to meet my Uncle Bobby, an ex-submarine commander, and his Australian wife, Zan. They had two boats, three horses and four daughters. Bobby was a passionate sailor, and I enjoyed his company, talking about all things nautical. He had a Sydney Harbour skiff, a hot racing machine with a sliding seat that allowed the crew to sit way out from the hull.

Sir Francis Chichester had just arrived in Sydney on his quest to be the fastest singlehanded sailor around the world, and he was actually racing the times of the 19th-century clipper ships that went around the Horn. No one had sailed round the world faster since those days. We saw him off on the second leg of his voyage to Cape Horn and England.

The Australians were talking about a howling gale on the way. A cyclone came down while we were staying at Whale Beach, and I admired the power of the waves as they smoked in. After the storm had subsided a southerly buster blew in; Bobby decided to take his other boat, a wooden dinghy, out for a sail and asked me to

---

2 Half of £1 sterling. Now around £11.

7

join him. We drove to the beach with the boat on the roof, and as soon as he'd undone the straps, the wind blew it off, and it tumbled over and over in the sand. Not to be outdone, we went out anyway, Bobby skilfully steering the boat through big seas and stormy winds.

Nuclear bombardment

I got a job at the Australian National University (ANU), Department of Nuclear Physics, in Canberra, following an introduction to one of the staff through my father. This led to more contacts, and I was soon building a computer. The project was managed by Wal Lamberth, one of the most dynamic people I've ever met.

'The nuclear accelerator blasts the targets, and instruments measure the results,' Wal explained. 'Problem is they're in analogue form, and the computer we use to analyse the results is digital. So we must build an interface to convert the analogue pulse height analyser signals to digital. That's your job.'

'I don't have any relevant experience,' I explained.

'Doesn't matter,' Wal replied. 'You can do it with intelligence and hard work. One thing, though – no mistakes. We can't afford to build something unreliable. It's got to work 100 per cent, as good as something sent into space. You'll get two dollars a week.' At that rate, I would have to work a month just to buy a pair of shorts.

I was soon making printed circuit boards connecting transistors together, and some of the world's first chips consisting of four transistors that made up components which switched a signal through or blocked it: a binary system. This was very intricate, detailed work, often completed under large magnifying glasses. Pulses were to travel at the speed of light, and I had to design boards that had the shortest possible copper links, so that signals would go through in a few nanoseconds. Light travels one foot in a nanosecond, so every inch counted.

Much of this technology was being developed simultaneously for NASA's Apollo moon programme. Their target was to compress the size of the on-board computer from room-sized to that of a shoebox. We were on the cutting edge, redesigning every week as new technology became available. Wal was engrossed in it and his enthusiasm was boundless.

Having got a driving licence, which was easy, requiring only four hours of lessons since there was virtually no traffic or junctions to deal with, I decided to cross Australia overland and try to get better paid work. Since most of the journey would be on dirt tracks, I needed a four-wheel drive. I could get a very old used Land Rover for about $200, but this would take me about six months to save up for, and I was due at Cambridge by then. I looked for evening work but got none. I placed an ad for myself as a gardener and got no replies. I tried to get a job as a cleaner – even that was turned down. Often, there were 40 applicants for one job. Then I discovered that jackaroos, Australian rookie cowboys, could earn $40 per week.

Crossing Australia

By 11 May 1967 I'd reached my target of $200 saved, and taken the computer project at ANU as far as it could go. I was now unemployed. A friend gave me the name of a sugar cane farmer the other side of Australia who needed labourers to cut the cane in a very remote camp. But how to get there? I decided to hitchhike west to Adelaide, and then north over 2,000 miles across country.

I announced my plans at a party. 'You're crazy,' I was told. 'There's no traffic in the middle. Been told you can wait days for a vehicle to come by.' Another student said 'Strewth, you'll be bitten by snakes, tormented by flies, you'll die of thirst. *Fair dinkum.*' I'd heard of a driver who'd driven past a backpack with a hitchhiker's skeleton beside it. Dingoes had finished him off. 'Out there, *yerron yerrone.*'

But nothing could put me off. I decided I'd buy a car in Adelaide and drive north. I was excited by this adventure, and nothing was going to stop me. I knew that I really needed a Land Rover, but I simply could not afford one.

I bought my supplies: a backpack, a big knife, a plastic sheet for collecting water, a trowel for digging my toilets. I decided against a sleeping bag or a tent so as to save money and weight. I hitchhiked west for two days then joined a group of out-of-work no-hoper drunks around a log fire under a tree. There I met a mechanic called Ken Liddiard. He had the auto knowledge, and I had the money to buy a car. We both wanted to get to Alice Springs as we'd heard wages were high there. As we got a lift to Adelaide, a storm came down, ending a seven-month drought, so we spent the night in the back of a derelict truck, trying to keep out of the rain.

In Adelaide, we found a 15-year-old Vauxhall open tourer sports car, which I got for $70. It was cheap as it didn't have a roof and was rotted from several years' rain each winter. We bought jerricans for fuel and water, and goggles for the dust. After a few hours the radiator boiled, so Ken flushed it out with compressed air at a garage and we were on our way again. A few miles down the road and the gearbox failed. Ken welded it up at another garage. We then had only third gear forward and no reverse. After Port Augusta, there would be no proper road, no towns for 1,000 miles, so I hoped the bugs would be worked out before then.

We saw three Land Rovers that had made it from the north – they were covered in dust and mud. How could we get across Australia in a beat-up sports tourer? It seemed unlikely. The desert ahead was a fearful prospect.

The car took a terrible beating as the track deteriorated into a rocky, dusty mess. The dust, known as 'bulldust', was as light as talcum powder and it got everywhere. When you hit it, you often went into a pothole at the same time – and those holes, plus the corrugations across the road, were terrible, hammering the car to pieces. Some areas were deep sand, and we had to drive on the ridge between wheel tracks so as to keep the bottom of the car from dragging through it. The car was not designed for this. Even if new, it would never make it.

We drove through the night, and reached the Nullarbor railway, crossing the south of Australia from east to west. There was only one train a day on this single-track line. There was no level crossing, just the two rails sticking up across the dirt track. I drove the car over the rails in the dark and it stuck between them. With only third gear, I couldn't get out. Then, to my horror, a light down the railway line told us a train was coming.

'You stupid idiot,' Ken yelled at me. 'We're gonna get run down.' I frantically revved the engine and was ready to jump out and run when miraculously the car bumped free and the train roared by behind us.

At the small settlement of Pimba we came across a hitchhiker. We picked him up, which turned out to be a mistake; he was big bricklayer and we were in soft sand, so the exhaust pipe kept filling up with the stuff. We would never make it – we needed to get rid of this guy at the next settlement. The night got cold, and we wrapped a plastic sheet over us, holding it down with rope and tape, to keep the wind and dust off. We charged on, bouncing and hammering over the rough ground, the plastic sheet billowing and flapping in the chilly night air. By dawn we were at Coober Pedy, where a few desperate men lived, digging for opals. This was a gravelly desert as far as the eye could see, with no vegetation. We dropped the hitchhiker off, saying we were going to a different place from where he wanted to go, then drove a detour across the desert to avoid seeing him again – but to my horror we came across him again, and as we drove past him his jaw dropped in disgust.

Stopped at Coober Pedy

The end of the open tourer

We thundered on across the desert. The oil pump quit, and we had to pour oil into the engine regularly. Two more days and nights, then we should reach Alice. Then while Ken was driving there was a loud bang. A lump of cylinder fell out. He reached into the engine block and pulled out one of the six pistons and con rods. 'She'll be right, mate,' he said optimistically. We had no option but to continue with five cylinders. The engine roared and smoke billowed from the hole. The car leapt over big bumps and crashed across riverbeds. The windscreen, covered in sand and dust, was impossible to see through – and then it shattered. I punched a hole through it. The chassis broke. Both doors – forward-facing with the hinges at the back – blew off. The bonnet flew up, obscuring

The end of my car

our vision. We roared on, desperate to reach Alice before the end came.

But the end did come. The engine seized up. A truck passed by and dragged the beat-up car to a cattle station, where we left it. Ken hitchhiked back south to get another engine. I decided to hitchhike north.

I walked the first 2 miles, then after five hours a huge Mack semi-trailer drove by. The driver wanted me on board as he needed the strength of two men to change a tyre, and he took me as far as a dirt track that led to Ayers Rock, which I wanted to see. When he dropped me it was dark, and even though the Milky Way spanned the sky in a huge white band the stars in the southern hemisphere were unfamiliar to me. 'People back in the UK won't believe what I'm doing,' I thought. I lit a big fire, then saw a dingo circling me in its light and I thought of the backpacker's skeleton. I tried to chase it off with a burning log, but it returned, its eyes reflecting the firelight. Unsurprisingly I slept fitfully; I was on my own here – no contact with anyone, no one for miles. It was the adventure I'd craved. The temperature dropped below freezing. I had frosty ice on one side of me and was warm from the fire on the other, so I kept rotating like meat on a spit. It would have been better if I'd built two fires and slept between them. In the morning, a cool wind sprang up and tumbleweeds rolled across the plains.

By the middle of the day, no traffic had passed and the heat was intense. Many dust devils floated by, swirling the dust in small tornadoes. Hundreds of flies tormented me, trying to drink water from my eyes; they were as thirsty as I was. At first I thought that if I let them have it, it would quench their thirst, but more flies came. I'd drunk all my water, since I'd used one of the jerricans for oil to keep our engine going. Now I was in a desperate situation, hundreds of miles from the nearest town. I recalled the story of the backpacker's bones. I dug a hole and laid my plastic sheet across it to collect water in a tin can. It produced an eggcup's worth an hour – at this rate I would soon die of thirst.

After 12 hours, a van came by and I took the offer of a lift – it was my only option. Soon the van hit a bump and the entire roof blew off, smashing to pieces when it hit the ground behind us. The driver's wife observed in a shrill voice, 'Arthur, the roof's gone.'

Alice was green, as they'd had some rain – the first in years. I checked into a boarding house and got a manual labouring job at Rudders, for $1 per hour. This was five times what I'd been earning in Canberra. 'Why get a degree,' I thought, 'when you can earn this kind of money?' I soon changed my mind. I was unloading trucks, manhandling huge crates among teams of strong men. It was backbreaking. I couldn't wait for a lunch break.

'No lunch,' I was told by the foreman, 'Boss'll run you off and get another worker for the afternoon. Lots of men want this money.'

I was getting cuts and bruises all over, guzzling pints of water and becoming weaker by the hour. We went to a refrigerated train wagon to unload frozen pigs. I climbed inside the gloomy ice box and ducked as a frozen pig came hurtling at me and smashed against the wall. It was the big hitchhiker. 'You bastard,' he shouted. 'Pommie bastard. Left me for dead. You'll pay for that.'

This was getting dangerous so I quit the job at the end of the day, and found work the next day making hot dogs, toffee apples and sno-cones at the Alice Springs Show, an annual agricultural event. Soon after I arrived, an announcer stood on a wooden box: *'Lies and Gem, It gives me grite pleasure to welcome you all to the Alice Springs Show …'* I got another $21 for two days of fast food manufacture and sales. This was good money and an easy job.

To the desolate north-west

After the show ended, I managed to get several lifts up to Katherine, a small town deep in the Northern Territory. Here I met an Italian New Australian, a labourer at the Rum Jungle uranium mine, not too far away. 'Left Italy to make my fortune in Australia. Been digging uranium down the mine eight years now. When I've saved enough, I'm going to start my own business. Hope I'm not dead from radiation before then. It's everywhere, in the mud, in the water, everywhere. It's hell there but the money's good.' He was built like a weightlifter and had a steely glare. Nothing was going to stop this man from achieving his dreams.

Taking a lift on this cattle train

Then I headed west, into the unknown. I'd never met anyone who'd been west from here, and I understood that the 'road' would often be just two wheel tracks. Would there be any traffic? Someone told me that six weeks could pass without a vehicle.

I started off okay, with a lift on a cattle road train with three trailers behind. This was along a 'beef road', a dirt trail for hauling cattle from ranch to slaughterhouse. There was so much dust that I didn't see the last trailer until we stopped sometime later, and I learned that around 10 per cent of cattle died from dust asphyxiation on these long trips. We passed another road train that had rolled over; the animals had all been thrown out of the top and were scattered all over the sand, some dead, some alive but squashed. The stench and noise were horrendous.

We stopped one night where there were some other trucks. I got an idea how tough these truck drivers were when I met one who was all bandaged up, blood dripping from his hand. It had been mangled in a winch. 'Gotta keep driving,' he said, 'or the boss will fire me. Throbs a lot, but a few beers kills the pain.' How he handled the heavy truck with that wound was unimaginable. Like everyone else around these parts, he was driven by the fear of someone else stealing his job.

Then I was on a big truck full of cement bags. I earned my keep by offloading these at a work camp. I was covered in dust; it was in my lungs, down my throat, in my eyes, everywhere, so I got a shower in the camp under a barrel with holes in it. 'Watch out mate, snakes in there,' I was warned.

I got another lift until sunset, then settled down for the night in the wheel tracks, as the bush was thick each side and I feared snakes. There would be no traffic to run me over. I kept a fire going in the dirt road all night, then baked a potato in the hot red sand in the morning. After 10 hours a ute came by, and I got to Kununurra, the largest town in far north-western Australia, where I had a contact named Warren Franklin. He worked at the Kimberly Research Centre, where they were testing crops next to the Ord River to see if an irrigation scheme would work. The sea was just 100 miles to the north.

Snakes and sugar cane

I walked into the labourers' mess hall. 'New face come in,' a big gruff man said. 'How did you get here?'

'Overland from Canberra via Katherine,' I replied.

'Here's a Pommie,' the man said to the others. 'Bus, train? Strewth, there's no buses and no trains. We all flew in. Sounds like BS to me,' and the others all laughed.

'I hitchhiked,' I said.

'No way, there's no traffic.'

'I'm looking for Warren Franklin,' I said.

'Warren! Want a job with 'im? In the sugar cane? You must be crazy; you must love deadly poisonous snakes.'

PC cutting sugar cane

PC in Northwest Australia in 1967

I had to get a job, any job, as it would take me two weeks non-stop to get back to Canberra, and I needed the money for food. It would be very hard to get any other work in such a remote region.

Fortunately, Warren was keen to take me on: 'G'day, mate. No one'll work in it 'cause of the snakes. But they'll slither off when they hear you coming. You'll get $25 a week and free boarding. Thanks for taking this on. We're having a barbie tonight – you'll need to get the men on your side. Bring your own grog.'

I had to get up at 5.30 am next day, and go into the cane, an almost impenetrable jungle 12 feet high, slashing my way through, to cut samples of cane, then crush them and analyse the juice, to see which type worked best. The main hazards were cuts from the razor-sharp cane leaves and giant lizards. At one point I surprised a perentie lizard just 10 feet away. It was bigger than me; we both froze and stared at each other, but eventually it scampered off. But the worst were the cane hairs: small thistles that made your hands go septic. Sometimes I would get thousands of them, and have to shave them off with my sharp cane knife.

One weekend, four of us went crocodile hunting on the Ord River. We took a Land Rover along dusty trails, across dry riverbeds, until we reached a large river. I was covered in dust and dived in for a swim.

The three Aussies, staying on the riverbank, were laughing at me. 'Feel anything nibbling you?' one of them asked.

Then I suddenly realised: all the crocs were in the river, not on the banks. I exited slowly, so as to save face. That night, there were dozens of them on the far bank, and we could see them in the light of our searchlight, scores of small red eyes. We took a few shots, but each time the crocs scampered into the water and didn't come out for several hours. Small wonder these animals had survived over 200 million years. We drove to Mistake Creek, then on to a gorge, where we found a cave with aboriginal paintings inside. We ate well, barbecuing 180 small steaks in three days, typically five steaks each per meal.

This region, East Kimberly, was three times the area of England but sparsely populated – England's population was over 30,000 times denser. The men that worked with me were a rough, hard-drinking bunch. My neighbour, Craig, kept dozens of snakes in his room as pets: 'No worries, mate, they don't bite me, they know who feeds them.' Sometimes they would get out under his door, and I didn't want them in my room. Some were poisonous, some constrictors. I found one outside my room, halfway through eating a rat.

Main track south across Australia

One of our pastimes was bull baiting, best done after a few beers. The challenge was to get a bull to charge you, then grab its horns and leap onto its back.

I knew the group was thawing towards me when one of them welcomed me with a 'G'day mate, have a schooner.'[3]

On dirt trails across Australia

After several weeks at Kununurra I said farewell to my mates, then hitchhiked south through high mountains and boab trees, identical to their East African cousins.[4] I was in anthill country, and the flies were even worse here, about 200 of them on me at any one time. After dark it was wonderful, quiet and peaceful. But in the morning before sunrise, I could see the flies all asleep, waiting for me. During the day, they built numbers to over 300. This was torture. I found that I could kill up to 20 at a time with a careful hand slap on my thigh, but after that although they would be cautious, buzzing angrily around me, still more came. I got a few lifts out of the area, then had a cold night without any firewood.

In the absence of my usual crackling fire, the night was totally silent. I don't think I had ever experienced true silence before. It was magical. The stars, as always in the outback, were much brighter than anything I'd seen in the northern hemisphere. There were millions of them in the crystal-clear air, the Milky Way a huge band of stars so densely packed that the stars blended together. I lay back on the red Australian dust marvelling at how lucky I was to experience this – the solitude and peace of a wilderness that few in the developed world ever see. This was a very remote part of the outback. No one lived here. I reckoned I was the only person in over 20,000 square miles. There were no tourists, either. I was doing a walkabout, what the aborigines did to get away from it all.

I came across a natural bush fire, burning the tall dry grass and scrub, but fortunately I was able to skirt around it. I'd been warned that a far bigger hazard was rain. Why? Because it turned the dirt trail into impassable mud, which could prevent any vehicles getting through for up to six weeks. I had been advised to climb a tree and learn some hunting skills, although there was not much to hunt. I prayed for an ongoing drought.

At 4 a.m. I lit a few twigs to thaw my feet, then got a lift after sunrise in the back of a pickup truck, sharing it with a big boxer dog. Then another beat-up vehicle came along with a couple of croc hunters – one white and one aborigine. The trunk was full of croc skins. The vehicle was on its last legs, a V8 firing on five cylinders. We were on the Great Northern Highway, just a narrow dirt track. I went through Halls Creek, a small settlement that was a major milestone for me. Full of rough-looking men, and anthills.

Then my luck came in. A Mack semi-trailer was heading to Perth. The driver, Barry, picked up a huge tyre from an earth scraper and put it on the back of the truck, and on the few occasions that we stopped for a break this served as my cabin. We thundered on, for four days and three nights down the west coast of Australia, past Eighty Mile beach, Pardoo Sands and a stretch of road that was straight for 120 miles. I earned my keep digging the truck out from the sand when it got stuck, and changing wheels. Barry drove 24 hours a day, on amphetamines so as to avoid the need for sleep, as he was paid by the load and wanted to do as many loads as possible during the year. Often, as sleep finally caught up with him, the truck would leave the dirt track and charge across the bush, terrified kangaroos scattering before us in the night. Many were run down by our runaway monster. We took a load of bulldozer parts several hundred miles. We travelled one stretch of 700 miles without seeing a building or settlement. We came across another vehicle, broken down with a burned-out clutch, and towed it to Port Hedland.

---

3 A large beer.

4 Also called baobab.

By now I was able to imitate an Aussie accent, as I'd found some of the truck drivers resented giving a Pom a lift. One had even dropped me off as soon as he found out, pretending he was not going my way. As we approached Perth, I decided to tell Barry the truth.

'Where were you before Canberra?' he asked.

'England.'

'Thought you might be a New Australian. You a Pom, then?'

' 'Fraid so.'

'Jeez, after all these miles, a Pom. Good job you didn't tell me before or you'd have had a long walk.'

I got to Perth, did some more labouring, then headed east: another 2,000 miles from the Indian Ocean to the Pacific.

It was midwinter now, and big storms swept in from the Southern Ocean, which separates Australia from Antarctica. A cold, wet front swept over me, soaking my clothes and all my belongings. I got ahead of it, then it swept over me again as it headed east. This happened a third time while I was overnighting under a tree. I nearly died from hypothermia, praying that I could stay alive until dawn. I got a lift next morning with the sole objective of getting into a hot bath before I shivered myself into oblivion. It cost me 20 cents in a cheap hotel in Coolgardie and saved my life. I continued on across the Nullarbor Plain in these wet conditions, passing Eucla at the halfway point. Back then, although Eucla was on most maps of Australia it consisted of only two buildings, one of them a petrol station.

Soon I was back in civilisation. I looked for Ken Liddiard near Melbourne, as he'd promised to buy the car off me, but he'd disappeared and his family knew nothing of his whereabouts since I'd last seen him. They were very worried.

One of the benefits of being back in populated areas was music. There was no source of music while travelling, as nothing was mobile – this was long before the days of walkmans – and we only had 12-inch vinyl record players and reel-to-reel tapes. We were usually beyond the range of radio stations, but one night, while I was travelling in a truck, Bruce Channel's 'Hey Baby' came on the radio at full blast, and we both sang along to it with the truck engine providing the percussion.

The weather was still cold, still wet, and one night I camped out in a phone box.

When I returned to Canberra, I managed to get my old job back at the Department of Nuclear Physics. Everything had fallen apart while I was away and they were pleased to see me back to finish the project. By now I'd hitchhiked 9,000 miles around Australia.

Afterwards, Wal Lamberth wrote a nice reference letter of thanks:

> It is possible that Peter and I were a lucky personality combination but I would still want to give Peter credit for 99 per cent of his successful stay here. His energy, drive, ability for fast absorption of knowledge, his natural confident personality left everyone who met him quite stunned. Quite honestly, I have never met a more promising young man in my life. If he maintains his present disposition to his life and work, there is no position in society that he could not reach.

He'd been a great boss and was one of those people who thought every hurdle had a solution. He also had nothing but praise for everyone around him. Most of the credit for my work goes to him.

Uneasy rider

In 1970, after going down from Cambridge, I was posted to Abu Dhabi as a petroleum engineer, drilling for oil in the sand dunes on the edge of the Rub al-Khali, the Empty Quarter. This was a fantastic opportunity in a truly magnificent desert. Hardly anyone in the UK had heard of Abu Dhabi at that point, and there were no roads to it.

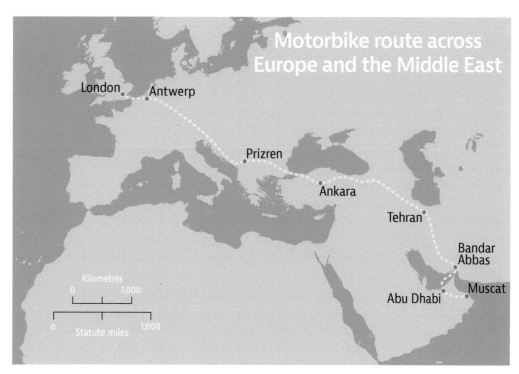

Motorbike route across Europe and the Middle East

I wanted to have a motorbike in Abu Dhabi so that I could join my geologist friends in their Land Rovers exploring the Arabian peninsula, including the dreaded Empty Quarter, which during the 1970s was surrounded by mostly closed countries with no tourism. But there were no large motorbikes to be bought in what was then little more than a fishing village, so I would have to ride one out there.

I was told that no one had ever driven a vehicle the 4,500 miles from England to Abu Dhabi before, partly because there were long sections of terrain without roads. To approach it from the west was impossible, not only due to the lack of roads but also because of the political isolation of Libya, Iraq and Saudi Arabia. From the north via Iran, the need to cross the Arabian Gulf by small dhows prevented cars from getting across. Access from the east, via Oman, was out of the question as the country was closed. And to the south was the Rub al-Khali, the world's biggest sand desert, with no roads across it. To get to Abu Dhabi from any direction, then, I would have to cross that desert, passable only by 4×4s or other desert vehicles.

But two of the things that I very much wanted to do were to ride across Europe on a big motorbike and to drive to Arabia by way of Asia Minor. The thought of riding day after day in hot sunshine and under blue skies, surrounded successively by plains, desert and rocky mountains, seemed so appealing that it would be well worth the high risk of not completing such a journey. As I couldn't afford a car, the motorbike was a better option. And it could fit on a dhow.

So I flew to London and bought a brand new black and gold Triumph Bonneville – too much of a high-performance machine for the sort of trip in mind, perhaps (at 50 bhp, it had more horses than many cars), but I had decided on this particular bike because of its engine design, which had changed very little since 1960, and because it had

Leaving the UK

15

achieved considerable success in endurance races such as the Isle of Man TT. It had also broken the motorbike land speed record.

I fitted the Bonny with a whole load of accessories and instruments (in particular an oil temperature gauge) and put in low-compression pistons for the low-quality fuel I would encounter on the trip.

A motorbike ought to be able to handle rugged terrain, but with a big load it would not be able to go where four-wheel drives could. So I had to plan my route carefully. It seemed my best hope was to ride to Yugoslavia, along a dirt track over the Montenegro mountains around Albania, then to Istanbul to take the ferry across the Bosphorus, then along the Black Sea coast and on more dirt track through the bandit country of the Turkish mountains to the Iranian border.

Then I'd go south through Iran for 1,200 miles to Bandar Abbas, where I'd take a small wooden dhow across the Persian Gulf to the Trucial Coast, and across the dunes to Abu Dhabi. Apart from getting stuck in sand or losing control of the bike in gravel, my main fears were getting knifed to death in Turkey if I had to camp out, and mechanical breakdown. How would I deal with bandits? Where would I sleep at night? What if the bike broke down? Would the bike make it through the soft sand on the south side of the Gulf, where there was no road?

My preparations for the journey included accumulating a huge quantity of tools, water bottles, fuel bottles, first aid equipment and spare parts, including gaskets, piston rings, cables, chain, clutch plates, brake shoes, electrical parts and so on. In the end there were over 180 items strapped on to the bike in various bags; I was leaving nothing to chance, as there was no possibility of any spares after leaving western Europe. I took a tent and cooking gear, and even a spare hard hat in case I came across a lone female hitchhiker. Most of the load was at the back, and this turned out to be a major problem as it made the front so light that on rough surfaces the bike would snake and I would lose control.

I could not get into Iran without insurance, and I could not get any in London, the insurance capital of the world. I was told I could try to get it at the Iranian border. Eventually, I found a tiny agency that would give me third party coverage as far as that border at least. This agency was in an extraordinary loft in the City of London, reached by getting into a water elevator, operated by counterweighting a barrel with water; to open and close the water valve you pulled a rope which passed through the cage.

My departure took place early in September 1971. It was the sort of day on which to appreciate the greenness of the trees and the fresh countryside smells that got forgotten down in the Gulf. At 8.15 a.m. I wheeled the machine out into the sunlight at the family home near Andover where, wet with oil where it should be and with paint reflecting the foliage around, it looked in perfect condition for the long ride ahead.

My parents, waving me goodbye, knew it was dangerous. I felt very much as I'd expected to feel – a mixture of excitement and apprehension. Apprehension for a number of reasons, but chiefly because of my familiarity with the temperamental nature of motorbikes. The Bonny was weighed down, its load of belongings – from Araldite to an Avometer – securely lashed on, weighing the machine down to over a quarter of a ton; really much too heavy and only just manageable. I swung my leg over and jumped on the kick-start. It was 8.30 a.m. Dead on schedule.

Motorbike across Europe

The new piston rings were run in on the journey up to London, but realising that the ferry might leave without us (Yogi bear, the mascot tied to the handlebars, Tigger, the bike, and myself), I decided that we'd done enough running in and hurried off to Ramsgate to board the hovercraft to France. Twenty-nine hours later we were in the Austrian Tirol, having spent the night in Antwerp.

We'd been battered by wasps all the way down the autobahn in perfect sunny weather, with the scent of the trees in the air and the roar of the slipstream at a steady 70–90 mph. I remember the signposts flying by: Frankfurt 320 … Frankfurt 318 … Frankfurt 316 … Frankfurt, Mannheim, Karlsruhe, Stuttgart, Ulm and finally across the Austrian border into the fringe of the Alps. We kept going hour after relentless hour, stopping only for fuel and wasp-wiping. The vibration was the main problem. Although all the screws and bolts were sealed up with locking compound, the innards of one of my cameras had shaken right out. On the autobahn, one of the wing mirrors had vibrated to pieces and the air horn diaphragm motor clip had cracked with fatigue. I lost my helmet peak in the slipstream and one of the Bonneville stickers was blown off. I was surprised that so much new gear was failing, but then I supposed that no one would go this fast for this long – around 700 miles in one day alone. My biggest complaint was an aching jaw from clenching my teeth for hours on end.

In the Tyrol I found a small hotel in Reutte and wheeled the hot, oily machine into the kitchen for the night. I had a welcome beer – in fact, several – with an Austrian who had driven to India the previous year. He told me lots of nasty stories about bandits and appalling road conditions in Turkey; and truck drivers who drive down the middle of

The Bonneville on a ferry in Yugoslavia

narrow mountain roads, especially if there is a foreign vehicle coming the other way. He advised me: 'Whatever you do don't kill anyone – a friend of mine ran one of the villagers over, so they chopped his head off and stuck it on the bulldog mascot on the bonnet of his Mack truck as a sort of retribution trophy.'

My route through the Alps was mostly along minor roads and involved climbing over several passes. I spent the next night in Cortina, then moved on through the Dolomites the next day. I had my first prang going steeply down a dirt road, and the bike slid over on its side. It was so heavy that I had to unload all the bags just to right it. The accident smashed off the mirror on the right side, so I did the next 1,000 miles without it – not so crucial when driving on the right-hand side of the road.

The Adriatic suddenly appeared just before Trieste, and the Yugoslav coast proved even more impressive than I'd expected. The road hugged the coast virtually all the way and was excellently engineered, cut into the rock in a continuous series of twists and turns. Apart from a few stretches of fallen rocks, the surface was good and I was able to ride the Bonny near the limits of its manoeuvrability for the only time on the trip, and in perfect weather. I covered almost the whole length of the coastline in eight hours, and at the end of it I wrote in my diary 'one day like this makes this trip worthwhile'. It was the sort of riding one dreams about, especially on a drizzly English day. Swinging in and out of corners with views of white rocky islands and the fresh smell of the sea, I never realised till then how good the Bonny's handling was, and I was often leaning over till the footrests scraped the road surface with the suspension pummelling up and down over the bumps. A well-designed motorcycle is a masterpiece of ergonomics, as all normal driving controls can be operated by moving no more than fingers or toes. For instance, dipping the lights while braking and changing down round a corner involves operating seven controls simultaneously, and would be impossible in a car.

That night I stayed on the luxury island resort of Sveti Stefan, now part of Montenegro, but before venturing near the reception desk I changed out of my leathers into my hotel kit in what I'd taken to be a Gents. Once inside, however, I realised I should have checked the sign in my Yugoslav phrase book, and it was ages before I crept out with my leathers and boots under my arm, hoping no more women would come in!

To a hostile world

What a contrast the next stage was. I started off up into the mountains, with superb views over the Adriatic, then along a new road blasted into the side of a gorge and on to Murino on a very narrow winding road. It was hard to believe that this was the road to Skopje, and as it went over the Čakor Pass it degenerated into an appallingly steep, twisting and loose-gravelled, rutted and potholed farm track. This was the E27! Although my AA guide had used similar epithets, plus 'notorious', 'hazardous' and 'unguarded' in its description of the road, I had naïvely assumed it was exaggerating.

Tigger was a lot trickier to handle on dirt than my previous machine, and I felt about as safe as on waterskis out in the ocean in half a gale. Logging trucks thundered down the narrow mud lane, forcing me off into the ditches, often with a sheer drop to a mountain river below. This was very dangerous, and I knew I should not be in such a place, but I was committed. Would it get any worse? If it did, I should try and go back.

There followed a brief magnificent view over Albania in the Montenegro mountains before the thick cloud came down, and with it the rain. After I'd summited the pass at over 6,000 feet, the clay surface soon became treacherous, slippery and rutted by fast streams. It seemed to me bad enough on a motorbike, but I later met someone who'd done this part of the journey in a car and at times had to reverse several miles to let oncoming logging trucks pass. I reached Pec[5] at last and looked back at the snowy range that loomed up as a formidable barrier.

The contrasts in Yugoslavia were quite extraordinary; while the coast had an air of affluence about it the interior looked like a forgotten corner of the world. I never knew

Main road across the Cakor Pass in Montenegro

such hard conditions of living existed in Europe, and at times felt quite an intruder among a sea of leaden Slavic faces. Once, while I was at speed somebody threw a stone at me, and it hit my foot. Fortunately my leather boot took most of the punishment, but the foot swelled up alarmingly that night, and I worried whether I would be able to operate the gearshift in the morning.

From Pec the road became cobbled, and passed through muddy countryside where the traffic was mostly horse-drawn, all the animals moving at the trot and leaving the road a slippery surface worsened by the steady rainfall. Soon the road joined the main route to the border and through to Macedonia, northern Greece and western Turkey, and my arrival in Istanbul after dark was dead on schedule. I could hardly believe that Istanbul was less than halfway in distance and about a third of the way in time on my route, as I seemed to have been on the road for weeks. However, I was expected in Abu Dhabi on 28 September, and a delay in getting new pistons in London had forced a very tight schedule.

Next morning I crossed the Bosphorus on a ferry to Asi – the only way across, as at that time there were no bridges. I was very conscious of the history here, the place where the former Roman Empire had had its capital city for centuries, controlling trade between east and west, and between north and south, making Constantinople the biggest and wealthiest city in the world.

A high-speed crash in Turkey

Fast driving on two wheels in Turkey was not to be recommended since most of the traffic was heavy transport. The only rule of the road which seemed to be obeyed was that smaller vehicles gave way to larger, and I saw the aftermaths of a number of quite spectacular head-on collisions between lorries of the same size. I found my headlamp flasher and ship's air horns invaluable, and tried imitating police tactics, with great success in overtaking.

I'd been expecting an accident as I'd had too many close shaves, and sure enough, on the run to Ankara I had a big one. The road was straight, and the light reflecting off the miraged surface made it difficult to judge distance and speed. My air horn would not operate against the 80 mph slipstream. At any rate, two trucks were

5 Now in Kosovo.

Crossing the Bosphorus by ferry to Asia

trying to overtake each other, barrelling down at me at a closing speed of 150 mph and taking up both lanes. As soon as I realised I was in for a head-on collision, I had no option but to brake hard and leave the road. I jumped off the tarmac into loose gravel above a forest and lost control of the machine at about 60 mph. I fought to keep it on the narrow strip of gravel without going into either certain death in the forest below or equally certain death back into the oncoming trucks. The bike snaked wildly from side to side and I fought to lay it over, as the alternative was to be flung over the top or squashed underneath it. My life flashed in front of me, and everything slowed down so that I was already trying to figure out how to get the wreckage home so that I could fly back to work. Somehow, by incredible luck, I landed on top of the bike, which skidded to a halt on its side in a huge cloud of dust and gravel.

When I could see again after the dust settled, I noticed to my amazement that the bike had made it in one piece. A number of parts had been squashed or bent, and some of my belongings, including my camera, had been smashed. The handlebars, horn, indicator, brake pedal, footrest and some electrics had been either bent or smashed. The tank was also broken off the frame and I was lucky it hadn't caught fire. My elbow ached, but the wonderful leathers had taken a terrible grazing and saved me from awful injuries. I later discovered that my elbow was chipped in the bone, and I did the rest of the trip with it broken.

Several people stopped to help me put the damaged pieces back together again. An hour later, I gingerly started off, and noticed the frame was bent as the bike developed a wobble at about 90 mph, but as it was okay above and below that the trick was to get up to 100 mph without pausing at 90. Since the bike could do the ton in third gear, it wasn't a problem.

My route took me north to the Black Sea coast and on to Ordu, where while trying to work my way through a hostile crowd in a narrow cobbled street in the dark, I drove into a huge pothole. This, after a very frustrating day, was the last straw, and I spent most of the next day – my birthday – getting a crash bar fitted by a Turkish gunsmith, after which it was a relief to head south and up into the mountains where the air was cooler. However, the roads deteriorated and so did the petrol, the normal grade available being only 65 octane.

Turks must have had a thing against Englishmen on motorbikes as most of the boys threw stones at me, often big rocks, usually as I entered a village. Fortunately they were poor shots and I would suddenly accelerate hard so the rocks would pass behind me. They must have been dumbfounded since most people freeze or duck when a projectile is being launched at them. The best technique, I found, was to wave just before they threw, which rather puzzled them. In fact they often ducked when I did this and I realised they thought I was throwing a rock at *them*, particularly when the slipstream yanked my arm violently back. But then maybe my reputation got ahead of me, as a wild foreigner on a huge motorbike, armed with rocks to pelt villagers. Other colleagues of mine who later followed my wheel tracks in cars told me of horrendous stories of vehicles, all their windows caved in by rocks by the time they reached the Iranian border.

By this stage of the journey there was lot of work to do on routine maintenance. I was constantly repairing things with galvanised wire, adjusting the chain, adjusting the carburettor for the changing altitudes, replacing cables, fixing electrics, adjusting the extra instruments and refilling the oil, which had spattered all over the machine allowing the dust to glue to it, meaning the Bonny was now pale brown instead of gold and black. The front forks were a constant problem, taking a terrific pounding in the rough terrain and emptying the oil all over the bike. The wheels needed aligning, nuts and bolts tightening, and everything needed to be checked. I couldn't afford to have something crucial fall off at high speed.

These big bikes could be temperamental, so every morning before setting off I used to spend a couple of hours on maintenance. This inevitably attracted a huge crowd, particularly when I was tuning, and people were curious and anxious to finger the controls. However, I soon learned a bit of crowd control. I would select the biggest man in the crowd, offer him a cigarette and then shout at somebody, 'Get your hands off, and …' The big Turk would then assume control and shout even louder in Turkish, whereupon the whole crowd would shrink back. Twice the crowds built up to such an extent that the police came along to disperse them and clear a passageway for me to get out and away.

My last night in Turkey was spent in Erzurum at 6,300 feet (1,900 metres). The next morning I found my mascot, Yogi, had been stolen, in spite of my having tied covers over the machine and tipped the hotel night watchman 20 cigarettes to keep an eye on it. I left in a very black mood, and to get out of the area I did a planned two-day journey in one, including a two-hour hold-up at the border.

Over mountains from Turkey to Iran

Most of the way across Iran was above 4,000 feet, which resulted in a marked loss in power that became very apparent when a strong headwind blew most of the way to Teheran.

There I had an extraordinary accident; I was in heavy traffic trying to get out of town when the cars either side of me squeezed me, and my wing mirrors smashed through their windows, one either side, leaving me jostling with two sets of angry Iranian teeth. Stopping would have been suicide, so I had no option but to carry on, wedged in and unable to steer, at about 40 mph. Eventually the traffic thinned and the two lanes either side of me opened up, whereupon the remains of my mirrors popped back out of the car windows and I sped off, not wishing to explain what had happened.

As I rode southwards the ride was taking on a surreal quality, and the arid desert surroundings floated steadily by. Whirlwinds drifting across the plains leaving trails of dust added to the dreamy nature of the surroundings. Hazy mountain ranges loomed up, one after another, and there was always the hot sun and cloudless sky, with dusty air so dry that my skin would crack and lips become glued together. Traffic and

At the Turkey – Iran border after dusty dirt roads

Crossing the Dasht-E-Lut, the
great salt desert in Iran

population grew sparse, for this was the Dasht-e Lut, the Great Salt Desert, one of the world's hottest. The surface was flat, grey gravel, devoid of vegetation, seemingly endless, quite majestic.

It began to dawn on me that the trip would soon be coming to an end and suddenly I realised just how much I was enjoying it. The thought of work ahead was depressing. On the last day's run the road down to Bandar Abbas was tunnelled, cutting through one mountain range after another as it steadily descended to sea level. My spirits descended with it. The inevitability of the end of the ride was difficult to swallow.

On a dhow from Iran across the Gulf

So to the Gulf, which looked so familiar. A yellow-green sea steaming in the sun. The strong wind across Iran had picked up a lot of dust, which must have caused the yellow haze over everything. By now it was so hot that if I stopped my leathers burned me. In this arid land I had to find shade before resting.

The next day the bike was manhandled aboard a small wooden dhow and we were off to Dubai, along with about three dozen Pakistani immigrants. In the evening the dhow was negotiating a way through a tide race when the steering wheel broke loose and we started going round in circles. Soon another dhow slid over the horizon and came up alongside, whereupon all but three of the Pakistanis leapt across the gap, complete with bedrolls and various other belongings. I never found out why, as my Arabic was as bad as the crews' English, but I guessed they were illegals. Fortunately I didn't have to join them, as I would surely have lost the bike in the deep blue between the rolling dhows.

The crossing was an experience in itself, and I certainly had an introduction to the primitive existence these Gulf seafarers have. The dhow was

Loading the bike onto a dhow in Iran

Dhow to Dubai

Bike aboard the dhow

completely open, with no beds or seats. The crew slept on the floorboards in whatever they were wearing, no mattress, no blankets. One of them slept on a 6-inch-wide plank 8 feet above the deck! Meals were usually rice with a bony, emaciated fish, eaten from a round tray with the only piece of cutlery, a ladle.

In spite of their piratical appearance, the crew were in fact very friendly, and we spent long hours drinking tea and coffee and exchanging views on what was good, very good or bad about things. It was quite fun chugging along under the stars, but the heat and humidity became oppressive, especially during the night and early morning. After 26 hours everyone looked a very sorry sight indeed, and the three Pakistanis looked as if they wished they'd never left Pakistan.

The head was simplicity in itself – a wooden crate lashed over the stern with the two middle planks knocked out. You had to crouch over the boiling wake while the Arab crew looked on with wide grins. The main problem was you had to stand on the remaining two planks nailed into the bottom of the box, which were just strong enough for my piratical friends, but as I was heavier they were not quite enough for me, and the nails came out with each large wave. I had visions of hitting a big wave and being tossed through the box and over the stern at night into these waters infested by hammerhead sharks. I remembered a strange statistic, that most drowned sailors are found with their flies open – was it because they had gone overboard during these crucial acts?

I didn't trust the skipper's navigation too much, as he kept waking in the middle of the night and ordering course changes. After some 24 hours at sea I got quite worried as I'd been told the crossing would take 11 to 14 hours, or possibly 20 in very bad weather. The weather was calm and the sea was rolling the dhow gently. There was nothing to see except dolphins, sea snakes and flying fish.

I was the first to see land – a water tower in Sharjah – and half an hour later Dubai showed up dead ahead. It was quite a while before any of the crew saw it. We were right on course, which was quite remarkable considering how difficult the dhow was to steer. Dubai was then a small collection of single-storey houses, some with wind towers to help cool them.

Stuck in the searing hot sand

As there was no surfaced road or even a gravelled track to Abu Dhabi from Dubai, I soon became bogged down in a lot of soft sand and I couldn't pull the bike out. This terrain was for 4×4s only, not for a heavily overloaded one-wheel-drive motorbike. I remembered my desert survival instructions and sat in the limited shade of the vehicle, sipping scalding hot water. Nobody came to rescue me, so after an hour I put a wet rag over my head and walked off with a water bottle, which was against our company rules, but better than dying of thirst. The first vehicle to appear was an

Stuck in the sand on the way to Abu Dhabi

Abu Dhabi Police Land Rover. Having hauled my bike out, the officers went ahead to tell the border officials to let me through, and I found a way round the soft sand to get to Abu Dhabi.

It was a relief to have made it, and yet sad to think that the trip was over. For days afterwards I woke up longing to get on the road again and to hear the roar of the slipstream, feel the heat of the sun and see the changing arid landscapes. The route I took for my long journey was one of the finest in the world, mountainous most of the way and passing through 12 interesting countries with four sea crossings. But if I did it again I would get myself an armed escort through Turkey.

My employer asked to write up the story for the company magazine. They titled it 'Uneasy Rider', after Peter Fonda's epic feature film *Easy Rider*, which had recently been released to the tune of $60 million at the box office. It was an apt title.

The bike had been hard to handle, with a heavy load of over 180 items, including:

- Maps, ferry timetables, phrase books and guides
- Repair and spares manuals
- Passport, visas, wallets, money belt, and paperwork
- Spares: oil, air and fuel filters, spark plugs, gaskets, piston rings, points, cables, bulbs, wire, chain and links
- Clutch plates, brake pads, coil, capacitor, carburettor spares
- Clothing: leathers, boots, gloves, crash helmets, goggles
- Washkit and first aid
- Tools: spanners, wrenches, pliers, glues, grease gun, special tools, puncture kit, tyre levers, pump, screwdrivers, pressure gauges, solder and butane bottle, tape, galvanometer
- Sleeping bag
- Cans of oil, water and fuel
- Tent and two backpacks
- Food, knife, fork and spoon tin opener
- Tyre inner tubes
- Chain and padlock.

Driving in the desert sand seas

I worked for four years in Abu Dhabi as a petroleum engineer, living initially at a bachelor camp on the coast at Tarif then in the drilling rig camps as they moved from well to well in remote sand dune areas on the edge of the Rub al-Khali. Our oilfields were mostly on the northern edge of these enormous sand seas, and there were a few camps. Further south, there was nothing.

Desert driving in Land Rovers was a challenging skill, and rather like sailing in that there were no landmarks, as the wind constantly changed the dune landscape. We didn't have any position-fixing equipment, however, as satellite navigation was yet to be invented, and without a clear and level horizon sextants were no use.

Driving across sabkha salt flats

So when looking for a specific location such as a wellhead, it was best to travel first with someone who had been there before, and then memorise the route by the shapes of the more memorable dunes. Finding one's way back to the camp was much more important, as if one got lost, or stuck in the sand, or broke down, there was virtually no chance of being found and rescued. The usual trick was to follow your own wheel tracks back. It was forbidden to leave the vehicle and try to walk to safety, as those that did try would die within hours.

But all this made for several problems. First, the layout of the dunes often dictated a different way back, avoiding steep uphill sections, especially up slip faces, which could only be negotiated straight downhill. This required a more complex and tortuous return journey. The dunes all marched south-east, so going over the slip faces in this direction was relatively straightforward, but coming back to the north-west was very challenging. Our camps were generally in the north of the country, and we were always pushing our exploration further south, so we had to be very careful to be sure we could drive back. Going out was rather like running before a gale at sea: beating back is sometimes impossible.

The second problem was that the wind could blow out our tracks in minutes, especially during the strong Shamal winds, which blew most of the summer days.

When I got completely lost, which happened several times, I just headed north across trackless dunes, 200–330 feet high on average: big red scarps with smaller white ones on their backs, and long treacherous slip faces. I would assess my direction from the shapes of the dunes and the angle of the sun, until I hit the coastal *sabkha* (salt) flats, where I would turn left and eventually find the camp at Tarif on top of its low *jebel* (hill). This strategy gave me a huge adrenaline rush and it was highly dangerous. I couldn't risk my Land Rover rolling over or getting stuck, as I would not be found. If I then tried to walk, I would most probably die when my 2-gallon water flask ran out – and if I lived, I'd be fired for leaving my vehicle.

All the drivers of the big vehicles were Bedouin, and they knew instinctively how to read the sand, to tell where it would be hard or soft, to know what was over a ridge, to know how to get out of an impossible cauldron of encircling white dunes.

I got to know the desert as the Bedouin did, reading the sand, the wind, the way the dunes moved. I spent a lot of time with them. I was always the only white man, the only infidel in a Moslem world, travelling with my Arab companions. Occasionally we would come across a black tent behind a dune, where friends or relatives of the driver lived in the traditional manner with their camels, their goats, their tents and their veiled women. I learned some of their customs, for instance always eating with the right hand from a communal bowl, never the left, which was a gross insult.

Coffee was a big ritual. It was ground up with a brass pestle and mortar, then into a big brass pot brewing on a fire of gorse bush twigs, with more herb twigs stuffed into the long snout. It tasted rough, but one was obliged to drink at least three cups: one for Allah, one for the host and one for the guest. Often the wind and sand would be blowing all around the tent, but none would blow in. I had to be careful not to look at the women who scurried about, dressed from head to toe in black, with heavy leather masks over their faces so you could only see their eyes flashing inside turquoise makeup.

The Bedouin were always friendly and hospitable, but once I had a memorable incident. I was driving alone, following my wheel tracks back, when a Bedouin appeared in front of the vehicle, waving me down. I stopped and began opening the door, thinking he needed water or transport. He developed a strange, contorted look on his face, and pulled a huge sword from behind his back, raising it into the sun above me. Thinking that I had half a second before my head was cut off, I slammed into gear and roared off, dragging him from the open door. I wasn't taking any chances. I was on the edge of the Rub al-Khali, where some Bedouin were outcast bandits, only able to survive by stealing, murdering and robbing from the tribes. While I felt sorry leaving him tossing in the sand behind me, I knew that it could easily have been him leaving me in the sand as he drove off in his new four-wheel drive pickup.

I learned to desert-drive like the Bedouin, and quickly improved, simply by constantly getting into the impossible dune country that we were advised to avoid. Most westerners were scared of the difficult sand after one bad experience of getting stuck under the summer sun or rolling their vehicle down the long slip faces. The geologists were the best of the westerners, exposed as they were to arduous journeys in remote locations where the exploration rigs were drilling high-risk wildcat wells in unexplored regions – but they had a notorious accident rate. I found that desert driving is like sailing, skiing or surfing – only practice and trial and error improves it. There are some fundamentals, but the key lies in reading the sand. The Bedouin did not want work in the oil industry that had just arrived in their land, but they did want to be drivers, and they were superb.

Driving across dune belts

I learned how to see where the soft sand was – in the lee of the dunes, where the particles were finer and whiter. The hard sand was in the windswept areas, where it was being blown away from the slopes, and the particles were coarser, often redder, with ripples. I learned how to drive down huge slip faces 1,000 feet high. They seemed almost vertical as the Land Rover flew over the knife-edge ridge at the top, and made a deep roaring noise as they avalanched down, with the vehicle sunk below its axles into the sliding slope. And I got stuck, hundreds of times, as the months rolled by. I was usually alone, short-cutting between wells where probably no vehicle had ever been before. I had to get out of the fixes I'd got into, particularly as my vehicle had no radio. I dropped my tyre pressures sometimes as low as 2 psi, so the rims were in the sand and the rubber was like tank tracks. After getting unstuck I would connect them with a rubber hose screwed into a spark plug socket in the engine, pumping them back up using petrol vapour and air, hoping they wouldn't explode.

Bedouin tent and tea

If that didn't work, it was a matter of digging, using the tank tracks that I carried in the back. Often it was too hot to do this and I had to wait till evening. I got stuck on knife edges, in troughs, in flat sand, on steep slopes and in the dreaded whirlpools of the desert: blowholes. Some of these were over 100 feet deep. I tried the spiral wall of death – any hesitation, and the vehicle would stop and roll all the way to the bottom. I watched how the Bedouin tackled difficult problems. They had a completely different approach from westerners. Westerners, including myself at first, would attack the desert aggressively, white knuckles on the steering wheel, lots of power, double declutching through the gears with teeth grating and jaws clenched; the Bedouin, in contrast, would drive gently, reading the sand a long way ahead, changing gear ahead of time, feeling the texture of the sand through hands lightly holding the wheel, weaving their way around the dunes. It was their environment, but to us it was a hostile moonscape.

Finally, I learned how to drive up small slip faces, going flat out at them at a place where they curved to the horizontal. Once I misjudged one, which had more of a V-shaped bottom, and bent my axles. I got stuck in sand so soft I couldn't even go downhill, and had to work my way forward, foot by foot, with the tank tracks. Frequently I would be digging for hours. I had heard that in Saudi Arabia they sometimes filled the tyres with water to stop the vehicles rolling over. I spent hours researching and trying different routes over unexplored desert passages directly between the wells. When I had discovered a way through I would mark the highest points so I could find my way out if my tracks got blown out.

If I got completely stuck, I would wait for the sand to cool in the evening, improving traction. But driving at night across unmapped dune seas was extremely dangerous, as I could only see a few yards ahead, so could easily get into a place I could not get out of.

Zararra in the Empty Quarter

Then I had a chance to fulfil a dream, to visit the second Zararra well, where a huge oilfield had been discovered by the first well. Zararra was well into the Rub al-Khali, in the 1,000-foot-high dune country, vast rolling sand masses a mile long each. No one lived here.

I drove out with a Bedouin and a Schlumberger engineer called Jeff. From Bu Hasa we headed south, following the wheel tracks of the giant Kenworth trucks that had hauled Santa Fe Drilling Company's Rig 68 into the Empty Quarter. The sand got redder, the dunes higher – 400, 500, 600 and 1,000 feet – as we worked our way from the last vestiges of civilisation into the world's largest sea of sand, stretching all the way south to Yemen. Engines raced, the Bedouin working both gear levers with deft skill, double declutching to avoid any jerking or pausing that could allow our tyres to slow and sink in. He spun the steering wheel wildly as he negotiated the tight corners forced on us by the walls of sand. It seemed more like powerboating in a hurricane, especially when the wind picked up and whipped the sand off the tops of the dunes in blinding sheets. In some spots the Land Rover had been polished clean to the bare metal by this windblown, abrasive sand.

En route for Zararra

After thousands of dunes – small ones, big ones, rows of small ones stacked on big ones, like waves on the backs of the Southern Ocean swells – we noticed recent tracks and knew we were nearing the rig. We were travelling in the same direction as the prevailing wind, so that as we crested each dune we plummeted over the top into what seemed like a near-vertical wall, the slip face. The driver, afraid to get stuck, would roar over the top in zero-G into deep blue sky. The effect was similar to driving off a cargo ramp of a plane 1,000 feet up. We would all hold our breath and the handles on the dashboard, waiting for impact.

On one dune when the front of the Land Rover crashed down, causing sand to fly everywhere, it started a big sand avalanche that roared like thunder all around us. It was now like white-water rafting in a muddy river, as we floated on top of the landslide, the driver deftly steering his front wheels like rudders, and throttling up to pull the vehicle left or right. He had to keep it pointing straight down or it would have rolled and tumbled all the way to the bottom, killing us all (a fate reserved for many in the Empty Quarter). We got to the bottom and looked back. I couldn't believe we had done it. There were no wheel tracks, as the avalanche had covered them.

A few more of those, and then we were weaving along a deep valley with huge dunes on either side. The air was now bone dry, more like an oven than a sauna. We rounded a bend and suddenly the rig was there, the mast laid down like a huge orange and white praying mantis. Saudi Arabia claimed this part of the desert and had warned us not to drill any more wells.

When the sun went down behind the dunes, we changed the tyres on the Land Rover, which had got shredded in the hot sand.

Next day, Jeff and I went to a blue steel unit to change some electronic equipment out. He was anxious to do it before sun-up. Inside was a mass of electronics on chassis from floor to ceiling, on all four walls and even the roof, like an aircraft cockpit. Unfortunately we didn't get it finished before the sun got over the top of the dune. As the metal expanded the unit started crackling and within minutes it was too hot to touch anything. We finished the work with our heavy leather work gloves handling delicate electronics. Within half an hour, the thermometer inside the unit read 65.5ºC (150ºF). This was quite something when at the time the world's highest officially recorded ambient temperature was 52.7ºC (127ºF). We had yet to get an 'official' thermometer in these parts. We had an unofficial weather station with a properly shaded thermometer allowing the wind to flow over it, and we measured temperatures up to 58.8ºC (138ºF) in the shade, as high as any worldwide. In the sun, thermometer readings were over 76.6ºC 170ºF. I measured 80ºC (176ºF) one day in the sand, enough to burn you badly. It melted the soles of my desert boots.

Coming back was even more difficult. We could not follow our tracks and took a completely new route. The driver was constantly getting stuck and following blind alleys. Often, he would get out on high ground and survey the desert, muttering quietly and curving his hands as he visualised the way through all the obstacles. We had the big balloon tyres at 6 psi most of the way. But in the end we made it.

Turned upside down in the dunes

While working on the rigs, I often used to teach the young geologists that came out how to desert-drive. We would start by following recognised tracks, then go off into the desert, then tackle the dune belts. On 13 December 1971, I took a geologist called Simon Budd out into the big dunes.

We stopped at the edge of a 300-footer and I explained to Simon how to get past it going into the wind. 'Obviously we can't get up the slip face, and we don't want to drive down to the bottom of the basin, as we may not get back out, so you should skirt along the edge, build up speed, change down into second and claw up the right-hand lip, then do a barrel roll over the top.'

Simon studied the route, mentally going through the wheel movements and gear changes, then confirmed, 'Got it.' He jumped into the driver's seat and took off down the bowl, building speed for the diagonal run up the slope on the right side, leaving the slip face to the left.

Big dunes near Zararra

However, as we went up, the Land Rover slowed in the soft sand and started digging in, leaning dangerously to the left, the slip face side. 'We're not going to make it,' I yelled at Simon above the screaming gearbox. The vehicle rolled over sideways onto its roof.

My main concern was that it would roll all the way to the bottom, hundreds of feet below, leaving us a pair of corpses inside, so I yelled to Simon 'Jump, get out!' – but if we'd done that while it was still rolling we would have been squashed. Fortunately, the vehicle stopped, resting on the corner of its roof. I was on the uphill corner, diagonally above Simon and hanging onto the seat to stop landing on him. 'Don't move,' I spoke softly. Not that he could, as his door was embedded in the sand. He went silent, and the only sounds were dripping noises. Soon an oil slick spread over the roof, fizzing and giving off sulphurous gases. The sump oil and battery acid were pouring out. There was an electrical smell as well, and I worried that a spark might set the petrol on fire. We had to get out. However the slightest movement would set the Land Rover rocking perilously downhill. I gingerly opened the door diagonally upward and squirmed over the uphill side, then leant out like a sailor on a dinghy to keep it as stable as possible while Simon escaped.

How could we get out of this?

It was the middle of the day, and we were a long way from anywhere – too far to walk, and also it would be against company regulations. The problem was that no one knew where we were. I had got so used to wandering off, developing my own routes through the dune belts, that I'd become overconfident and never believed I would get into a situation I couldn't get out of. Also, this dune belt would hide a vehicle from air search unless directly overhead. Besides, I didn't want all the adverse press of a full-scale air rescue. We had no radio on this vehicle and even if we'd had one the aerial would have broken off anyway. It was a choice of either getting the vehicle upright, walking, or arranging a land rescue.

The first option ended when we couldn't find a way of rolling the Land Rover uphill, as there were no bushes to tie a rope to. In the evening, I walked to the top of the dune to look for the nearest rig. Fortunately, the dune was very high and visibility good. I could make out the black spike of Rig 55's 140-foot derrick, some 10 miles away. I had a mirror designed for flashing the sun at a chosen target, and spent the rest of the day doing just that. At sundown, I unscrewed a headlight and managed to get the battery out. We installed it on top of the dune and dug a hole in the sand to sleep in shifts, buried for insulation against the cool winter night.

By the early hours of the morning there had been no acknowledgement from the rig and a fog had descended, so we decided to wait out the night and try the mirror again in the morning. But then, much to our surprise, we heard a vehicle coming out. One of the Bedouin parked a short wheelbase Land Rover on top of the ridge; he had seen us flashing and driven out from the rig. When the fog came down, he had driven in a wide circle, eventually crossing our wheel tracks and following them until he found us. We all went back to 55, and again I was amazed at the Bedouin's driving. We were in thick dune country, at night, in fog, and cutting a new route against the slip faces. The short wheelbase Land Rover could be spun on a dime, which we did often, on top of ridges and in tight corners hemmed in by slip faces on three sides.

When the sun came up, we took a bigger pick-up truck and attached ropes between the vehicles to haul the Land Rover upright. After cleaning the oil off the plugs and petrol system, we jump-started it and got it back to the rig.

Soon after that I was working in the remote Asab field, which didn't have any camps, as it was still undeveloped. When I drove out, which was six hours diagonally across the wind direction, I nearly didn't make it. I had taken a short cut through a dune belt, got stuck and overheated the engine so it wouldn't run. No matter what I did, I couldn't get enough power to get out. This time I was on my own and 50 miles from any camp. It was much more serious than anything I had encountered before.

Eventually night came, but the engine still ran too hot and I was still stuck. I unbolted the bonnet and doused the engine with water from my three jerricans. It worked and I limped to the rig, apologising for being late. We had a tent for eating, and inside it, even at night, the cutlery was too hot to hold. We had to eat wearing our heavy safety rig gloves.

Climbing Abu Dhabi's unclimbed Jebel Hafit

I also took up mountain climbing again, learning from my friend John Pooler. There was only one mountain in the country, Jebel Hafit, which had formed when huge forces thrust the limestone from deep underground in our oilfields up above sea level and into tortuous shapes, and it had never been climbed. The Bedouin, believing the devil was up there, were thought to have never climbed it. Several British Army expeditions had attempted it, but all had failed on the rugged hot parched limestone terrain.

John and I decided to be the first ever to climb it. We went up on our motorbikes and camped at its foot. We started up one of the wadis that we had identified in aerial pictures, but eventually we got to an impossible cliff and had to turn back. However, we had got higher than anyone previously.

A few months later, a geologist, Ken Fellowes, and another keen climber, Dave McKinnell, succeeded on their second attempt, and left a book in a plastic box on top for later parties to fill in. However, it turned out they had left it on the lower of the two summits, so John and I decided to climb to the top and move the book to the correct summit.

On our second attempt, we followed Ken and Dave's route, which involved climbing several dry waterfall pitches. On one of these, we had to belay across a vertical smooth limestone wall. The only rope we had was a piece of line for herding camels, and when I fell off the wall the rope snapped and I crashed to the bottom. I was scraped rather than broken, and I carried on. It was a gruelling climb, up steep limestone slabs under the hot sun, and across rocks so razor-sharp that they cut our boots. But we made it to the top.

PC climbing Jebel Hafit

Waterskiing in Abu Dhabi

Back to Zararra

My final desert adventure was to go back to Zararra. I went with Mohammed Thani, a legend in his time. He was an old Bedouin who knew the desert better than any, and he was Santa Fe Drilling Company's chief truckpusher, with all the drivers reporting to him. It was he who found a way through the worst terrain for the huge Kenworth trucks with their massive loads.

In his Land Rover was another Bedouin; in mine was my colleague, Dave McKinnell. Nobody had been down there in three years and our task was to locate and list all the equipment we'd left behind.

The route taken by the big Kenworths had been blown out years before, so we had to pick our way south through the dunes to the Liwa, a wonderful crescent of oases uninhabited during the fierce summer but occupied during a few weeks of the winter by Bedouin, who harvested dates there. The oases were always at the bottom of big slip faces, where the winter rain would collect in a shallow freshwater pool above the salty brine that was found below the sands. A shallow hand-dug well and a bucket and rope system were all that was needed to irrigate the date palms.

We then crossed into the Empty Quarter, our Land Rovers taxed to the limit as we negotiated our way around the dunes. Mohammed's skills in this tough country were awe-inspiring. And then we came to the rigsite I'd visited four years previously, a sad place without its rig, and without even a well. Just rows of steel casing, sacks of mud chemicals and cement. We counted it all up, and then started back north.

Motorbike across Oman

In 1973 I settled into my life in Abu Dhabi town. Work was mostly organising drilling operations for a nine-drilling-rig operation: both exploration – looking for new oil – and development wells to produce oil. I commuted to work on the Bonny along the sea front. One morning, the road was slippery from sea salt and I dropped the bike, skidding along and grinding areas of skin off my arms. The company medic patched me up and I was able to bend straight the damaged parts of the bike. I had some repairing to do, but much of the time there was thick dust both outside and inside my accommodation. The solution was to put the painted bike parts in the fridge while they dried, as this was the only dust-free place. One of my guests got a surprise when he was looking for a cold beer, and could only find black painted motorbike parts.

I did a lot of waterskiing and scuba diving, sharing a boat with my good friend Chris Rivett-Carnac, who had been rig geologist on many of the rigs I had worked on.

One winter, a couple of years later, 11 of us left Abu Dhabi on two bikes and in three Land Rovers and entered Muscat and Oman to explore an unknown land. We also wanted to look at the geology of the cliff faces, which related to the underground geology in Abu Dhabi. This was the plan: me on my much-travelled Bonny, John Pooler on his much-crashed 350 Honda, and then Rick and Wendy, Ken and Penny, Stuart and Jane, Chris and Sara, and Dave in the Land Rovers.

The first snag was securing visas, as Oman was closed to tourists. The official answer was 'no', but perseverance and string-pulling via the diplomatic channels eventually won the day. So after weeks of planning we were finally on our way at the start of Eid al-Fitr, the four-and-a-half-day Muslim holiday celebrating the end of Ramadan.

Oman would prove to be one of the most breathtaking and inaccessible countries in the world, Land Rover country that we dared to enter on bikes. It was 800 miles of gravel plains, tracks over bare rocks, riverbeds of pebbles and finally skirting the very edge of the Rub al-Khali.

Our route began along the road from Abu Dhabi to Al Ain and Buraimi. This was the way to see the desert in style, winding through 300-foot sand dunes, grabbing ice cold beers from the Land Rover on the move.

The bliss came to a sudden end when the Bonny quit on me. Its electric wires had all sawn through each other from the vibration of dirt tracks. Then another short circuit meant I went into a river with no lights and with my air horns blazing, bouncing from rock to rock in pitch-black with the river. I fixed it on the spot; there was no other option. Then, as the sun went down we found a campsite. It was dry and firm but with a lot of

The bike near Khorfakhan

waist-high camel thorn bushes – painful to ride through! After a meal by the campfire, we turned in under a clear starlit sky and were rewarded with the magnificent sight of a meteorite with a long flaming tail.

Next morning was an early start for the mountains. Soon we were travelling between pinnacles of rock. Then suddenly we were in Land Rover country. Crossing wadis of loose stone, the track consisted of two deep wheel ruts with the intervening space spliced off to fit a Land Rover exactly. The roads were now impassable to any four-wheeled vehicle with less ground clearance than this vehicle. On two wheels we were restricted to one rut or the other; John dropped his machine several times when changing between the two.

Down the Wadi al-Jizi

The bike on main road along the Indian Ocean

The valley narrowed and we were at the border post. We were met by the border guards, dressed in long white robes and armed with ancient rifles, ammunition belts and *khanjars* (silver daggers). The border post was well into Oman but was strategically situated where the mountains rise steeply each side of the track. This was the entrance to the notorious Wadi al-Jizi.

Ken and John were both able to conduct a conversation and translate the visas and passport numbers into Arabic, which proved priceless because no one there could read or speak English.

We crossed the barrier – a thin wooden pole between two drums – and immediately the road dropped at one in three (33 per cent), with a loose rocky surface. Fair warning of what was to come. After 150 yards the track levelled out and we were in water. Thereafter we went through what must be one of the wildest tracks in the world. Winding down slopes of bare rock, we crossed and recrossed a cascading stream, across soft gravel, over slippery pebbles, picking our way through boulders. All around us the sides of the wadi rose in ascending towers towards the deep blue sky. And so it went on for five hours.

We reached the coastal plain and the track became corrugated, both bikes spewing oil over us from the forks, providing goo for the dust to stick to. We stopped once at a Bedu camp to refill the jerricans with water from a hand-dug well. The water was hauled up a couple of gallons at a time and tasted delicious. We left a few tins of food in exchange.

We spent the night on the beach in soft sand – no problem for the Land Rovers with their balloon tyres for the Abu Dhabi desert, but hard work on the bikes, especially John's Honda with its low ground clearance. The headman of a nearby village had invited us to coffee and tea, and we returned to drink the customary three cups.

The sun rising in the morning over the Indian Ocean was superb – its own reflection in the sea joined by a mirage so that it looked like an hourglass that became more and more stretched, until it finally snapped in the middle. John had work to do on the Honda, soldering up the throttle cable over the primus petrol cooker. He had ended up the night before driving with the inner cable wrapped round the handlebars, causing acceleration round every left-hand bend. That on top of a 1-inch clutch handle, the rest of which had been left behind in the Wadi al-Jizi. He had also lost the innards of both silencers.

The coast of Oman had been a Portuguese stronghold 400 years ago, and their fortresses survived. We explored one on the seashore, now being slowly eroded away with a forgotten cannon lying on the beach.

Finally we reached fabulous, fabulous Muscat. The mountains swept round in a curve and Muscat lay where they were cut off abruptly by the sea. Deep sheltered coves, high ridges and rock faces falling sheer to the sea. A series of natural fortified harbours. Every prominent rock topped with a castle, every high ridge fortified with a wall. Ancient cannons peeping out everywhere. The inner sanctuary of the town had its own wall, and until three years ago the gates had been closed during the hours of darkness. Anyone on the streets after dark had to carry a lantern.

Into the mountains

The next day's travelling was for all of us the most memorable. Twisting along a graded track through the Sama'il Gap westwards into the mountains with the 11,000-foot Jebel Akhdar towering up to the right. Water crossings, mud villages and forts, date gardens, people waving, *Salam Alaikum* ('Peace be with you'). Omanis wearing their khanjars and belts of .303 bullets round their waists and over their shoulders, and the clear blue sky and hot tropical sun overhead.

John and I crossed the Tropic of Cancer cruising at over 60 mph, riding abreast on the deserted track and setting up a shower of flying stones and dust behind us. Bidbid, Sarur, Sama'il, Mati, Izki to Birkat al Mouz. Then a long wait for the Land Rovers to catch up.

Here we made a detour into a dry wadi. The river had cut a canyon with walls rising 6,000 feet. The strata dipped steeply and all the Middle East rocks of geological interest were displayed in turn. We stopped by a village that was set, complete with its date palms, on a ledge 20 feet above the canyon floor and ancient irrigation channels. At that point the canyon forked and we walked up the smaller and steeper branch. We were soon on bare rock, with snakes scurrying away before us into the nearest pool. We rounded a corner – and there, glistening in the sun, was a deep pool of clear water alongside a flat slab of rock. Hot and dusty as we were, this was the place to be, snakes or no snakes. I was bounding down the wadi like a skier with the big Bonny doing rhythmic parallel turns. John tried to catch up but bent both his wheels.

Back in Birkat we had a look round a ruined fort. John was in a small room taking a photograph when he noticed next to him a tribesman kneeling on a prayer mat. Seeing another and realising he was in a mosque, he decided to get out quickly. He smashed his head on the low ceiling. The resulting gash with its radial drips of blood was a fitting addition to the cuts, bruises and burns he had collected in the Wadi Al- Jizi.

On to find a campsite, the main problem being water, as all the wadis in the area were dry and the wells were usually in the centre of a village. We plumped for an area of dying date palms and I went off into the street of a deserted village to look for *fallajes* (irrigation channels), but all were dry. After a painful encounter with a thorn bush while trying to negotiate some steps, I finally emerged to join the rest to move on up a wadi. The track into it was nigh on impassable, descending as it did on a 30-degree sand and boulder slope. Meanwhile, in the gathering dusk we noticed glints and flashes of eyes and armaments further up the wadi. A group of Bedu were watching us, and not

Track down a Wadi

Wadi in Oman

coming forward to greet us with the customary hospitality. There was a history of rebellion in the area and with the mystery of the deserted village we decided to go back. During tribal conflict, wells were often poisoned by throwing in dead animals. We had to be very careful.

In an attempt to get back up the sand and boulder slope, I crashed the Bonny and had to be pushed up it with the engine racing and the rear wheel showering Penny in sand. John made it – soaring over the top with just his hands clutching the handlebars and the rest of him flying in the breeze.

There was a water well in the dead palms, so we spent our final night there. Everyone slotted into their responsibilities, Ken and Penny getting a fire going, Rick and Chris trying to get a bucket to fill in the well, myself setting the bar up on a Land Rover bonnet, Dave fiddling with paraffin lamps, and Wendy, Sara, Jane and Stuart all hauling boxes of food around. The starlit night was our last. We didn't carry tents, so every night we had fantastic starscapes.

Skirting the edge of the Rub al-Khali

Off again to an early start, as we were to get back to Abu Dhabi that day. Jebel Akhdar was still on our right, more majestic than ever in the long morning shadows. The Rub al-Khali we knew was over the horizon on our left. The air was dry and clear. We sped on at a mile a minute. Now we were climbing and the road started to deteriorate. Rick's Land Rover blew a tyre in a bulldust hole. It had already lost its silencer, had a leaking radiator and a slipping clutch. Chris's had sheared a locating pin on the axle and the rear wheel had worked forward on the spring, causing it to travel diagonally like a crab. Ken's had fractured a hydraulic line and lost its brakes. This country was taxing even Land Rovers to their limit.

The road deteriorated to two ruts in a boulder-strewn slope. The sun was now well up and the temperature rising. We pressed on, crossing many dry shallow wadis and travelling through sparse vegetation. For the most part the bikes travelled together with the Land Rovers behind. I stopped to film John crossing a particularly soft and dusty patch. John's camera by this time was so full of dust it had to be operated with a pair of pliers.

The track became softer and we were soon in sand. One of slides on the concentric 930 carburettors on the Bonny jammed. A quick strip-down and copious quantity of penetrating oil freed it. Half an hour later we had lost sight of the Land Rovers. A 15-minute wait failed to establish contact, and we thought we must have split. In fact the bikes were far faster than the Land Rovers on this surface, and we didn't realise we were in deep sand surrounded by small but active dunes. We were now on the very edge of the Rub al-Khali, without water or spare petrol – the first two rules of the desert violated. We also had no food, tools or spares, as everything was in the Land Rovers. We had no radios, so our only communication was line of sight, mostly by looking for the dust trails. But we had to keep moving fast in the soft patches to avoid sinking in.

At As Sunainah we found a freshly graded gravel road to the border, so we stopped there. The others, battered and bruised by the Land Rovers, met up with us an hour later. They were annoyed that we'd separated and gone on, as they'd spent a couple of hours looking for us. The story we heard was that they'd spent most of the time drinking tea in a village where they had been offered 1,000 riyals (£1,000 approximately) for three of our four girls. Who was the unlucky fourth? They would all like to have known!

Through the border there was the wildest ride of all – leaping from bump to bump and sliding on the sand in the dark. I was following a Land Rover's tail light very closely, in the thick dust – like dense fog, with visibility down to a few yards – and John,

PC in dusty terrain in Oman

who'd been following my tail light as his headlight was askew, narrowly missed a tree and went clean through a bush instead.

We made it back to Abu Dhabi at ten at night to face electric lights and air conditioning. The end of a dream and back to work again. I was lucky to have survived 25 accidents, mostly at low speed on sand and gravel. I always managed to get on top of the bike as it laid over, avoiding injury.

We'd travelled deep into the desert and back again. We'd seen amazing beauty and history untouched by modernisation, before it opened up to visitors. But beyond the sands lay an entire world, and I was planning on exploring many more mountain ranges.

3 Mountaineering in unexplored ranges

The volcano was closed off, as it was erupting and too dangerous, but we managed to get on board a helicopter with a government geologist who was here to take temperature measurements on the lava flow. We flew over the top of the eruption and quickly turned away, as the heat was too intense. Red lava pools were bubbling below us. Then we landed on top of the flow so the geologist could take his measurements from a gap in the skin above the lava. It poured through like a burning river and we had to be careful not to break through the crust. The sheer power of this lava flow was awesome.

The Himalayas

When I was working in the camp at Tarif in Abu Dhabi, we had a regimen of 96 days' non-stop work, often 24 hours a day, followed by a 32-day break. I decided that in my next break I would fulfil a lifelong ambition to explore the Himalayas. However, I only had tropical gear, and I couldn't find any shops selling climbing gear. I wasn't planning on going via the UK or USA, where I could buy all the kit I needed, but fortunately, a geologist, Mick Storey, had some boots and weatherproof clothing, which he kindly lent me.

In 1971 I flew out via India, and saw the Himalayas from 300 miles away – an immense white wall of rock and snow to the north. I stopped in legendary Kathmandu to buy provisions. I was introduced to an English mountaineer who lent me his rucksack and rented me his tent. I stayed in a cheap hostel, which was memorable for its huge rats scurrying among the guests sleeping rough on the floor. Marijuana was legal in Nepal, and it was sold by the kilo on large weighing scales; as a result in the evenings, many people were stoned, singing traditional songs with incense in the air.

I flew in an old DC-3 to the (then) small village of Pokhara – a delightful place with, at the time, no road access and therefore no vehicles. There I met up with a contact, and was introduced to Tsultrim, a Tibetan porter who would show me the way up to Annapurna. The Annapurna massif was to the north, reaching 26,545 feet, the world's tenth highest mountain. It had only been climbed three times by that point, and until 1970 just once. Most of these high peaks were unclimbed. Even today Annapurna is the world's most dangerous high mountain, with a summit-to-fatality ratio of 3:1.

When I travelled to the region in 1971 very few people had visited the area, and no foreigners had been there until just 15 years earlier. I was hoping to get to a big basin known as the Sanctuary, which was sacred to the local people, the Gurung. Eggs, meat and women were prohibited from the Sanctuary.

We bought local food, mainly rice and dhal. And then we started climbing, up 60-degree stairs cut into the hillsides, and I rapidly learned how hard life was for the Nepalese. The villages were connected only by paths.

Icy river crossing on the way to Annapurna

PC at Machapuchare, Nepal

Whereas at lower elevations pack animals could be used, higher up everything had to be carried on foot. Tsultrim had a big basket with a strap around his head, and a 45-lb load. We swapped loads for a while, and I found that the compression on my neck was agonising; the load on my legs, and on my heart, was huge. No wonder life expectancy was only 24 years here. We climbed from 2,500 feet to 6,000 feet, welcomed by children in all the villages we passed, with their hands together, saying 'Namaste'. That night we slept at a tiny farm, in a small shed for the animals.

Next morning, the path took us over a ridge, then down to Landruk, to cross the raging Modi Khola river on a rickety log bridge. We then climbed another 2,000 feet up an endless staircase to Ghandruk. The views were staggering. We were invited into another tiny farmhouse, belonging to an ex-Ghurkha soldier. He proudly showed me the photos of his days in the British Army. The Ghurkhas had – and still have – a fearsome reputation, especially due to their use of the big *kukri* knives, which incorporate a notch to stop blood dripping onto the handle, making it slippery.

We joined the family for dinner prepared over a wood fire. Popcorn was cooked in a large frying pan suspended from the ceiling on chains. The next day, we climbed up to 7,300 feet, down to 5,600 feet, up to 7,700 feet, down to 6,300 feet, and up again in steady rain, above the highest village, where we set up the tent in a terraced field 4 feet wide. From here on we would have to carry all our food with us, and we had a live chicken in a sack in Tsultrim's basket. There was bamboo here that we could use for firewood. Over the glowing embers, Tsultrim told me of how when he was a baby his mother had escaped from Tibet, carrying him in her basket over a high pass in the Himalayas, when the Chinese invaded in 1951.

We were now in the Modi Khola Gorge, 18,000 feet (~5,500 metres) deep, reputed to be the deepest in the world. On the other side was the sacred Machapuchare, at 22,943 feet (6,993 metres) the world's highest unclimbed peak.[6] It was majestic, with a sharp, sheer look to it, shaped like a fishtail, hence its name. Swirling clouds were tinted red in the setting sun. We climbed up this narrow gorge to 10,000 feet and then slept under a huge boulder. During the night, a frozen drizzle came down and it was too cold to sleep, so we huddled around our bamboo fire.

Next we collected firewood, as there would be none above us. As we had no cooker, the wood we carried was for cooking as well as surviving the night. River crossing was dangerous – one bridge in particular had four parallel logs with flat boulders laid on top, no handrail, and thick ice where the river had splashed over it. Crossing this bridge with a pack was a scary balancing act; Tsultrim slipped and his basket lost a lot of its contents, which crashed thousands of feet down the scree to the Modi Khola below. We lost some supplies, but fortunately retrieved the tent, which was now essential for survival.

We climbed over a boulder field, as the gorge opened up to reveal the staggering views of the Annapurna mountains. We were up with the glaciers now, at 13,600 feet. Tsultrim, deeply concerned about the cold, refused

Tsultrim at Annapurna

6 At the time of writing this is still the case.

to go any higher. We pitched the tent between two boulders, to trap some heat. After our dinner, I tried to get a little sleep in the tent, but it was too cold. I wore all of my clothing but still shivered all night. I pulled my spare underpants over my head to act as a scarf, and I wore my shorts over my head. Ice built up steadily inside the tent. Tsultrim kept the fire going all night, but everything more than a foot from the flames was frozen solid. I swigged some hot coffee but it froze solid in my cup as I drank it.

I knew we should not be this high without mountaineering equipment, especially during winter. We had to get down quickly, and we descended 6,500 feet. We got back to Ghandruk and spent the night in another village house not high enough to stand in – yet with, proudly displayed in a back room, a photograph of the Queen of England. When a thunderstorm came down and carpeted the high gorge in deep snow, I knew I had Tsultrim to thank for our not having been stuck up there with our rudimentary and inadequate clothing and equipment.

Soon we were back to the busier footpaths of the lower elevations. One morning the rising sun lit up the whole Annapurna in a magnificent spectacle, gleaming with its fresh snow. At Pokhara I said farewell to Tsultrim and wrote him

Tsultrim cooking below Annapurna

a certificate of recommendation. I went to the field where the DC-3 was due to land, to find that cattle were being cleared off it. There was no terminal building, just a set of scales for passengers and luggage. As there were more passengers than seats, it was a mad scramble to get on board, the crowd chasing the plane as it slowed to a halt.

After this incredible experience, I flew on to Thailand and Japan, then took a ship across the straits from Honshu to Hokkaido in heavy snow and a howling gale. I boarded a train to Kuchan, sitting next to a Japanese student who had been studying English for 10 years. He had never spoken to a foreigner before. I spent a few days skiing in the deepest, lightest powder I had ever encountered – so light that I sometimes skied in it over my head. I stayed in a Japanese youth hostel for the week, learning the culture and eating only with chopsticks – even fried eggs, steaks and soups. Kuchan was buried under 15 feet of snow and people were constantly shovelling the stuff off their roofs. The town was connected by steam train, which made a magnificent sight as it ploughed its way through the powdery snow. But sadly for me, the time had come for me to head back to work in the desert.

Mountaineering in the Wild West

In 1978, while I was working for BP on their projects on the North Slope of Alaska, I was living in San Francisco. This gave me a chance to do some more demanding mountaineering. My first big climb was with Mike Davidson, a BP geologist, on Mount Shasta, a 14,179-foot (~4,300-metre) snow-covered smouldering volcano in northern California, at the southern end of the Cascades. We climbed a ridge made up of loose volcanic debris cemented with ice, then camped at 11,000 feet, cutting a ledge for my little tent out of a steep ice field called Avalanche

PC on Mount Tamalpais

North Palisade and the U-notch in the centre

Ice climbing up a frozen waterfall

Gulch as a blizzard set in. We got to 13,000 feet the next day, where there was a volcanic fumarole, but Mike had a bad case of altitude sickness and we had to turn back. A thunderstorm was rumbling below us, too. We glissaded down, sliding on our backs using our ice axes as brakes, dropping 6,000 feet in a few minutes into the blackness of the storm.

Bill Bredar, a geologist friend also working on the Alaskan projects, joined me on a climb up Mount Whitney, at 14,505 feet (~4,420 metres) the highest mountain in America's Lower 48,[7] in what we believed to be the fastest-ever round trip from San Francisco – 48 hours – not because we were trying to set a record but because we were only allowed a two-day weekend. It was a gruelling trip, much of it done at night, and in the last 1,000 feet I got acute altitude sickness due to the rapid drop in pressure. So we ran all the way down, much of it in the dark – and then I couldn't find my backpack, which I'd stored in a crevice in the rock. I thought a bear might have stolen it, so I slept with my feet inside a small pack in the sub-zero cold. When day eventually dawned, I saw my pack with its nice warm sleeping bag in it right there, in a crack a few yards from me.

Bill was from Colorado. He was a real mountain goat, and if he hadn't become a geologist he would have joined the Mountain Rescue. Although I had done a lot of mountaineering in Scotland, the Himalayas and

---

7 The contiguous states, ie excluding Alaska and Hawaii.

Bill Bredar at the top of the U-notch on North Pallisade

PC and Bill on North Palisade summit

the Andes, I had never done anything seriously technical. We practised on rock crags on Mount Tamalpais, above my home in Mill Valley, and in winter I learned to ice-climb on frozen waterfalls in the High Sierra.

My biggest test was joining him on a climb of North Palisade, a technical climb whatever route you take. First, we climbed a 55-degree ice gully

Bill coming down North Palisade

40

called the U-notch. Every few minutes, a huge rock would come thundering down, dislodged by the sun melting the ice further up. I saw one of them heading straight for Bill, and he ducked behind a crag as it exploded into a million pieces. Next, we had to climb a long, vertical rock section, installing chocks and wedges as we went up. It was incredibly satisfying to put all our training into practice. A long traverse across a cliff face, then an ice field, and we were on top at 14,242 feet (4,341 metres). I had a blistering altitude headache. We abseiled down the vertical section, which would have been exhilarating except for my thumping head, and I was especially careful not to make a mistake.

Mountaineering in Patagonia

In 1979 I fulfilled a lifelong ambition to go to Patagonia. I wanted to see Cerro Torre, reputedly the world's most difficult unclimbed mountain, shaped like the Eiffel Tower but ten times higher, and often crowned with a huge mushroom of ice where the Roaring Forties swept over it, freezing snow onto its summit. I had seen a picture of it and was intrigued.

I started off on an Aero Peru flight, which failed to take off and had to be towed back off the runway. On a second attempt it took me to Lima, where I saw the remains of the Spanish conquistador Pizarro, the man who with 150 soldiers and three muskets conquered the Inca army of over a million with a combination of daring and treachery, thus destroying one of the most fascinating cultures in history.

Then to Buenos Aires, where on New Year's Eve I had a close brush with death. I had been drinking alone in a bar to celebrate the *Año Nuevo*, when I went to settle the bill and took off my money belt to get some change out. The barman saw my two $100 bills and decided the bill was $200. I was amazed and refused, whereupon the bouncers started roughing me up, giving me throat-cutting gestures. I was planning to run for it when two gangsters entered, wearing leather holsters. I had no illusions as to my fate, so bolted for the door and mingled, James Bond style, into the carnival atmosphere outside on the hot summer night. I hid in doorways and changed

Fitzroy in high winds

41

PC swimming below Fitzroy

Glacier below Fitzroy

my route down narrow, crowded streets. Buenos Aires was notorious for murder and kidnap, and I had no desire to be another unrecorded unsolved statistic – 95 per cent of murders in Argentina were never investigated.

South to Rio Gallegos, an oilfield town, where I tried to find a bus or plane to El Calafate, at the foot of the Patagonian Andes; but there was no public transport, so I hitchhiked for the first time since my student days. I slept at night in a bivvy sack, much smaller and lighter than a tent. I cooked chicken soup on a candle. Traffic was sparse, and once I waited 13 hours for a lift, then travelled with a group of geophysicists doing a seismic survey for oil. We crossed La Pampa, the dry and windswept plains that the gauchos roamed on their tough Patagonian horses; the wind was so strong it blew stones through the air, and vehicles had stone guards over their windscreens. Halfway across, in the middle of nowhere, I got another lift, this time with a wedding party; a red-haired Argentinian with Welsh roots was getting married at a crossroads consisting of a gas station and a Justice of the Peace Station. 'I'm going to shoot myself today,' he said. 'A bad day is a wedding day.' His family of origin were all McDonalds and Davidsons, and his bride was Italian – a typical Argentinian mix.

Next morning I was waiting at the gas station in case a vehicle came by, when an American got out of a truck coming the other way. 'Geoff Radford,' he said, extending a hand by way of introduction. 'Been hearing about you the last two days. Been looking forward to meeting you.' He'd thought I was a famous English solo mountaineer, so I was sorry to disappoint him. In fact Geoff and his colleagues, Chris Blatter and James Jennings, were planning to climb Fitzroy, adjacent to Cerro Torre. They'd been driving from Alaska for a year, and had had some of their gear stolen. Geoff had been sent east by the others to find a high-altitude cooker, and when he turned up I decided to join his expedition, trading my petrol-burning stove for a 350-km ride in a rented truck from El Calafate to Fitzroy, and agreeing to help backpack their gear across the rivers to set up their base camp.

When I headed west with Geoff, I soon saw a thin silver line on the horizon – the Andes, over 100 miles away in this crystal-clear southern hemisphere air. All four of us then headed north on more dirt tracks to Fitzroy, where we pitched camp. For me this was the height of luxury after several nights in my bivvy sack. We started hauling 80 lb (36 kg) packs across deep, raging mountain rivers, and up the foothills. Sometimes we crossed the rivers at night, which was extremely risky. These rivers were fast and dangerous, and had reportedly drowned a previous climber. However, we later heard the true story: he had been caught sleeping with a gaucho's woman, and shot.

Then there it was – Cerro Torre, the sky tower – a rock needle thousands of feet high surrounded by swirling storm clouds roaring past, its top in the clouds. Next to it were several smaller, or broader, versions of these volcanic cores, including Fitzroy. The range was absolutely magnificent, the most spectacular mountain scenery in the world.

I became aware of a distant periodic roaring and rumbling noise, getting louder as we gained altitude. It sounded like glacier ice, but falling. We clambered to the treeline and pitched the base camp, hanging our climbing equipment on ropes slung between the short sparse trees. Above the treeline any tents would be swept away by the gales so there would be only one way to survive the night: in snow caves. We carried ice axes and snow shovels.

I helped the other two above the tree line and across the big glacier. Crevasses were easy to see, as loose snow had been blown away, leaving hard ice edges with blue chasms between. Most were small enough to step across. The roaring noise was close by now, seeming like a mountain dragon in this far-off land. We came over a ridge to see a stupendous sight, a glacier rolling down to a 1,500-foot cliff, where it cascaded over the edge, dropping huge icebergs off that crashed against the rocks at the bottom and landed in a lake full of broken chunks of ice. It was primeval.

We summited a peak but could not stand on it, as the wind would have blown us off the mountain. On the way back, we had to jump a chasm over a stream, and as I was in mid-air a huge gust of wind blew me hard, nearly dropping me into the lake thousands of feet below. We found another lake, full of icebergs, and I went for a swim in the zero-degree water.

Then I left my friends on their lonely journey up the glacier. I later heard that after ten attempts Geoff had finally made it to the summit, coming across the remains of a frozen climber on the way.

I continued south to Ushuaia, the southernmost town in the world. The first 300 km (~185 miles) was in a truck with no brakes. It stopped at a little house to deliver provisions to an alleged Nazi war criminal in hiding. Later, I dropped in on a bar full of drunken Argentinean soldiers, preparing to fight a war with Chile over three disputed islands. When they heard that I was English, they started shouting 'Malvinas!' I realised that they meant the Falkland Islands, and rashly said so, whereupon there were some throat-cutting gestures. The men were bristling with grenades and machine guns. I left quickly.

I melted into the forest and hid my backpack in a crevice in the rocks, then climbed through dense rainforest, which was exhausting, as rotted tree trunks formed a hollow floor with the solid surface often 30 feet below. A fall through a crack there would be as deadly as falling into a crevasse. I was able to make some progress where a forest fire had cleared the trees, then I found a better route over an avalanche trail, which had swept the trees away. I got to a ridge, where the wind was blowing rocks into the air. Later, above the treeline, I saw it – the Cape Horn island group, on a beautiful summer day with the gentlest of winds. It was not what I'd expected from my childhood seafaring stories of the great clipper ships, but I could imagine the storms.

I returned to San Francisco with memories of this beautiful land – Tierra del Fuego, 'Land of Fires', where Joshua Slocum, the first person to sail singlehanded around the world, spread carpet tacks on his decks to ward off the natives who one night had attempted to board before leaping back into the water, howling.

Jumping out of aeroplanes

One day, four of us decided to form a parachuting club, calling it 'The Laid-Back Flyers'. We ran off some T-shirts with our logo: 'Try it in the Sky'. We went to Pope Valley in the Napa valley to learn how to do it. We practised on an aeroplane in the hanger, and I noticed grooves on the wing struts where reluctant beginners had tried to hang on in their moment of truth, scratching the paintwork. 'Once you're out the door there's no turning back,' said the instructor. 'You can't come back in. I've got a hammer for your knuckles if you don't let go.' To simulate the landing we practised jumping off a 12-foot cupboard onto concrete. Then we went to see the parachutes being packed – rather moth-eaten Second World War military surplus, with sullen-looking students doing the packing. I hoped they liked us Brits, and weren't on drugs.

We went up, and the higher we went the more a horrible truth sunk in: there was now only one way down. I suffered from vertigo, and was doing this to try to get over my fear of heights. Simon Dance, a petroleum engineer who worked for me at BP was first out, screaming 'Ahhhh!' as he dropped away. Then there was a banging on the tailplane next to me. I thought he was caught on the tail and trying to let us know. I was later told it was just his static line shackle.

I was last out. I crawled to the door to the right of the pilot's seat, where the roar of the slipstream off the prop drowned everything. I checked to make sure my static line was attached to something solid, and to my dismay saw it tied to the pilot's seat, which was a lightweight aluminium lawn chair sitting on the floor without any bolts. I had visions of my static line pulling the pilot and his chair out of the plane on top of me, then getting wrapped around the tailplane.

'Put it onto something more solid,' I yelled at the instructor.

'What?' He looked annoyed. 'Can't hear you. Get out of the plane.'

My legs were dangling over the edge as the countryside passed a mile under my boots. I now had to do a stunt like a flying circus: get across the wheel, 5 feet out. I grabbed the strut, this one also with fingernail grooves, and swung across to put my right foot onto the wheel rubber. I let my feet go, flying in the breeze horizontally in the slipstream. The only reason I let go was that I was convinced this wasn't happening and that it was probably just a bad nightmare.

However when I dropped like a stone, I realised this was for real, and I started counting to five slowly. If I got to five and the chute hadn't opened, I had to jettison the main parachute and release the reserve – a tricky business, as the two chutes could tangle with each other if not done properly, with only 10 seconds to go before hitting the ground at 120 mph. 'One thousand … two one thousand … three one thousand … four one thousand.' My shouts sounded hollow and I reached to my shoulders to hook into the rings to release the chute. Suddenly I was shaken violently and pulled to a stop. I looked up, trying not to move in case something released itself and I fell out of the harness. The pale khaki parachute was billowing gently and I noticed several patches in it. I had just dropped about 1,000 feet – the same as the Eiffel Tower. The plane was a dot overhead, and I couldn't see any novice parachutists being dragged behind the tailplane.

As soon as I got used to it, it felt wonderful. It was quiet, and the sight of California's lakes and mountains was stunning. By pulling on one side or the other, I could change the view, and even spin through 360 degrees. However, the ground was coming up, and I steered for the circle with the target flagpole in the middle of it. Suddenly, I realised I was too accurate and might impale myself on it. I landed a few feet away, and shared stories with the others. They'd had their share of fun, a knee twisted during landing, a narrow escape from a 33,000-volt power line, and in Simon's case, a damaged groin.

We dared each other to do a second jump, but nearly changed our minds when we went to the clubhouse, where a whole lot of skydivers were sitting by a swimming pool, complete with crutches and slings. Indeed, while we were there, we saw an accident. A skydiver's parachute failed to open properly, and he tumbled thousands of feet out of control. When he finally popped his reserve chute, he was falling so fast that most of the strings broke and the parachute was only partly open. He hit the ground with a tremendous thud, as everyone raced off to see if he was alive. Fire engines and ambulances arrived to haul him off to hospital.

My WW II military surplus parachute

We all did the second jump anyway. Mine was just as terrifying as the first, as during the freefall I ended up head down rather than in the proper frog position. Later, the club was closed down, after six people were reported to have been killed among rumours of malfunctions, suicides and dares to pop the chute late.

Over unexplored mountains: Alaska's Brooks Range

'We can drop you off at Last Lake, but we can't pick you up from there. It's not long enough for us to take off with a load.' Tom Olsen, manager of a bush plane outfit with the impressive name Air North, was shouting down the phone from Fairbanks.

'Okay,' I replied. 'We'll be going from south to north, then. Can you pick us up from Schrader Lake?'

'Sure, but don't be surprised if we're a few days late. The weather's often bad in the pass.'

In northeast Alaska there are no roads or footpaths, so our only access to my next climbing destination would be by floatplane. I was planning to realise a lifetime dream: to cross an unexplored region of a mountain range. I got my chance in 1980, while working on the Arctic Alaska North Slope oilfields.

Last Lake to Schrader involved 100 miles of walking and climbing over the continental divide, which separates the watersheds that drain into the Pacific and the Arctic oceans. Keith Gordon, a BP engineer, and I were planning to cross the range. We were headed for the eastern part of the Brooks Range, the highest mountains of the North American Arctic, and we hoped to do an ice climb on Mount Chamberlain if there was time.

'I've borrowed a Colt Python,' Keith announced over the phone, 'and I've got 50 rounds of .357 Magnum bullets. They're supposed to be okay for grizzlies.'

Good. We had all the gear we needed. At Fort Yukon, Nick, our Cessna pilot, flew us off from an oxbow of the Yukon River. Forest fires caused by lightning were everywhere, and the air at 8,000 feet smelt of wood smoke 'Visibility's been down to 2 miles most of the summer,' Nick shouted across.

We saw no sign of humanity all 150 miles to Last Lake. And then, when Nick had dropped us off and pressed the starter button to take off again, nothing happened. Fortunately, another floatplane flew in and agreed to relay a message for help. Nick had no tools, no sleeping bag and a useless radio. I was amazed. 'I'll just sit and enjoy the scenery,' he said, and we left him swatting mosquitoes inside the plane. He was the last person we spoke to until we got to Schrader Lake.

The journey started with an unpleasant flavour. Liberal rubbing with mosquito repellent failed to stop us breathing and swallowing hordes of bugs. Our repellent was the strongest in Alaska and the directions warned it would dissolve plastic. But the summer was still here, unfortunately. Then recent digging marks and wet mud by a riverbank told us a grizzly was around, so I blew my whistle and jiggled my pack to ring the bell attached to it. And we practised with the revolver.

The first three days were hiking up mostly unnamed river valleys and across two major rivers, the Sheenjek and the east fork of the Chandalar. Bog blueberries and alpine bearberries supplemented our diet. Keith grilled a couple of grayling over the ashes of a twig fire for breakfast one morning. The size and remoteness of this vast land gradually sank in. 'How about a brew of cocoa and Jello before the climb?' Keith suggested. 'Sounds good. I can't make up my mind whether to take this glacier valley to the left or the dark V-shaped one up there. I think we'll need the compass.' We had many surprises in the navigation as the only map showed 36 square miles in 1 square inch, and many mountains,

One of many river crossings

lakes and rivers were simply not mapped – probably never surveyed from the ground before, either, as the maps had been derived from aerial photographs.

We plumped for the V-shaped valley. But then the river sank into a canyon and we were forced to go up the side on a fragile scree of shale, mud and coral limestone. We had been following tracks of bear and moose to get through the scrub willow in the riverbeds, then caribou trails on the tundra and now wild Dall sheep tracks over the scree.

Only now there were no more tracks. I had the feeling we shouldn't be here. We were both setting off big rockslides and had to keep moving to avoid being carried down with them. In one place the whole slope had clearly slid over the edge of the cliff recently, into the canyon thousands of feet below. This route was extremely dangerous; we could easily disappear without trace.

'We've got to get off this stuff,' Keith shouted.

'I know,' I agreed, 'but I don't know about the river crossing.'

We descended carefully, as if on an avalanche. When we reached the river, Keith had a long stick he'd brought up from the Chandalar and he jammed it in a rock then pole-vaulted across, complete with 50-lb pack. He threw the stick back and I had to do the same. Thereafter we referred to it as Pole Vault Creek; since nothing in this area had been named we gave them our own based on our experience of them: Gym Shoe River, Devil's Toothbrush, Hanging Glacier Peak and so on.

First to go over an unnamed Arctic pass

'I don't think we're going to make it to the pass today.' We were both dead tired, and the weather looked mean. At least there was no problem with darkness since there was none. I needn't have brought my miner's lamp.

'I hereby declare this Camp Three!' Keith announced, jamming his ice axe into a piece of peat moss among the rocks. Soon the petrol stove was roaring and a dinner of freeze-dried food was on the way. We buried our food in caches some distance from the tent so that grizzlies would not interrupt our sleep.

PC approaching the pass in Brooks Range

Keith Gordon and Romanzof mountains

A light patter on the tent increased during the night and the wind got up. By midday, we kept hearing noises like thunder. I thought it was landslides and rock falls on the other side of the pass.

When the storm started to abate I ventured out into the barren, grey, foggy scenery to collect water. The mountains had a fresh sprinkling of snow. The river had swollen enormously and its water was too thick to drink. Huge boulders were rolling along its bottom in the flood – it was these that had been creating the thundering noises. It was a good job we'd crossed it the night before.

At the pass we paused to take a photograph of ourselves holding a tea towel with 'Drink at Jack Mann's Exeter Inn, Thorverton, Devon' emblazoned across it. Jack had given it to me on condition that I send him a photo of it in a suitably remote part of the world. Keith and I lingered there, savouring the moment; we were probably the first westerners to have travelled here. Since the central Brooks Range was quoted in *The Book of Lists* as being the most unexplored of the ten most unexplored parts of the world, I felt that this was just the spot. We were 300 miles from the nearest bar, and probably the only people in a 3,000-square-mile radius. Our only company was a lemming, and a few Dall sheep up in the clouds. Actually, I'd felt honoured to receive the tea towel and I hoped that our photograph would end up in the till, along with the Mount Everest and Empty Quarter ones.

Downhill at last. No scree or marsh for a bit allowed progress up to our maximum speed of 1.5 mph, passing unnamed mountains and unmapped glaciers. The temperature plummeted, signifying the end of the Arctic summer and emphasising our progress northwards. The browns and reds of autumn intensified.

Miles and miles of trudging through marshy tundra and past endless pingos brought us to views of glaciers and the wide expanse of the North Slope. By this time we were both suffering from old leg injuries playing up – Keith's right knee from a rugby accident and my right foot from a bad parachute landing. There were crunching and grinding noises coming from my foot, which seemed to have tendon and bone failures. It had better not fail, as Keith wouldn't be able to drag me, and we were too far from help. This was still before the days of mobile

Keith Gordon at the pass, a first

Keith keeping the Colt 357 Magnum dry

phones and sat phones, which today have taken most of the risk out of this type of expedition. Then we found our way was blocked by a river too high and fast to cross, so we set camp in another gathering storm.

Next morning we headed up the river looking for a crossing place while lots of marmots clucked at us from the entrances to their burrows. This area is free of snow and ice for only two months a year, and the marmots were feverishly gathering food in preparation for the first snowstorm, due probably in a week or two. A bear had been around, judging from the way these burrows had been ripped up. Then the river sank into a canyon and we had no option but to backtrack and go down into the gorge.

We usually did our river crossings with our pack waistbands undone to allow a quick release in case of a fall. Not this one – we couldn't afford any wobbling, since below us was a roaring mess of white water disappearing between the two cliffs. A slip would have been fatal. So with ice axes plunging in for balance, feet delicately feeling the shapes of the boulders, and fast, icy grey water hip deep we tackled it – quite an experience.

To Alaska's North Slope on foot

Another storm hit us. The wind raged and the tent flogged all night, preventing sleep. We were worried about our food blowing away in the caches, so buried it closer to the tent, considering the wind a bigger hazard than the bears. Snow built on the mountains and new avalanches poured down.

Rain, grey skies and a great sense of space accompanied us on a magnificent walk across brown tundra moors. We set camp in a decaying pingo by Schrader Lake, and next morning we caught four grayling for breakfast.

Then we headed off for Peters Lake, wondering whether the research station we had on our maps was still there. We'd been told it was abandoned. Thoughts drifted to how we would survive the winter if Nick didn't turn up. We decided that the best option would be to build stone walls and hang the tent over the top, insulating it with layers of moss and living off grayling caught through the ice in the permanently dark winter. We didn't want to be dead heroes.

Lo and behold, a radio mast … the sound of a generator … a man walking between two huts … three more huts alongside …

PC on Mount Chamberlain

PC on the North Slope of Alaska at minus 40 degrees C

I banged on the door of one of them. It opened and an Inuit peeped through, brandishing a sawn-off shotgun up my nose. Needless to say, he'd not been expecting to see anyone, and had initially thought we must be grizzlies. He said we could stay in one of the five huts. It had a paraffin stove. Fabulous … our clothes were soon drying out, and we went over to talk to the Inuit. His gun was quite a weapon, able to fire four large slugs simultaneously.

He was called Ralph and had been on his own for two weeks. His job was netting and tagging fish for the Fish and Wildlife Service. He was expecting a visit from his boss to bring provisions, but couldn't raise anyone on the radio. It rained for three days and nobody came. We finished our food. We yarned a lot and Ralph told us tales of his wild life. The knife scars on him indicated that some of his stories might be true.

We ate mostly from the lake: the Arctic char were the best, poached in butter on a heavy cast iron pan. Ralph told us that two weeks ago a woman had lost her eyes, nose and thigh as a result of an encounter with a grizzly where we'd last camped. The Latin name for this animal is *Ursus arctos horribilis*. It seems an apt description.

Nick failed to arrive on the appointed day, or the next day. As he'd never been to Schrader before we thought he might be lost, or even still stuck at Last Lake, swatting mosquitoes and enjoying the scenery.

While we were waiting a spell of good weather allowed us to climb up to the summit ridge of Mount Chamberlain (9,000 feet/2,740 metres), leaping over snow-filled crevasses and cramponing up a 50-degree hard green ice slope. The view from the top was stupendous – the greens and blues of the ice on Chamberlain, cliffs dropping away to an ice field below us on the other side, the glaciated Romanzof Mountains along the eastern horizon, and the Arctic Ocean a dark blue line 50 miles to the north. Keith could see the pack ice beyond the blue (or so he claimed). We came down fast, glissading the last bit in a couple of minutes – it had taken us hours to climb. Keith came to an abrupt stop in a crevasse, and I practised ice-climbing on the crevasse walls.

Ralph's boss finally landed on the lake with the food and flew off to Kaktovik to try and get us the one and only available floatplane in north-east Alaska (an area four times the size of England). We were lucky – a week later the station was to be abandoned for the winter because freeze-up was due in a couple of weeks. That would have been the end of plane access until December, when the ice would be thick enough for a ski-plane. But there were no plans for any planes until summer, so if we'd arrived late we could have had a nine-month wait.

I rang Air North to ask about our pilot, but he had not been heard of for two weeks and never returned. I was told that in Alaska many pilots don't come back, and that this was to be expected.

Ski mountaineering

In 1980 I got into ski mountaineering, which combines cross-country skiing, downhill skiing, rock-climbing and ice-climbing into one sport. I'd tried it in Scotland, and during a short equipment test at Zermatt, using free-heel alpine bindings and downhill skis, but it was very hard going on the flat or uphill. I needed to be able to ski downhill on flimsy cross-county skis that would go fast on the horizontal, so I practised the telemark turn, a technique that had been developed in Norway at the turn of the century for skis without heel bindings. It had been all but forgotten except by a few backcountry skiers. I practised on California's ski runs, much to the amusement of puzzled downhill skiers. Twenty years later the technique would become commonplace, and even fashionable.

There were some memorable trips. The first was at Mount Lassen, a snow-capped volcano in northern California, with Bill Bredar and John Moreland, a rugged Glaswegian mountaineer/geologist who I'd known in Aberdeen from working in the North Sea. John was a world-class mountaineer, with experience on huge vertical rock walls in Baffin Island, way up in the Canadian Arctic. We were unable to climb the volcano, as a huge snowfall dumped on us, and our tents were almost completely buried by morning. It was good to see Bill and John lapping up the challenge as if it was everyday business. But as the going was too slow, the snow was too deep and the visibility was low, we kept to lower elevations.

I then learned to ice-climb on a frozen waterfall near June Lake, just south of the small mountain town of Lee Vining, due east of San Francisco. The night before was rough, as we all slept in the open on the tarmac in a car park in (−17°C) −1°F. But the climbing was exhilarating, hanging from two ice axes or from the tips of my crampons on near-vertical ice.

Trans-Sierra blizzard

Crossing the High Sierra on skis
at Cloud Canyon: a first

Next was the big one, a high-altitude traverse of the High Sierra in 1980, across the highest mountains in the Lower 48 states. This expedition was led by David Beck, one of the world's top ski guides and avalanche experts. There were ten of us, including Susan Beck, a lightly built woman with the most incredible strength and endurance; Andrea Mead-Lawrence, alpine skier and double Olympic gold medal winner; and her nephew Matt, holder of the world record downhill skiing drop – at something like 50,000 vertical feet (15,250 metres) in a day – using heliskiing techniques. This is approximately three Mount Everests, summit to base camp. Compared to them and the six others, I was a relative novice.

I learned that the High Sierra in this region had only been crossed in winter a couple of times before we had got there, the first time only five years previously, by David Beck and Bob Couly, and that we were going to try a new route. There were nine high-altitude passes to cross, each at about 13,000 feet (4,000 metres). Such a place in the Alps would have been well visited, but here it was still pristine. David had brilliantly found a way across that could be mostly covered on skis downhill, with minimal dependence on ice-climbing or long cross-country slogs through snow. This was his territory, and he knew it like no one else. This was only for leading skiers, and I wondered if I was up to it.

Trans-Sierra camp in evening

I got some new gear: steel-edged cross-country skis, thin for fast travel, but very difficult on steep terrain, and stiff leather double boots that were good for rock and ice, and which added some stiffness for the skiing.

Tent at Desolation Wilderness

PC telemarking

PC on Mount Lassen

Plus they were well insulated and comfortable. I weighed everything over and over, getting the pack as light as possible, and bought a tiny Minox camera.

We started with some gruelling climbing through a forest, with our large backpacks. One of the party could not make it, and had to be escorted back down. We camped among bristlecone pine trees, the oldest living things on the planet, some individuals over 4,000 years old. To put that in perspective, it's twice as far back as when Christ was alive, and it's getting close to the age of Stonehenge, construction of which started in c. 3000 BCE. These trees were really gnarly, with twisted trunks caused by the branches growing towards the sun in the south, then the westerly wind blowing them into an anticlockwise corkscrew. Above the treeline we put skins on our skis.

But soon after, we were hit by a blizzard that kept us tent-bound. But we had good tents, looking rather like those of Antarctic explorers such as Scott in the early 20th century, held up by a single ski in the middle so as to save the weight of tent poles. Then we went on a steep traverse, about 50 degrees, to Milestone Pass. This was dangerous, as a fall could be unstoppable, so we roped up and put on crampons, with our skis on our packs. One of our party slipped and triggered an avalanche, sliding hundreds of feet down. David had brought two avalanche rescue dogs, which wore dark mountain goggles to prevent snow blindness. One of these took off after our mountaineer in case he was buried, but thankfully he'd settled on top of the snow and did not need digging out.

After Milestone Pass, I had a desperate time with altitude sickness. I climbed down a steep rock and ice slope, and then skied a steep section with a blinding headache. Skiing was incredibly difficult. We had three-pin bindings and no heel clamps, so it was almost impossible to perform downhill parallel turns. The telemark technique I'd practised was graceful, but now, with a 40-lb pack on my back, and crusty, icy snow ahead of me, it was very difficult to pull off.

As I got to lower elevations, my headache disappeared, my confidence returned, and I was able to do some sweeping telemark turns, pack on my back, gazing at some stunning views over snowfields and craggy mountains. But the sun glare was blinding, even with my very dark glacier glasses, with their round lenses reminiscent of those used by the Everest team in 1952. We covered up with glacier cream, hats and bandanas, but got burned in places hard to reach, like the roofs of our mouths and inside our nostrils, as the glare bounced back off the snow.

Then Colby Pass, Triple Divide Peak and Glacier Lake, followed by a long traverse round the top of Cloud Canyon, to Glacier Ridge and Dead Man Canyon. Some of these places had only been named in the previous five years. Past a cliff to a V-shaped notch called Farewell Gap, and then we were over the high mountains and dropping into a long, wide meadow. Skiing was idyllic; the air temperature was now above freezing, so we had the superb 'corn snow' – sugary and loose on a still-frozen base. The slope was perfect, and we skied for hours in a swooshing noise, gradually getting into trees again, without the need to pole along or do the difficult telemarks, which usually involved some serious 'crash and burns'.

We were on top of a river flowing under the snow, and came upon a place where it surfaced, at the bottom of a 10-foot-deep snow crater. We all stripped off our foul-smelling clothing and jumped into the freezing water under the hot sun, then sat on our packs to dry off.

However, when we got into the trees the snow became patchy, and we were sliding our way over pinecones and streams. My skis stopped dead on a rough surface and I did a monumental face plant, as there was nothing to stop my boots twisting forward, and my pack buried my face into the ground. Soon we were back in inhabited land, to hear that the US military had suffered a blow in trying to rescue the American hostages in Teheran, suffering an accident that had crippled the effort. It had been a refreshing break to have been away from this sort of news, in the beauty of the mountains, where our world was ice, snow and rocks, with the camaraderie of friends, and the challenge of skiing with our thin skis and huge packs.

Volcanoes

When I visited Santorini in 1974, en route to the idyllic island of Folegandros in the Greek Aegean, I became intrigued by volcanoes. There was a caldera where a Minoan city had once been 3,500 years ago, its disappearance probably the inspiration for the legend of Atlantis. During the 1990s my wife Bonnie and I took a series of holidays to visit some of the world's most famous and interesting volcanoes.

My first exposure to an active volcano had been in the 1980s, when I flew over Mount St Helens over 100 times while commuting between San Francisco, Seattle and Anchorage. It was a beautiful, classic snow-white stratovolcano shape, with the blue Spirit Lake at its base. It reminded me of Mount Shasta, which I had climbed with Mike Davidson.

In 1980 I flew over Mount St Helens five days before it erupted, blowing the top off in a huge explosion of ash, poisonous gases and rock that killed more than 50 people and flattened forests for miles. Ash fell out over much of North America. The eruption had been well forecast, with altimeters and tilt meters monitoring the growing mound of viscous lava under the mountain. The forces that caused the explosion are deep below in the Pacific Ocean plate, which grinds under the North American plate to a depth where heat and friction cause the rock to melt. Because it's an ocean plate the moisture embedded in it melts the magma, which then forces its way upwards through a combination of buoyancy and fracturing.

Two months prior to the explosion, the snow on the mountain started to melt and earthquakes grew in intensity. However, even though it was clear that an eruption was imminent, the volcano blew out sideways instead of upwards, so the destruction was far greater than forecast. For the next two years, there were beautiful red sunsets over the Pacific as the last of the sun's rays caught the ash high up in the stratosphere.

My next flight over Mount St Helens revealed a different volcano, the top blown off and a huge crater inside with the north side breached, where a combination of a colossal landslide and the violent eruption had allowed all the debris to be ejected. It was now grey and smoking, as was the flattened forest surrounding it. The same effect would have been achieved by a nuclear bomb. In successive years, I noticed a new peak building inside the crater as a mound of viscous lava built up inside. Eventually, it will renew its classic volcano shape, and then erupt again.

While living in San Francisco I had been acutely aware of the movement of the tectonic plates. While there I went through four major earthquakes, one of which cracked all the walls in my office and caused the reflection of our skyscraper in the building opposite to sway back and forth. My property boundaries at 645 Sequoia Valley Road were off by 20 feet, the distance that the San Andreas Fault had moved in 1906 in the space of a minute. It had thrown all the survey data off.

Colombia, where I worked off and on from 1983 to 1990, was another active earthquake and eruption area. The earthquakes were smaller in magnitude than those in California, but more dangerous, as Colombia's brick buildings could not survive as well as the steel skyscrapers and wooden houses of the American state. While I was there, the Nevado del Ruiz erupted, causing a huge mudslide that destroyed the town of Armero, killing over 30,000. Some of our team went to help in the rescue efforts.

My time working for BP in San Francisco had been memorable for more reasons than one. It was then that I had first met I met Bonnie Rollyson, a petroleum geologist finalising her degree in Fairbanks, Alaska. She would cross the Pacific and Atlantic Oceans with me, and work with me on a big project in Colombia. We married in 1989, and we went on to share many more adventures together.

Active Krakatoa

Krakatoa, off the west coast of Java, had fascinated me since I was a child. The entire island had blown up in 1883, with colossal loss of life, mainly from the 150-foot tsunamis which devastated the local coastline then circled the world seven times and were recorded as far as the UK. It was regarded as the most violent volcanic eruption in recorded history.

In 1992 I was working in Indonesia for Trident Petroleum, where we were drilling a wildcat well in Borneo. I travelled west on Java and chartered a fishing boat to the islands; we left from a dirty volcanic-sand beach in the pitch-black before dawn. I was surprised that such a large population

On top of Krakatoa

could live on this low-lying land, which had been destroyed 100 years before and would surely face destruction again. After several hours in the hot tropical sun, the islands emerged from the mist, and we entered the huge amphitheatre where Krakatoa had once been. There was now a crater over a mile wide, open to the sea and filled with deep water. When it had erupted, the island had blown clean away, taking with it most of its foundations from below sea level, a total of 20 cubic kilometres of rock. The rush of sea water into the gigantic red-hot abyss caused a colossal explosion of steam and debris which rose 60 km (~40 miles), into the fringes of outer space.

In the middle of the caldera was a new Krakatoa, which the Indonesians called Anak (Child of) Krakatoa. We landed on its barren ash beach, and I hiked up the smouldering slopes with an Indonesian who knew the mountain. The rock was light, loose and hot and the soles of my boots burnt my feet. Sulphurous fumes were wafting in the heat, and we often had to reverse tracks to find breathable air. Holes in the mountain vented poisonous gases and steam, and were ringed with yellow sulphur. The ground was unstable and collapsed slightly every now and then under our weight. It was clearly a highly dangerous place, and I wondered how far the magma was below us. The island had risen over 500 feet above sea level in less than a century, over 5 feet a year. There was a sensation of pent-up energy waiting for release.

Iceland: fire and ice

In September 1991 Bonnie and I travelled to Iceland. The Land of Fire and Ice is perched on the mid-Atlantic ridge, which splits apart along its length, leaving cracks through which lava erupts frequently. Because of this, the island is only some 10 million years old (many of the youngest parts are less than 10 years old), compared with much of the world's land surface, which averages some 200 million years. Little surprise, then, that Iceland is the scene of possibly the biggest volcanic eruption in recorded history: Laki's 18th-century blast caused several years of severely cold winters worldwide, along with droughts, floods and crop failures.

Iceland is one of the most beautiful and rugged islands, a land of huge waterfalls, glaciers, lava everywhere, volcanoes hissing steam and geysers. It has appalling weather, with howling gales much of the time, which fortunately keeps away the mass tourist markets, lager louts and clubbers.

Our first river crossing of many river crossings in Iceland

The only road across Iceland

PC on lava bridge at Ófærufoss

Skogafoss waterfall

Dettifoss waterfall

We climbed up the world's third-largest ice cap and watched chunks of ice crashing off a cliff from a hanging glacier. Under the ice cap is a volcano. When it erupts, it melts the glacier, which comes loose and crashes down the valley, scouring it out and destroying everything in its path to the sea. There were reports of bigger eruptions in times past causing icebergs to be thrown high up in the sky. We went to a place where hot water poured out of the end of a glacier in a tunnel. I found a hot lake and went for a swim on my own in this majestic landscape.

We crossed the middle of the island in our 4×4 on a dirt trail that is only passable for six weeks a year, crossing deep glacier rivers that threatened to carry us away down the icy rapids. Mostly there were only two wheel tracks across the lava boulder fields. Sometimes the tracks disappeared into rivers and we had to chance it, hoping it wouldn't be deep enough to stop the engine or float the vehicle. I'd been advised not to put on oversized tyres, since they're too buoyant; many an adventurer had been swept away over raging waterfalls.

A violent storm came down, closing visibility in, and we passed between two lighter areas in the clouds where we glimpsed icefields on either side of us. Then we came upon an area of steaming streams and vents. It was surrealistic in this wintry, icy landscape. We saw no one and no vehicles on this long crossing. We had no radio or communications, so had to be very careful.

Iceland's fantastic waterfalls are the biggest in Europe. We were always the only people there. One of the falls, Ófærufoss, featured a slender lava bridge high above it, spanning 100 feet. I ventured onto it, but backtracked, worried about the 200-foot drop. Two years later the lava bridge fell.

Above a rainbow in Hawaii

Landing on a live lava flow

In 1995 Bonnie, our son Michael and I went to the Big Island of Hawaii, home of the world's biggest volcano, Mauna Loa, and its offspring Kilauea, the world's most active volcano. These behemoths are on a mid-Pacific hot spot, heating basalt, which rises continuously as the Hawaiian chain of islands moves over the top of it at a few inches a year, causing new volcanoes and islands to form. Basalt is more liquid than the andesite of the stratovolcanoes, and thus less explosive. The islands of Hawaii have been entirely built up by layers of volcanic basalt, typically 12 feet thick, and flowing down to the sea in all directions. The Big Island is only a million years old and growing daily. Its two peaks rise 32,000 feet from the ocean floor, making them the tallest[8] mountains in the world.

One evening we drove down to the coast and carried Michael, aged two and in his 'off-road' pushchair, over the new pahoehoe lava, which was itself only two months old and had crossed the road, closing it. Pu'u Ōʻō, Kilauea's vent, was disgorging lava at a rate fast enough to cover a football field 100 metres deep every day. The lava was mostly travelling from three hot orange lakes down through a system of lava tubes several miles to the sea, where it was lighting up the steam, hissing in great pink clouds. Up above us, the lava was glowing as it worked its way slowly down. It had destroyed 160 homes. Michael slept through the rough ride over the lava, but suddenly woke up and saw the red glow in the dark: 'Look! Fire on the hill!'

Next day, Bonnie and I chartered a helicopter piloted by a skilled Hawaiian, Paul Darryl. That morning the US government had shut down due to a budget dispute between President Clinton and the Republican Congress. So all national parks, including the Hawaii Volcanoes National Park, were closed until the dispute could be resolved. The volcano itself was closed off, as it was erupting and too dangerous to ascend. But travelling with us was Carl, a geologist from the US Geological Survey (USGS). The budget cuts had prevented the USGS from being able to charter helicopters, and as he'd joined us this meant we got right into the middle of the action. He was particularly interested in visiting several specific areas of the volcano, as there'd been some earthquakes in the night, and the volume of lava flow had increased.

The helicopter flew over the crater of Kilauea, which had been an active lava lake for most of the 19th century, prior to a massive eruption in 1924; it attracted visitors from all over the world, who stayed at the Volcano House on the rim of the crater, where we too had stayed. Paul flew us then to the erupting caldera of Pu'u Ōʻō, where steam and smoke were billowing out. Bonnie sat in the front, in the bubble, and Michael sat between her and the pilot. I sat behind, next to Carl, who had a crash helmet and microphone. Bonnie and I could listen in to the conversation between Paul and Carl.

'I want to look out for some landslides in the crater that could have accompanied the seismic tremors', Carl said.

'Can't see anything new,' Paul replied, as we hovered next to the steam cloud, directly over the crater and about 150 feet above it.

Suddenly the steam shifted and the bottom of the crater was clear, the most majestic sight of three red lava lakes bubbling away. One of them was very active, pouring lava into its edges and upwelling in the middle from the mantle of the Earth. It was primeval.

---

8 'Highest' is altitude above sea level; 'tallest' above the base of the mountain.

Flying over erupting volcano in Big Island Hawaii

Flowing lava tube on the Big Island Hawaii

'First time we've been able to see it in seven months,' Carl told me. 'There's been too much steam to see in there. But the level's been pistoning up and down and we're not sure what's going to happen.'

I was worried we'd drift into the white cloud and be asphyxiated. Meanwhile Bonnie's feet were being roasted by the fire below. I'd heard a story of a helicopter's bubble melting when it got too close to an eruption.

We flew down to the coast over a line of steaming vents marking the rift or dike where the magma was escaping from the volcano, then along the lava tubes. The coast was boiling with steam over hundreds of yards as the red lava disgorged itself into the sea. On the way back, Paul put the chopper down on the skin over the flow so that Carl could get a thermocouple from a vent where the red-hot flow could be seen underneath.

'The crust's 18 inches thick at most, so I'm keeping my hands ready to lift off if we break through,' Paul said reassuringly.

Carl hopped out onto the skin. The searing 1,125°C (2,220°F) heat blasted into the chopper cabin. He ran to the hole and retrieved his instrument, shielding his face. He started staggering about, and I jumped out to help him back in.

'Bad gas there, took a big hit of sulphur dioxide,' he said as he clambered back in. 'Thermocouple's gone; lava ripped it off.'

Then we flew to another open vent, like a cave entrance, where we witnessed the most amazing sight; inside was a huge torrent of lava, roaring along like an underground river. 'That's the whole 500,000 cubic metres a day in there; that's where it all comes from,' Carl told me over the headsets. This was an even more primeval sight, to see the workings of the lava under the ground. These processes had been going on since the dawn of time, and the volcanoes had provided the water, the atmosphere, and much of the land of Planet Earth – the very essence of life. It was wonderful to see it so close, at first hand.

4 Crises at sea

We were in Calypso, my 16-foot Wayfarer dinghy, about 20 miles off the French coast. But something was ominous, not right. There was a big swell running, and the sky was black to the west; it looked like a huge, menacing squall. This had every aspect of the Atlantic in an ugly mood. We should not be here.

Suddenly it hit us. We were knocked down, and I let the sheets fly. The sails were flogging uncontrollably, shaking the boat violently. Night was coming. If we capsized, we would not survive. We had to get out of this, but how?

Offshore voyages in an open dinghy

While I was a teenager I was intrigued by the open sea and the oceans, and sailed our family Wayfarer dinghy, *Calypso*, offshore on many adventurous voyages.[9]

Huge waves offshore

In the 1960s we had no GPS, no EPIRBs, no mobile phones, no way of calling for help. We navigated mainly by sextant and compass. Boats and fittings were not as strong as they are today. Calypso was made of thin plywood, which sometimes split in two when we hit a big wave. We could not risk the slightest contact with a rock. Fittings were mostly bronze. Things broke often. Plenty went wrong: a dismasting, two capsizes, nine rudder breakages, getting lost and arriving at islands we mistook for other ones.

Dinghies are not a safe means of transport on the open sea: no keel, so they are easily capsized; no cabin, so no shelter from foul weather; no motor, so no means of propulsion other than oars when unable to sail; no electricity for navigation, communications or lights.

When awake, we were often like tightrope walkers, trying desperately to avoid a capsize. When asleep on the floorboards, the spray would still be flying at us. We did many overnight passages, up to three days non-stop in the Atlantic, and fatigue was a huge risk. Dropping off to sleep while helming, with the crew asleep, could lead to a gybe or a capsize.

In summer 1966 I was sailing with George Greenwood, a friend from school. Setting out from Poole, and longing for the adventure of the high seas, we decided to head west to Weymouth. The chief danger on

---

9 These were written up in my book *The Sea Takes No Prisoners*, published by Adlard Coles, an imprint of Bloomsbury Publishing Plc, in 2018, parts of which are summarised here.

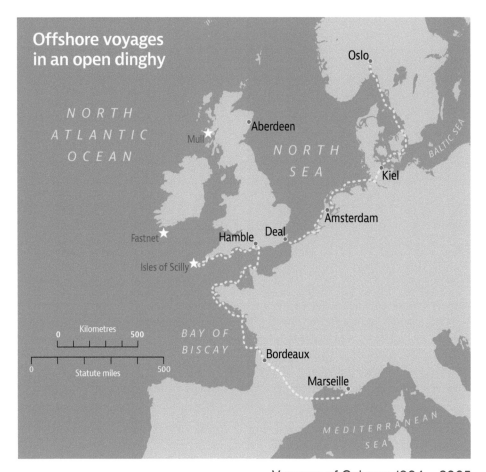

Voyages of Calypso 1964 - 2005

this coastline is the area of overfalls near St Alban's Ledge. In addition there are various tidal races, notably the Peverell Ledge/Anvil Point race. I was pumped up with curiosity. How would our little dinghy fare in the big waves and open sea? I was 17 years old and keen to build experience carefully.

The 0640 shipping forecast on 29 July was wind up to force 6. We had planned to take St Alban's Head at slack water at 1545, when the dangerous tide rips and overfalls were at rest. This meant going outside the Handfast Point and Anvil Point tide races, which on a spring ebb stream would be creating violent waves and swirling waters. When we were out of the lee of Handfast Point, the wind was WSW and force 6, so we dropped the jib. The seas were gradually getting larger as we sailed south, and by 1330 we were out of the lee of Durlston Head with America the nearest land to windward of us.

As we went further out into the open sea the seas grew until they were truly huge. George was sitting out at the front of the cockpit, trying to keep the boat upright with his body weight, hanging onto the shroud so as not to be swept off: 'Watch out, Peter, some really big ones ahead.'

Calypso's bows were being lifted as we were drawn up a steep wall of water. A crest was curling over to land on us. It hit the boat and George like a rugby tackle, knocking us back and breaking over the boat, then into the cockpit, half-filling it.

'Hang on, another big one,' I warned George. It broke in, and then we were on top of the wave as it roared underneath us. We crashed into the bottom and stopped dead. There was no wind down here – but I could hear it roaring overhead.

'Another big one, must be as high as the mast,' shouted George. 'White breakers ahead' – he was pointing – 'worse than here.'

'Can't be worse – these are very dangerous right *here*!' I shouted back. But then I saw what he had seen. There was a line of white water extending from the cliffs out to where we were going, and with every wave it grew closer. I remembered that the tide would be pulling us into this.

'Is this a tide race?' George looked very worried.

'The boat can't handle any more than this,' I said. The mast was 22 feet high. The waves were about that big, but it wasn't the height that worried me – it was their steepness. They were black on their steep faces, white on top, and white where breakers had left a trail of spray.

'We must go back,' said George.

But could we? The boat would be running with the waves and surfing them. They were moving so fast. We'd be out of control.

'I can't turn back here,' I said. 'It's too dangerous.'

'And it's too dangerous to carry on,' he replied.

I was fighting to overcome increasing fear. The sea was roaring. The air was shrieking. We had no place here. There were no other boats out here. No one could rescue us. We had to be very careful. The waves were tipping *Calypso* over as they hit us.

'I'm going to raise the centreboard,' said George. 'Maybe we'll be tipped less when we're broadsided.'

He raised it halfway. Another breaker hit us near the top of the next wave. We slipped sideways instead of being rolled.

'If we go much further, we'll get close to the race off St Alban's Head,' George yelled. 'The seas could be monumental there.'

George Greenwood driving Calypso in 20 foot seas

He was pumping flat out. The problem was removing the water faster than it came in. We were being tossed about like a rubber duck in a washing machine. We were mesmerised by the phenomenal roar of the breaking waves, the terrifying power of the sea. This was beyond an adventure – it was turning into a nightmare, potentially a disaster.

The sea was a mass of huge white breakers. And with each passing minute the waves grew ever bigger and steeper as the tide ripped into the dark Atlantic rollers. The boat could be flipped over at any moment, and we would never be able to right her in these giant waves. The tide would then sweep us further out into the grey, open, boiling sea.

'We've *got* to go back!' I yelled. We had to do that before we had a fatal accident. George raised the jib and dropped the main, so now we had only that tiny jib up. I hoped we'd not surf out of control on the faces of these big, near-vertical seas. The wind was now force 7, gale strength. We had to get back to land, fast, before it got any worse and before we were rolled. No one knew where we were, and no one would know we were in trouble.

Between waves I pulled the tiller in and bore *Calypso* around until the wind was behind us. Under jib alone she flew before the wind. I looked back. A huge wave was towering astern of us. I had to take it square on. This exhilarating surf ride lasted maybe ten seconds, then *Calypso*'s bows pointed up as the crest frothed underneath and we glided down the back of the wave. In the bottom of the trough, there was very little wind, as it roared overhead from crest to crest, while the sea made a sound like rolling thunder. Then we were lifted by another huge wave; it happened again and again. It was an adrenaline rush. Sometimes a wave would tower behind us with a curler that looked as if it was going to land right on top of us, but the boat, lifting her stern, would start surfing down the wave front, then the wave would break and we'd be sailing on air in the froth.

We arrived back in Poole Harbour shaken and relieved. The gale was screaming through the rigging of the boats at their moorings. Trees were being whipped back and forth in the gusts.

'Shall we have another go at Weymouth tomorrow?' I asked.

'Why not? We survived today. We'll probably survive tomorrow. It was a wild ride, and we're learning as we go.'

There was virtually no shelter on the rugged Dorset coastline – mostly cliffs – ahead. The next day we got within 2 miles of St Alban's Head before deciding to turn back and head east for the Solent.

At 1505, we decided to risk putting up the main and lowering the genoa. What a mistake! When we bore away, there was a loud crack astern.

'Rudder's gone!' I screamed at George.

Now we *were* in trouble, wallowing broadside on to the seas and risking being rolled. We had to get bow on. Fast. George streamed the drogue sea anchor from the bows and we pulled the rudder out and had a look. A quarter-inch bolt had sheared, causing the two arms of the rudder head to be bent outwards and split. We repaired it with long screws and a G-clamp as the boat heaved and swayed in the big seas as they roared by, and we got back to our base at Hamble.

The next year, 1967, we sailed from Falmouth to Hamble along the south coast of England. The rudder broke again and we had to learn to steer with an oar, which turned out to be a useful skill. We capsized, too. And by sailing overnight for the first time we developed yet more skills.

Desperate times off France

In 1968 I sailed with Barry Hunt-Taylor, a university friend, from the UK to Brittany, and then on with Peter Jesson to the Mediterranean.

Much of this journey would be along the wild Atlantic coast of France, so we would need to be offshore, out of sight of land, much of the time. The North Atlantic has a fearsome reputation for storms. For centuries it prevented Europeans from reaching America. Its westerly winds build big seas which dash against the rocky west coasts of Europe. This would be more like ocean sailing than sea sailing. What challenges would it throw at us?

I had crossed the Bay of Biscay before, but that had been in a troopship. A fearsome Atlantic storm had hit us as we sailed south. The ship had heaved, rolled and shuddered from end to end as it fought the storm. That ship had weighed 14,304 tonnes: our 16-foot Wayfarer was a quarter of a tonne.

I had learned from seeing rough weather that the sea takes no prisoners. On land, in a difficult situation, you can normally stop or go back; on a mountain, you can go back down. You will probably have the opportunity of finding somewhere safe. But at sea, everything is in motion – tides, waves, wind, storms – and you have no choice but to be carried along by that motion, adjusting to whatever nature throws at you. You cannot stop. You cannot just go where you want: not dead downwind due to the gybe risk, nor directly into the wind, and in heavy weather you can only go on a broad reach. The sea anchor can help, but you are still carried by tides and drift, often in a direction you do not want.

We were ready to cross the Channel on 24 June 1968, but several days of gales followed, so we moved *Calypso* into a derelict shed to finalise preparations. Then, after five days of waiting, we finally got a good weather forecast.

The *Sunday Mirror* interviewed Barry on the dock, and then we were off, sailing through the first of two nights at sea. While out of sight of land, we used a sextant for celestial navigation. When we picked out the French coastline at 2030 the next day, I felt much more at ease, and expected an easy passage to Guernsey. However, in the next few hours we were to go through a set of alarming experiences. The sky clouded over before sunset and became grey and murky as the light faded – dramatised by lightning flashes and distant rolls of thunder, which emphasised how exposed we were.

The wind was backing and increasing. We were approaching the race too fast and too soon. At 2300 we reefed down and reached north for half an hour while Barry fixed our position. By 2330 we were 10 miles north-east of the race. I was very fatigued – and, hallucinating, I was sailing in zigzags, trying to avoid fluorescent coils of barbed wire in the sea.

When Barry woke me at 0430 to come on watch I felt lousy – shivering, and stiff from cramp and cold. We were rolling round in a big oily swell with the gaunt shape of Cap de la Hague on our port beam.

'Well at least it's France,' Barry said, in an effort to raise morale.

'How was your watch?' I asked him.

'Fast sailing.'

The tide had been under us, too.

The sky at dawn looked ghastly – a tangle of red cirrus above us with several cumulonimbus clouds rapidly changing shape and blotting out the yellow sun, and a black horizon to windward. The ugly weather situation, and the strong tides, were giving me the feeling that we were in a trap. We were soon hit by a series of intense gusts coming from all round the compass and were forced to drop the main. The thunderstorms were coming at us. It was horrifying and threatening.

The sea was a strange sight – most of it smooth and glassy, but with areas of tidal whirlpools and overfalls, and occasionally darkened by a gust descending from nowhere – and the surface perpetually undulating as the big grey Atlantic swells marched in from the west. If the tide was running true to form then we had clearly missed it to Guernsey, so we decided to try and reach shelter in Alderney before the weather broke.

'I'll start rowing,' Barry said. 'This is not a good place to be.'

I looked up and gasped, horrified, to see in the distance a white wall of breakers advancing rapidly across the sea towards us. 'What's *happening*?'

'No idea. We'd better be ready for it.'

I suddenly realised that the breakers were stationary, and we were being swept onto them by the tide. The swell was meeting an underwater ledge extending off Alderney.

'We're going to have to go the other way, or we'll be swept through the breakers,' I said.

It was touch and go. They were curling over and roaring. Barry's knuckles were white on the oars, and he pulled like he was training for the Boat Race. I clutched the distress signals in one hand and the tiller in the other. Would we manage to make it round the breakers, or would we be drawn into the danger? Barry managed to pull hard enough to get to the edge of the worst breakers, and there were steep, dark waves ahead now. Our bows pointed up towards the sky and crashed down. A couple more, and we were through.

We'd missed disaster by a few yards, but still I felt very frightened. The roar of the sea reminded me that we were in a dangerous place. There was no wind, just breaking waves. *Calypso* was sailing fast but only just gaining on the increasing tide (we were later told that it runs at over 6 knots through the rocks). We were in desperate need of a rest, so decided to land on Herm to wait for the tide to turn.

We beached at 1130 and pulled her up on boat rollers with help from a couple of bikini-clad sunbathers. It was turning out to be a hot day, and we must have looked an extraordinary sight, staggering about in thick layers of night clothing, oilskins, lifejackets, lifelines and boots, and slurring our speech through fatigue.

Barry collapsed exhausted on the beach and I feared he might have been put off sailing for life. Hundreds of sandflies were eating him, but I couldn't wake him up. He eventually rose in the heat of the afternoon, surrounded by incredulous children. Neither of us had had more than three hours' sleep in the last three days. He too had suffered from hallucinations in the night watches and we had both needed caffeine pills to keep going the last few hours. We were lucky not to have gybed or capsized during the worst of it.

We continued to Brittany. Once there, Barry had to leave for work and I was joined by Peter Jesson. From there, Peter and I sailed west and rounded the edge of the French coastline, then on down the coast into the Bay of Biscay and the eastern side of the Atlantic Ocean. One evening, we had an emergency.

Calypso beached in Channel Islands after a 39 hour passage

The Atlantic throws an ugly night at us

We were about 20 miles off the French coast, getting ready for sailing on through the night. But something was ominous, not right. Peter was normally unflappable, but he looked worried.

He asked loudly, above the sound of the rising wind, 'What do you think's going to happen?'

'I don't know. There's a big swell running, so there must be bad weather coming at us.'

The sky was black to the west, and it looked like a huge, menacing squall. This had every aspect of the Atlantic in an ugly mood. The shipping forecast was imminent, so we hove to. I unstowed our waterproof RDF, which we used also for the weather forecasts, and tuned in. The forecast should have started at 1758, but I could hear nothing but crackling. And then, when sea area Biscay came up, I could make out just one word: 'seven'. That meant a force 7 gale, way more than our little boat could survive.

I gave the RDF to Peter to re-stow, and set the boat back to sailing on a beam reach. The black sky was upon us. White foam was being blown off the waves as the wind picked up to our weather side. Suddenly, it hit us. We were knocked down, and I let the sheets fly on both sails. The sails were flogging uncontrollably now, and shaking the boat violently. I could not luff up as the wind was too strong. I dared not bear away, as we would take off like a rocket out of control. We couldn't stay as we were, either – we'd be blown over and could never right the boat in such conditions. Night was coming. If we capsized, we would not survive.

'Down main!' I yelled.

The halyard had been carefully stowed so that it would run out with no delay. This precaution paid off; Peter got the sail down and into the boat in seconds. We now had just the jib up, but the rising wind still forced us over, with water washing into the boat. If the boat filled up, we'd lose our stability. What to do now? We let the jib sheet fly and it flogged ever more violently. The sea was too rough to risk going onto the foredeck to take it down but it was either going to shake the mast to pieces or tip us over. We were at the mercy of the sea. This time, it was merciful, and the wind dropped a little. Peter hauled the jib sheet in and we sailed on. But the seas were getting rapidly bigger, and the wind was blowing the tops off the waves in sheets of white spume. The noise went to a high-pitched shriek. What choices did we have?

Sailing on like this, with the waves on our beam, would be very dangerous after dark, as we would not be able to see them coming and could easily be filled up or rolled over. Running for shelter was risky, as we'd be surfing huge waves in the pitch-black of a stormy night and closing a lee shore without any shelter, with the risk of being wrecked on rocks or reefs. We could try to ride it out, lying to our small sea anchor, but this was also risky. If the weather got worse, the sea anchor wouldn't save us. Also, we'd drift on to the same lee shore about 12 hours later, without being able to choose which bit we wanted to be wrecked on. On this 100-mile stretch of coast, there was no shelter within reach.

'What do you think?' I yelled at Peter.

'We've got to get to shelter before it gets any worse,' he said.

'But there *isn't* any shelter!' Then I had another look at our chart inside its waterproof case. To our lee was the Île de Noirmoutier, which had a bay on the side facing the mainland. But by the time we neared safety it would be dark, and the waters between the island and the mainland were strewn with rocks and reefs. There was a lighthouse on the lee side of the island, and beyond this a beach, and if we kept in the white sector we'd be clear of the rocks. We'd have to head up hard on the wind and drive into this gale. We'd then have to beat into the gale to get into the island's shelter. But by then the waves would be huge. A Wayfarer could not beat into a force 7, even in flat water. In big seas, at night? We'd never done anything like this before. I looked again to the west, where the Atlantic weather was coming from. The horizon was still darkening and the rest of the sky becoming uglier every minute. We had to get out of this.

There was another problem. The boat could not beat with just the jib; we needed the mainsail. But we couldn't set it when the wind was this strong, even if we reefed it to a quarter of its size. However, I'd made what I called a 'trysail adaptor' to cover such a situation. It allowed the jib to be hanked onto it and then hoisted up the mast as a small mainsail, or trysail. But it had never been used. Would it work? Our lives would depend on it.

We unstowed it and lined up the holes with the jib hanks, to make sure we could set it up while effectively blindfolded in the dark.

So at 1850 we bore away and *Calypso* began surfing down the steepening waves in the fading light towards Île de Pilier, which guarded the north end of Noirmoutier. Soon we were surfing up waves as well. *Calypso* was in danger of driving her bows under, or being pooped by the large seas. The wind was rising inexorably. I was expecting the jib to be split in two any moment. The sky was black to windward, above us were red streaks of cirrus and to the south it was a sickly green and yellow. Soon, ragged brown clouds scudded low overhead and the rain began as the light faded. It was a frightening sky.

Calypso, under only 46 square feet of canvas, was planing continuously up and down waves like a speedboat, and the safety line on the rudder blade was screaming. We couldn't risk going any closer to the rocks. We had to try to beat off them. Everything depended on being able to sail to windward into the lee of the island. It was dark now. The sea was breaking around us on rocks and shallows. Ahead were more breakers. We had to turn and try to beat. Would the trysail adaptor work? Could we escape the rocks downwind of us? Could we control the boat on this stormy night? Would we be able to see the lighthouse and its white sector light? Could we point high enough to get to the beach? Would we capsize? Or hit a rock?

When we headed up, I was amazed to find she would point towards the lighthouse, flashing at us through pelting rain. She was driving through sheets of spray in the howling wind, and the self-bailer was working overtime. The flashes of the light loomed higher and brighter in the rain, which was by now heavy and pelting horizontally. Soon we were round the back of it, where we found a mooring, got the tent up, unstowed sleeping bags and slept.

Barry on Calypso leaving the UK for Norway

To the land of the Vikings

Barry joined me again in 1969 to sail from Deal in England to the Kiel Canal, where he disembarked to start work in Hamburg. From there, Tom Moore joined me to sail on to Norway.

In the Danish waters of the Baltic, the rudder broke. This time a reinforced stainless-steel gudgeon just snapped in two. Steering with the oar was, however, something we were skilled at, so we decided to continue for our original destination – Copenhagen, 60 miles away.

When I came on watch at 1550, the wind freed, so we unreefed and had a tremendous sail, planing on a beam reach. Using the oar, however, meant it was shocking hard work: in order to balance the helm we were constantly adjusting sheets, sail area, centreboard, kicking strap and trim. When we arrived at the next headland, we found that *Calypso* had averaged nearly 7 knots. I thought it might be a speed record for steering with an oar in modern times. The Viking ships may have done better.

After this the wind headed us, and it was a long beat to Copenhagen, steadily reefing down as the wind rose. The trouble with steering with the oar was that the helmsman needed two hands for it, so the crew had to do everything else. There was no chance to get any sleep.

I came on watch again just before midnight. I took over the oar. We were in a very dangerous situation: reefed down in pitch-black with the wind rising, and no rudder. We had to get to shelter, fast. I was very scared. We had to focus intensely to avoid losing control of the boat and capsizing.

There was a loud blast right next to us.

'What's that?' I yelled above the howling wind.

'Huge ship!' Tom shouted. We looked astern to see a large tanker heading straight at us, 100 yards away. It must have just altered course; they could not possibly have seen us.

'Quick, flash the signalling torch. Blast the fog horn. Bear away.' Its bows were now above us, as black as the night between its red and green navigation lights, a sight held up in navigation classes as one you never want to see. We flashed our hand torches and bore away sharply. As we escaped – just – we reflected that this was a sharp lesson on what a moment's inattention can lead to.

The shipping was now heavy, and as the wind freshened further we had to let the sails flog until there was a safe gap that would allow us to heave to and reef down again. Soon we had nine rolls in the main, which reduced it to about a third of its full area. Fifteen minutes later we were again overpowered, having to let the sheets fly. By now the wind was roaring in the rigging and *Calypso* was slamming into some steep seas – it was impossible to see them.

Copenhagen was now to the west of us, but our chart was far too small-scale to be any use and in the driving spray we couldn't read the Pilot. The approach was a hair-raising one, with hydrofoils crossing our bows at 50 knots not knowing we were there, and numerous unidentifiable lights and unlit buoys. But suddenly I identified the harbour entrance lights. We were safe.

We decided to sail direct from Copenhagen to Gothenburg so as to have more time in the islands further north. We spent all day beating up the Sound[10] between Denmark and Sweden in a light northerly, and hot sunshine. After sunset I went through the normal routine of preparing for a night's sailing: cooking up a Vesta curry on our homemade gimballed oven; crawling into the bow locker to unstow the waterproof sleeping bag; unstowing extra clothing from the stern locker; assembling the compass light; hoisting the navigation light up on

---

10 Also known as the Øresund (Danish) and Öresund (Swedish)

the burgee halyard; checking and replacing batteries or bulbs on our pocket torches and the powerful signalling lamp. As the shipping was heavy, we decided to erect the radar reflector as well – a complicated operation involving five ropes and the spinnaker pole. We could see ships altering course for us a couple of miles away as they picked us up on radar – in these waters, they were keeping a radar lookout, which they didn't usually do in the open ocean in good visibility.

We passed within a few hundred yards of Kullen but now, in fog, I never saw it, which was a pity as it is apparently an impressive headland. We heard several ships sounding their fog horns. One dead ahead of us seemed to be getting slowly closer, and I was answering its blasts. It seemed to take ages to get nearer, and I woke Tom to help look for it. Then we could hear its engine-room telegraph. It must be just a few yards away – but where? The first we saw was the top of its bows; it was a big liner, doing about 1 knot. They must have seen us; the ship got under way and by the time the stern was in view the bows had slid out of sight. Neither Tom nor I had realised how thick the fog was – we had been expecting to see something near the horizon, not halfway up in the sky above us.

The next ship must have done a complete semicircle around us, judging by the blasts from its fog horn. I heard the bow wave before I saw it pass abeam of us – another liner. The value of the radar reflector was very well demonstrated, but I felt a bit guilty, as the ships' helmsmen, thinking we were big enough to be taken seriously, must have been as worried about us as we were about them.

By mid-morning the fog had lifted but the shipping still altered course for us. The only one that didn't was a very rusty Russian trawler covered with radio masts and full of grimy sailors. It looked like a classic Cold War spy ship, and was probably reporting the ships going through the Sound. We sailed on to our destination, completing another three-day passage.

On 20 July we left Gothenburg and sailed some 30 miles north to an uninhabited island called Ussholmen. Navigation in these waters was demanding because of the number of rocks around, so we sailed well offshore, clear of the maze of islands. It was thrilling sailing – reefed, in a fresh westerly and bright sunshine. The water was clear and reflected the deep blue sky. Big Atlantic swells were coming up the Skagerrak – there must be bad weather out there to the west.

Calypso at Ussholmen offshore Sweden

I looked at the chart, searching for an anchorage. There was a good one in a deep cove on the lee side of the island. When we got there, it exceeded expectations. The island was about 400 yards long, uninhabited and completely deserted – just bare rock boulders, moss, seagulls and the sound of the waves breaking on the rocks to keep us company. There was no sign that anyone had ever been there. There were grooves in the granite where glaciers had ground their way across. It had an Arctic feel about it, in stark contrast to the woods and fields of Denmark. This was really what we had come to Sweden for. But we couldn't stay for long, because if the wind swung to the east, we'd be trapped and could be dashed against the rocks. We spent the night with our bows tied to these rocks, and our anchor out astern, to keep us a safe distance from them.

It was in these surroundings that we listened on the radio to the first moon landing. It was easy to visualise the sense of desolation the astronauts must have felt. The moon was shining on the granite around us as Neil Armstrong spoke from Apollo 11. It was a fantastic feat of technology and adventure, needing both brilliant organisation and plenty of good fortune. I was fascinated to learn later that the Apollo missions used a sextant for astronavigation en route to the Moon. They also had a groundbreaking minicomputer on board, which was the foundation for today's digital world – just one of the many benefits to modern civilisation deriving from the space race and the Apollo programme.

Rough weather and fog

The next passage was the hardest *Calypso* ever did. It was blowing half a gale, with fog. To avoid going in among the thousands of small islands and rocks, we decided to sail to seaward of all of them, and go from one to the next. But, like Apollo, we had to be exact in our navigation. Too far west and we wouldn't see the next island, lost in an area where we couldn't expect good RDF fixes. Too far east and we'd be among rocks and surf, unable to beat back out to sea in the big waves.

We'd be sailing outside the main archipelago, picking up the westernmost islands, which were about 8 miles apart. Visibility was such that we had to steer a course accurate to 5 degrees, almost impossible in heavy seas in a dinghy. We

Tom Moore taking a sextant shot

needed faultless teamwork between navigator and helmsman – the navigator to plot our DR course, and the helmsman to steer accurately, so that when all the tortuous sailing around big waves on the beam was averaged out, we would have gone in exactly the right direction.

It was a rare day of force 6 winds and fog occurring simultaneously. We rounded Paternoster, and at 1505 I asked Tom to take a bearing on the lighthouse before it disappeared in the poor visibility. It was the last landmark for the next 10 miles, so I wanted a good fix as we were off a rock-strewn lee shore. He was soon busy unstowing the sextant in its Tupperware box under the foredeck and wedging himself in the driest place in *Calypso* – on the windward-side floorboards by the centreboard case. It was virtually impossible, as the seas were too high and the lighthouse soon disappeared in the mist. Every now and then Tom would duck and protect the instrument as I shouted, 'Watch it!' when a crest broke in. These were big seas from the Atlantic.

The wind was steadily freshening. An hour later we were planing most of the time. Grey skies, and large grey seas, but it was exciting sailing. From the log:

> 1615. Seas on the beam – much larger and some breaking heavily. Difficult steering as some need luffing, others bearing away to take astern – usually last-minute decision – heavy strain on rudder. Centreboard nearly up to allow her to slip sideways if hit beam on. Course must be within 10° to pick up island ahead – too far west and we miss it, too far east and we are on submerged rocks.

By 1630 Tom's DR estimate put us within expected sight of the island, but there was no sign of it. I was beginning to think that I could have steered a course inaccurate to at least 20 degrees. I was looking around for breakers but could see nothing except grey, heaving seas – breaking but definitely deep-water waves. There should have been a fog signal on the island, but we could hear nothing except the sound of the sea and the moan of the wind in the rigging. I thought I heard breakers, but couldn't see them. I had two fears: first, that we wouldn't see any rocks and be lost, with a risk of being wrecked later, especially after dark. Second, we might see the rocks but be unable to beat clear and be smashed against them.

Suddenly we saw breakers close on the starboard. The entire island emerged from the fog. There were more breakers to starboard. Which island was this? What were these extra rocks? Now we could hear the fog signal: a Tyfon and very loud. It was the right rock! The wind was still gradually rising and visibility deteriorating, but there was a group of islands 12 miles ahead where the chart promised us shelter. From the log:

> 1715. Hove to. Put three more rolls in mainsail. Wind WSW 5–6. Planing hard on beam reach with seven rolls in mainsail. *Calypso* taking seas very well rolling if steep ones not luffed, but not dangerously. Some seas sweeping in over quarter. Self-bailer doing a grand job.

Tom's helmsmanship was proven when Bonden Island emerged at exactly the time and place expected. I took a rough fix as we passed it, then we set a course for the next one.

We passed to windward of that one as well, watching the breakers shooting up the cliffs a cable to starboard. Tom was not in possession of the chart and looked very worried, staring ahead intently when not lining up on a steep wave astern. 'There's another island dead ahead and I think there's another one fine on the port bow – yes, there is, definitely. I can see the breakers,' he said.

A large wave was rearing up on the beam, but Tom got our stern into it in time. 'Sorry, didn't see that one. They're all coming from different directions.'

'Bouncing off the cliffs. I'd better assemble the oars in case anything goes wrong. The entrance looks pretty narrow. There will be one hell of a sea in it.'

This was a desperate landfall. We were committed to a narrow cut between high cliffs, from which there could be no escape. The right one and we'd be saved; the wrong one and we'd be smashed onto the rocks. I started going rigid with fear and hoped Tom wouldn't notice. I stared hard at the gap. There were vertical granite cliffs either side. In the middle was a boiling sea of white water, shooting up the cliffs. What was on the other side? There wasn't a cliff, so it looked like we *would* come out the other side. But how could I be sure there were no submerged rocks? There was no way of telling, except that the chart showed none. If we were wrong, we wouldn't be able to beat back out. It was getting late in the evening and there was no way we could thread these narrow gaps in the dark. This was our last chance to find shelter for the night.

We entered into the gap, with granite cliffs a few yards either side of us, spray shooting up them as the Atlantic waves broke. Five minutes later we were safely through the gap and found ourselves in calm water surrounded by about six islands. We tied up on the lee side of an island called Tan.

Nearly wrecked at night

As we travelled north, the boat was nearly wrecked one night. We were anchored close to a rocky island, with our bows tied onto the rock. The wind had freshened and the anchor holding our stern off the rocks dragged. The bows were still tied to the rocky island and I was woken by the boat banging against the rocks. I woke Tom, who stowed our sleeping bags and cooking gear, while I pulled in the anchor and tried to fend off. I went ashore to cast off the bow line, then shoved off and leapt onto the boat as Tom started rowing, sitting inside the tent. I had made a major mistake in not taking the tent down before casting off, but we had to get away from the rocks quickly. At least the tent would keep the sleeping bags out of the pelting rain. We'd just have to row like Roman galley slaves, unable to see the blades of our oars.

Then we lost an oar overboard. It was a dark night, blowing half a gale and raining, and we were drifting towards a lee shore – rocks and cliffs about a mile away. What could we do now? We couldn't control our course or direction. We'd be wrecked within half an hour. One oar was as good as none.

'I'll try to cast the anchor,' I suggested.

'It's too deep,' Tom replied. 'The warp's 120 feet and the water's deeper than that.'

'It's our only option,' I said. 'It might get shallower as we close the rocks.'

Calypso was making fast progress backwards under the windage of the mast and the tent. I leaned over the bow to cast the anchor on its full length of 120 feet of warp. It never gripped; it was just getting dragged along under the boat. I tried three more times, each time hauling in all 120 feet of warp before casting again, and each time it failed to grip. We could see the rocks in the darkness, with the surf breaking on them. It would be the end of the boat, and of our voyage.

'I'll jump over and swim for it,' Tom shouted. 'You should do the same. You might survive even if the boat is destroyed.' His voice was drowned by the roar of the breakers. We'd be smashed any second now. My fifth cast would have to be the last.

I felt a tug on the anchor warp. 'It's touching the bottom, Tom!' Then it tugged hard and the boat spun round. When we were about 20 yards from the rocks it gripped. We were saved!

Catamaran racing on the Pacific coast

In 1978, when I was in my twenties, I moved to California, and I couldn't wait to get sailing on the San Francisco Bay with its strong winds, tides and wreaths of fog. I bought a North America Catamaran Racing Association (NACRA) multihull; it was 17 feet (5 metres) long and the fastest sailing boat of its size worldwide; I was shown pictures of people waterskiing behind it. It turned out to have a hair-raising performance in strong winds with one person hanging on the trapeze.

The first few times we went out we had alarming experiences, burying the bows at 20–25 knots and pitchpoling, often in a strong tide ebbing out through the Golden Gate into the huge Pacific breakers over the Potato Patch shoal. The problem was intensified by the sudden stop resulting in the crew on the trapeze being catapulted forward in front of the bows, whereupon the boat would cartwheel on top of him. When Keith Gordon and Mike Davidson pitchpoled one day, Mike was trapped under the boat for about a minute, with lines knotted tight around his ankles from the force of the impact. Fortunately he was a trained scuba diver, and this saved his life as he methodically untied the knots before coming up for air. We eventually solved the problem by installing a line from the trapeze crew to the transom; we called it the Geronimo line, per the rapid escape line from an oil rig derrick.

I joined the Multihull Racing Association and we took on the Californians, the best sailors in America, and in fact the world – they had won many Olympic golds and America's Cups. Fellow member Randy Smyth had several Olympic gold and silver medals on the Tornado catamarans.

Gradually we worked our standards up, and started winning races: in the windy bay, offshore in the big Pacific swells in Monterey Bay, central California, and at Lake Tahoe, 6,000 feet up in the High Sierras, where the air was cold and thin.

Sailing accidents

I wanted to build up my experience so that I could achieve two goals: crossing an ocean singlehanded; and breaking records. I would go out with a friend, and we had some exciting times. At Monterey when two boats had capsized a quarter of a mile offshore, we sailed straight over one of them, raising our daggerboards and rudders as we flew over their mast and sails. The other one was broken into tiny pieces in the 20-foot breakers. Another time, my boat, *White Lightning*, was standing empty on the beach at Lake Tahoe before a race and a sudden gust of wind blew her off. I jumped on board another cat and chased her all the way to Nevada, where she had piled up on the rocks.

A few years later I was sailing with a friend of mine, Andrew Pitcairn, in very strong winds at dusk on the bay. Andrew was on the trapeze behind me as we shot through the waves at breathtaking speed. Suddenly the boat leapt out of a trough, through a crest in a shower of foam and upwards as if a rocket was under her. She felt very strange, much lighter than normal – and then I noticed Andrew had gone. A frayed trapeze rope was flogging in the wind where he'd been. I got a glimpse of him behind and tried to tack around but couldn't, as to do so I needed his weight to hold the hull down. Even so, in trying the boat heeled over almost horizontal and I crawled over underneath the trampoline, praying that it wouldn't go over, as I had to rescue Andrew; I knew he had about 15 minutes to live in these chilly waters before hypothermia killed him. He had a wife and two children, and had been a close friend of Britain's top offshore sailor, Rob James, who had just died in a similar accident. I *had* to get Andrew back. Miraculously, the hull came down again and I was able to sail north, where, intercepting a yacht, I gesticulated to them to go and rescue him. It worked.

White Lightning was eventually rammed in a race in the Pacific and destroyed. While I got a replacement boat – a faster one – from the offending boat's insurance company, I felt that having survived seven years of thrills and spills it was time for me to move on.

So I got into windsurfing, which was at the time in its infancy. I remember once crossing San Francisco Bay and being swept out through the Golden Gate on the ebb tide as the wind dropped at sunset. The Pacific waves were big and breaking, and I knew that if I stayed out there I would not survive the night. Fortunately a yacht went by, and picked up my board – but then took off, leaving me in the water, at night, with no chance of anyone seeing me. On the boat was were a group of lawyers, all drunk. Fortunately they circled and heard me yelling at them. I was saved. One of them gave me his business card in the hope that I was a potential client, albeit in a wetsuit.

Keith Gordon driving the Nacra catamaran

Offshore in the North Pacific

While I was in San Francisco I started getting some practice crewing on racing yachts, leading towards getting my US Government Coastguard Certificate to operate as a professional operator and captain. One of the yachts I crewed on had a wealthy owner with very little sailing experience, so unsurprisingly we had some hilarious escapades. First we managed to capture a big red steel buoy, entrapping it between our spinnaker pole, the spinnaker guy and the hull. We couldn't get free of it, and hoped none of the other yachts could see us and get us disqualified. We completed the race – but the game was up, as there was loads of red paint all over the port hull topsides.

Next, we were racing along the San Francisco waterfront, where the America's Cup was to take place in 2013, in foiling 72-foot catamarans sailing at 50 mph. We were beating and on the port tack, trying to sail behind another yacht, which, on the starboard tack, had right of way. However, the skipper misjudged it and our spinnaker pole, which stuck out in front of our bows, shot through their pulpit, ripping off lifebuoys and other gear and sending their crew diving for cover. So then we had all this gear torn off the other yacht hanging off our bows, and next we lost control coming towards the exclusive Saint Francis Yacht Club, which was a few feet in front of us as we tacked at the last minute. There was a wedding reception going on outside on the patio, and all the guests ran for cover, thinking we were about to ram them …

Fun in the Caribbean

I was also keen to gain more keelboat experience, as I was planning to buy an ocean racer. In June 1980 I headed to Saint Lucia in the Windward Islands, with Carolyn Sasser and Keith Gordon, a good friend from my time at BP in the North Sea and Alaska. We chartered a Peterson 44, a big sloop. Our first anchorage was deep in Marigot Bay, a 'hurricane hole' where ships would shelter from storms. Spanish, French and British fleets of warships used to hide there, with palm fronds tied to the masts for camouflage.

Next stop was a wider bay, below the twin points of the Piton mountains. All these places were paradise, at the time little visited. We sailed on southwards to the next island, Saint Vincent. However, we were advised not to stop there, as several yachtsmen had been murdered, one of them beheaded. As we sailed past, a dark vessel shadowed our every move and we suspected pirates. Fortunately, our boat was faster and we got away.

We had an open passage to the next island, Bequia, with big squalls, rainbows and dark blue Atlantic seas. After dark, two boys with a homemade guitar in a little dinghy serenaded us with Caribbean calypso songs. The following morning I visited Customs, which turned out to be an experience from centuries past. First I had to declare our liquor on board in gallons. Then I had to declare how many people had died on our voyage. Finally, I had to report if there had been any noticeable decline in the rat population on board, an indication of plague.

On our next passage we caught a 6-foot kingfish which fed us for the rest of our voyage. We sailed to Tobago Keys, a windswept anchorage exposed to the Atlantic, where the water was a bright pale green, then we went on to Union Island, to fill up our fresh water. Here the natives were hostile, and reluctantly sold us water supplied in buckets by Land Rover. Union Island was rarely visited, with serious poverty. Marine cargo was still transported by sailing boats.

I'd enjoyed my time sailing offshore and navigating in races from Europe to the Caribbean, and I had learned a lot. But now it was time to realise a dream I'd had since I was a boy: singlehanded transocean racing, which would test me to and beyond my limits.

5 Transpacific solo

I am in mid-Pacific, competing singlehanded in my 38-foot ocean racer, *Alliance*. I pluck up enough courage to set the 1½-oz small chute in the fresh conditions, and have a ghastly time of it. It takes me two hours to do a ten-minute job. The sock wraps itself around the forestay, the spreaders and any running rigging it can get hold of. When I finally raise the spinnaker it has a monstrous hourglass in it. This is where I need my other eight crew members. … 'Okay, don't panic,' I shout at myself as a squall descends. … We roll in a series of broaches, then I rush back to take the helm.

The next two hours are a pure adrenaline rush, as *Alliance* surfs down 10–15-foot waves in roaring sheets of spray. I can't leave the helm, as the wind is too strong for the self-steering; we would either broach or gybe, risking being dismasted. But as the wind is far too strong for the chute and getting stronger, I'll have to go back onto the foredeck to drop it. 'How am I going to get this monster down?' I ask myself out loud.

The Pacific Ocean

In 1982 I started looking for my dream yacht. Soon, I found her, a Canadian C&C 38 offshore ocean racer, moored on a private dock at the bottom of her owner's lawn, in the Sacramento Delta that feeds into the San Francisco Bay. It was love at first sight. She had raced in the Atlantic, and in the Transpacific race, and she needed a crew of eight to handle her 17 sails, including 5 spinnakers, controlled through 16 winches.

I named her *Alliance*. With some friends, I started racing in the bay, and then went for an offshore sea trial in the winter of 1982. We sailed south off the north Pacific coast to Santa Cruz. On the way back, we were nearly wrecked. I was asleep down below on a pitch-black night, when I heard a yell from the cockpit: 'Breakers!' We had drifted into the surf and were between two great waves, on the point of being rolled and washed up ashore. There was no wind, so to escape we started the motor. Success! Then we sailed on to Half Moon Bay, and back to San Francisco, in big winter seas up to 15 feet.

We campaigned offshore for three years, and got our crew trained up for all the complex sail handling. I did the Doublehanded Farallones race a couple of times, with Jim Parrett. This required the helmsman to do the work of three crew, and the foredeck crew to do the work of five. It required a lot of agility and strength, and was especially difficult when hoisting or dropping the big spinnakers. The wind was often strong, and the approach to San Francisco Golden Gate was rough, often with a 5–6-knot tide ebbing against the breakers, which could be 10–20 feet high. We often surfed this 7-tonne yacht at 12 knots or more on these steep waves. We lost control of the boat many times, usually due to broaching. One of my crew, an ex-American football defensive line-backer, was a tough cookie. Our crew was celebrating a race in our jacuzzi on the patio overlooking a 30-mile view when he accidentally ran through a plate glass window in the dark, wearing only his swimming trunks, shattering glass over 400 square feet. We called for four paramedic teams and an ambulance, and he ended up with 96 stitches. He handled all this as though it was a minor accident.

One of our crew was Peter Bird, who had just become the first person to row across the Pacific, a fantastic achievement that took 294 days. Peter had a great sense of humour, which kept him going all those months. He made videos of his days at sea, including him interviewing a seagull that had landed on his boat.

When I introduced him to Jim Parrett, he said: 'Another Bird … part of my species … you must be a good fellow. We'll have great crew with two birds in it.' He popped a champagne cork before a race start, and a seagull caught it – 'Another bird,' he said. 'A good omen.'

Another of my crew was a marketing director, and when he said he thought ocean rowing was a bit pointless, Peter swiftly replied, 'It's my profession, I get paid for it, like a stuntman. And I'd rather be rowing than marketing.'

Sadly, Peter died in 1996 while rowing eastwards across the Pacific to set another record. His boat broke up during a storm. I was asked to say a eulogy to him at the memorial service. Peter was a great pioneer of ocean rowing, pushing the boundaries in a way that entertained people. Every adventurer has their own motives. For Peter, it was that ordinary life was just too boring. Also, he was sponsored by Sector Watches, and so, as he had so succinctly stated, it became his job, his career, his means of making a living.

My heart was set on the Singlehanded Transpacific race, from San Francisco to Hawaii. Having tried the Doublehanded Farallones race, I now wanted to go it alone, so to develop more experience of solo sailing I did the Singlehanded Farallones race a couple of times. I'd installed a self-steering vane, which freed me up to do the work of seven crew. It was tremendous fun, developing new technology and being at sea alone. I had to be careful not to get overpowered, though, since it was really tough getting sails down even with an eight-man crew, and to do this heavy work on my own I needed to take a series of carefully measured steps.

Great Pacific Longitude race origins

The Great Pacific Longitude race, or LongPac, as West Coast singlehanders affectionately call it, was the brainchild of Graham Hawkes, whose profession designing one-person submarines seems particularly relevant in retrospect. The singlehanded race runs from the Golden Gate out into the open ocean and back. Graham's idea had been to create an ocean race without the hassles of a return delivery, and without the effect of handicapping being unknown until all the boats were home. His concept is one that could be applied to a race off any open ocean-adjacent coastline. The difference between this and a conventional race is that instead of all boats sailing the same distance and being corrected on their time around the course, each boat races out over a distance based on its handicap, the fastest boats going the farthest. At each boat's specific designated point in the ocean, it turns around and races back. The result is an exciting sprint to the finish, boat for boat and all the way, both for line honours and for corrected time results, as in class racing. The LongPac also acts as a qualifier for the Singlehanded Transpacific race.

An additional factor is that, unlike a conventional race such as the Fastnet, boats are not sailing to a specific mark but to a longitude line. The skipper can therefore choose the shortest course, or go north or south of it. In the LongPac, most decide to stay as far north as possible, to find favourable winds and tidal streams.

Preparations

For me, this was a dream come true. For decades I had read the accounts of ocean races by singlehanders, and I held them in awe. Now I would be joining their ranks. How would I manage the solitude? Would I enjoy it, or would I be terrified? How would I get the big spinnaker down in strong winds – would I be overpowered? Most importantly, would I avoid falling overboard to certain death?

Alliance beating out of San Francisco Bay

Pre-race preparations for me revolved around the concept that this was likely to be a medium-air sprint of 4–5 days. *Alliance* was by far the heaviest boat in the fleet, and to have any chance of winning she would need to be stripped out. We removed the comfort items like cockpit cushions and floorboards, and we filled only the starboard water tank, as ballast for the beat out. At my longitude line I would dump this, and two large bottles would do me for the run back.

Sailing inventory was kept to a minimum and again piled up on the starboard side. For the beat out, I had a reefable No. 1, also furlable, and a No. 3 as backup and for booming out for heavy-air running. On a reach back I would use a 150 per

The Alliance racing crew

cent high clew full-cut reacher. If the wind were freed enough, there was a choice of a ½ oz chute, or two tri-radials prepacked in modified North socks: a full size ¾ oz and a small 1½ oz. There was also a drifter to take care of anticipated light air off the Golden Gate. This was about 400 lb lighter than the complete racing inventory.

For self-steering, there were three systems. For light air, I would use an Autohelm 3000 on a compass heading. For moderate to heavy air wind upwind I had a Monitor windvane self-steering system, and for moderate to heavy air downwind I would use an Autohelm 2000 driving the vane on the Monitor on a compass heading. This was homemade, and unique at the time. The Monitor on its own was too slow to control the boat on a fast spinnaker run.

There were a few other modifications to make the boat easy to singlehand. I rigged jib car traveller lines to allow continuous tuning with the furler. The North spinnaker socks had internal and external control line loops, a continuous red stripe, swivels and jam cleats, all to allow easier snuffing and ensure less chance of a tangle. The reefing controls were all led to the base of the mast, and I could put a reef on in 30 seconds. Two spinnaker poles allowed easier heavy-air gybing. Most of the lines led back to the cockpit, where a battery of winches, including two giant Lewmar 65s, and nine sheet bags awaited them. I used North's sailing shape guides to help with the sail trim, determined to sail the boat as fast as with our regular crew of eight to nine.

Safety items included two EPIRBs, a life raft and continuous jacklines, which would allow me to sleep in oilskins with my safety harness on and to get from the helm to the bow without unclipping. But I left behind the crewmember overboard pole and horseshoe life rings; they have no place on a singlehanded boat. I also left behind my storm jib and trysail – something I was to regret.

The Singlehanded Sailing Society required mast-climbing gear, so I had a three-part tackle system that Peter Bird, the Transpacific solo rower, had successfully used on his own singlehanded TransPac sailing race the previous year.

Also on board was a trusty, even though corroded, Zenith radio that I'd lent to Peter; twice it had been the only navigational device that survived on his TransPac boat, allowing him to find local radio stations and fix his position. Peter had sold me two solar chargers, which had an interesting history. They had been on his rowing boat, *Hele-on-Britannia*, and had still been attached to the bow and stern when the boat had broken up on the Great Barrier Reef. Several weeks later the Australian Navy recovered the bow and stern, which were displayed in a Sydney museum – minus the solar panels, which still worked for Peter's TransPac under sail and would be tested again on *Alliance*. I have seen the bow and stern of Peter's previous rowing boat in a museum in England after they had met a similar fate on Maui, and it was a reminder of what can happen on a lee shore.

For food, there was canned food for light going, and dried ramen cup-soups for heavy conditions. These would be filled from a thermos of hot water bolted upside down in the aft cabin bulkhead. This system would prove to be priceless.

The LongPac start

The start of the inaugural race at 8.00 a.m. on 31 August 1985 saw nine boats beating out of the Golden Gate: for me, there were 400 miles to go. There were singlehanded monohulls, and one doublehanded catamaran, in a class of its own. The catamaran was Peter Hogg's *Tainui*, a Newick 40 in which he had won the 1984 Singlehanded Transpacific. Hogg's boat was unbeatable on a reach or a run, but would suffer on the beat out. Graham Hawkes was sailing an Olson 40, *Aquila*, which would be a tough boat to beat in heavy air downwind. Bud Fraze was in a Capo 26, a slower boat than *Alliance*, so sailing a shorter course.

Manoeuvring prior to the start, I was somewhat impressed at the amount of high-tech sails on show, and could see spinnakers packed and poles ready for a windshift. My pulse quickened as the countdown went to zero, and then at the gun I was in hot pursuit as we beat out of the Golden Gate before the fleet split onto either side of the approaches and the flood tide. I went north: I didn't want to risk a repeat of the Singlehanded Farallones race, when I'd had to short tack inside all the rocks at Mile Rock with my big No. 1. Bud and I got away, but the rest got swept back in, some of them anchoring.

Leaving the Farallon Islands behind, at 27 miles out, was a weird feeling, having in previous races always turned there and raced back. It was somewhat akin to venturing into the deep end of the pool. Out here the water was about 3 miles deep and an inky black colour.

In the evening the wind freshened. I put in both reefs, and then, as the wind hit 30–35 knots apparent, reefed the genoa to storm jib size. I was surprised to get seasick as I had on a scopolamine patch, which I'd applied before setting off, and they'd proved effective in the past. I'd always been concerned about getting sick singlehanded because of the effect on morale, but was relieved to find that in the event it had little effect on my attitude. Besides, I wasn't the only one feeling sick at this stage in the race.

The self-steering gear broke

Suddenly there was a loud crack and the boat came up into the wind. I found that the self-steering blade had twisted around and was dragging sideways through the water. So despite the Autohelm not being not suited to these conditions, I switched it on. The rising wind would demand the Monitor overnight. I went over the stern and saw that a bearing had popped out. Fortunately, there was a spare on board and I was able to get it in, complete with tiny circlip, neither getting my fingers crushed by the gear as it swung wildly around, nor getting swept overboard.

Alliance and I had the sea to ourselves in a ragged sunset and what looked like a rising gale. A huge breaker appeared a quarter of a mile to starboard and I felt seriously alarmed, thinking it was a rock, but it must have been a whale jumping or a freak wave. *Alliance* was charging to windward at 8 knots in 30–35 apparent wind speed; she was taking the conditions very well, and if this heavy air kept up, we'd do well. After three years in the charter business, *Alliance* was now idiotproof and almost indestructible. I put in the log: 'Very wet and noisy down below. Everything requires superhuman effort – even putting on oilskins or getting a piece of cheese.'

In the morning porpoises came by, and their presence did a lot to lift my soggy, cold spirits. Later the wind moderated, the sun came out, I hung wet clothes out to dry and took a few sun shots to check the LORAN. For the calculations I used an HP41CV computer; it can even tell you where 80 stars are in case you don't have your almanac. You don't need to do any paperwork at all.

The next night was beautiful under a nearly full moon, and I drove the boat hard as I saw a sail on my port quarter. It turned out to be *Aquila*. At 1800 Graham, Bud and I all got in contact with each other on the VHF. The wind had backed, pushing us south, and Bud was 20 miles north on the other tack. There was a 2-knot set to the south and we were all clawing our way to windward as high as possible. Bud had done remarkably well in the conditions, and was going to be the boat to beat. But it seemed I was in the lead for now. Graham had had a rough night and a wet time, and had thought of turning back. Meanwhile I constantly tuned the sails, reefed and unreefed, furled and unfurled, looking for that extra 1/10th of a knot.

The halfway point turnaround

On Monday morning at 0850, I reached my line at 127°27'33"W. I took a photo of the LORAN in both TD (Time Difference) and Lat/Lon mode before and after turning, then gybed around and headed back into the rising sun: 200 miles to go. It was a big moment, out there without a visible mark. As it turned out, *Alliance* was the first boat to turn. It might, I thought, be a new first in the history of yacht racing – the first yacht ever to round a longitude line as a mark.

I'd expected the run back to be easy and fast, but progress across the chart was still painfully slow. The LORAN showed that we were cranking along at 9.6 knots average. By sunset the wind was back up to 30 knots and had swung north, putting us back onto a beat. This was good for my race but predictably miserable. The wind was gusting to 40 knots apparent, and *Alliance* was severely overpowered with a full main, but I didn't want to reef it, as all the controls were on the starboard side which was often under water. I prayed that the wind would abate after dark, but it did the opposite. The going was bumpy and rough.

Suddenly there was a huge bang and the boat shook like a dog coming out of the sea. The jib, which had previously been 50 per cent, storm jib size, had unfurled to its full 150 per cent[11] and was threatening to do something very nasty, like knock us down or shake the mast to pieces. I crawled up with two lifelines attached to the jackline, and found that in just those few minutes the furling line had chafed through on the final rail block. I had to do something quickly before major damage was done. Getting the No. 1 down was out of the question unless I was prepared to convert it to a sea anchor, which would do little good to my race result, or indeed my bank balance. I could tie a knot in the furling line – but then how could I lead it through the rail blocks, and how would I stop it happening again? The foredeck was going completely underwater and I hung on for dear life. The boat would not slow below 8 knots and I knew that if I went over the rail I'd never pull myself back on board.

'Okay, don't panic,' I shouted at myself. 'One thing at a time, okay.' That made me feel I was in charge again. I crawled back and got a spinnaker snatch block. I could snap it over the line after tying the knot, and it would chafe less than the one it replaced.

I slithered back, my heart hammering and the adrenaline pouring. These were the heaviest conditions *Alliance* had ever seen at sea, and here I was, singlehanded with a full sail. I thought of the storm jib but I could have never got it up. What if I couldn't furl the No. 1? I thought of cutting it loose with a knife, but the wind and waves were stronger now, and trying to lower it would have been extremely dangerous. I needed two hands for the knot, but was getting airborne on the bow – I'd never tied such an ugly reef knot. I undid the next rail block, which was by now under water, and went back to try to furl the jib.

Would it, or wouldn't it? Slowly I winched it in and got it back down to storm jib size. The next block stopped the knot, so it wouldn't go any smaller than that unless I took the bolt cutters to the block to free it from the rail. I was not about to unfurl the jib again to release the strain on the shackle, nor was I going to try to loosen it with the load on it under the water.

The next thing to do was rest for an hour before reefing the main. I put both reefs in at 10 p.m. under the foredeck light – and this took me over half an hour compared with the usual minute or less. It was quite the most desperate foredeck work I've ever done, with two very short life harnesses on, both feet standing on the buried lee lifeline, and my head about 6 inches off the deck to avoid getting it taken off by a loop of wild flogging rope, and with the water pouring over the deck trying to sweep me off.

When I got back to the cockpit the wind speed was showing 45 knots, and I sheeted in as *Alliance* leapt off at 9½ knots on a close reach. When I transferred control from the Autohelm to the Monitor I marvelled at how she sailed like a dinghy, dancing over the waves in the moonlight between the clouds. She seemed to have shrunk in the gale, keeping company with my now somewhat shrunken ego. I went down below to crash in the quarter berth, as all the other berths were swimming in the water pouring through hatches and tracks – previously tested as impervious under a high-pressure hose. My log entry reads: 'V fast, big moon, terrifying.'

---

11 Relates to the area enclosed by the forestay, the mast and the foredeck.

Anchored in Polynesia

Suddenly, there was a deafening crash and brilliant flash of light. A thunderbolt? No – there were no burning smells and I was still alive. Just another big wave, which had been enough to trigger the large 'shipmate overboard' strobe light. It happened a few more times, so as I couldn't stop the light being triggered by the g-forces I threw it into a cupboard. It wouldn't be any use to me anyhow, unless I took to the life raft, and that was extremely unlikely since I couldn't imagine being able to control the raft in this amount of wind. It would be like setting a storm spinnaker.

I thought of trying to get the main down but decided it was too risky; I probably wouldn't be strong enough to control it and lash it to the boom. The wind was now gusting 50 knots, storm force 10 and backing, which was not a good sign. I had to steer 30 degrees north to get 60 degrees north over the ground on the LORAN, due to drift and leeway. The drift was over 2 knots south. There was an infernal din of squeaks, cracks and bangs everywhere, much of it from the hull flexing against the bulkheads.

Storm force 10 at night

There was an interesting noise coming from the ice chest. It sounded like a bunch of bottles in a tumble dryer. I opened the top and found that the gale had mixed an enormous eggnog; the beer bottles were swimming around, and their tops had all unscrewed themselves, along with all but one of the soft drink bottles. A box of half-and-half[12] had been pulverised to nothing, along with raw eggs, whose shells had been ground to dust. Some old cheese and ham added to the aroma. The boat was heeling more, and this lot was threatening to spill all over the cabin, so there was nothing for it but, strapped in with the safety harness and two stove straps, to bail it all out.

Afterwards I rested, ready for action with oilskins, harness, boots and gloves on, all soaked through from the foredeck work. Every few minutes, *Alliance* felt as though she'd hit a concrete wall, and I worried that she

---

12 Thin cream with about half the fat of single cream.

might split the hull or a bulkhead. I decided that surviving was more important than winning, so went on deck to bear off. It was 3 a.m. and the wind was still steady at 50 knots, force 10, on what was now a broad reach. I made a humble request for a favourable consideration from the Powers That Be, and also called the Coast Guard to let them know my position, and to ask them to tell the marine weather people what was happening, since they were still forecasting 10–20 knots. No response; we were probably out of range. The moon was out, and the waves hissed and roared by. The Monitor was doing a fantastic job and I prayed that the bearing would hold. There was heavy water going over and into the cockpit. *Alliance* was beautifully balanced and just roaring along in masses of boiling foam.

I later heard how the others had fared. Bud had turned an hour after me, and got to double-reefed main in the gale, but could not hold the boat on a reach, so he ran off south, holding 17 knots steady. His knot meter then hit 20 and broke. He steered by hand all night, with one safety harness tied to the base of the mast inside the cabin, and the line jammed in the closed hatch and another clipped to the rail, while drinking cans of Classic Coke for the caffeine and sugar. His boat had two broken bulkheads and a broken companionway latch where he'd been thrown against it. She'd been knocked down horizontally once with mast and boom in the water and inside the curl of the breaker, with Bud hanging from both hands from the lifelines. He said he was too scared to try to get the sails down.

Graham had broken two ribs and had gone down below to ride out the storm, averaging 11 knots on his LORAN. Peter Hogg, having been forced way south, broke a backstay, causing the mast to shoot forward and catapulting the masthead light 200 feet ahead. Linda Webber-Rettie lost her mainsheet block and both autopilots, so hove to in seas estimated at 15 feet, landing up at Point Sur. Buzz Sanders got through, but only by regular pumping as his keel was breaking away from the hull and a big crack was letting a lot of water in. Paul Steinert had lost all his electrics and was unable to fix his position, so returned as a DNF at his own request. Jim Fair was unable to hold a double-reefed main and ended up under bare poles trailing warps; we had all been worried about him, as several boats the size of his Merit 25 had broken up and been lost with all hands in recent races off northern California. The pilot charts show the area off San Francisco to be the roughest in the North Pacific. The number of incidents would certainly seem to bear this out.

Sprint to the finish

I crashed again and slept through my usual one-hour alarm. I came on deck to see the wind down to 25–30 knots and porpoises jumping out of the curling crests of the waves, then surfing down the wave faces. Suddenly ten of them leapt out of the backside of a wave, coming straight at my starboard beam, and when I rushed down below to get the camera I could hear them, through the hull, squeaking at each other.

A little white sail was behind me about 5 miles away and intermittently visible on the waves. I remembered Errol Bruce's advice that races are often won or lost after gales, so I unreefed and unfurled everything and started to surf the boat. The Monitor got her surfing too, and I couldn't help a few yahoos as this old displacement boat put a big bone in her teeth. The sail behind me disappeared.

By afternoon, the sun was drying everything out – but no peace for the wicked, or the singlehanded sailor. It was spinnaker time. A haze came down, and I spotted the Farallones a couple of miles off. And then a spinnaker right behind me, about a couple of miles back. I felt I might be in the lead, as I doubted that any of the other boats would have pushed through the gale in the way that *Alliance* had done, so this could be a sprint to the finish for first place. I decided to reach up

Bora Bora in swells from the Southern Ocean

and go between the Farallones to get more VMG and avoid the hole on the south side. The spinnaker behind disappeared. *Alliance* was slipping along faster than if she'd been fully crewed (being 1,400 lb (635 kg) lighter in weight), and was doing 6.1 knots in 5 knots of apparent wind.

At sunset the wind suddenly died completely and I cut Southeast Farallon Island much too close; I was only carried clear of the rocks by the strong surface drift. The Autopilot had died, and a battery check showed both banks dead, presumably due to salt water shorting out the wiring. The wind was too light for the Monitor, so I no longer had self-steering or lights. The engine almost started with a blast of ether, but not quite … it would be quite a night.

The night, as it turned out, was eerie. Sea lions (or something else?) were breathing heavily nearby. There was only a knot of wind and I couldn't keep the big ¾ oz full. It was overcast, dripping a very light drizzle, and pitch-black. The spinnaker was so badly wrapped around the forestay that I had to take a knife to all the ropes in the snuffer and cut it loose. Up went the drifter as I desperately tried to keep awake with the boat doing 360-degree circles. I gybed the drifter back and forth in vain, running up and down decks with my miner's light on, stumbling over a cobweb of lines, the boat continuing to pirouette without self-steering or indeed any sense of direction within my own mind. I promised myself that next time I'd bring a spare battery and a generator. The others had them, and I cursed as I continually lost control of the boat while trying to work both ends at once. Down with the drifter, and up with the ½ oz spinnaker. Amazingly it went up right first time. Then the wind filled in from the south, so up went No. 1, and down with the ½ oz. Wet sails filled the dark cabin down below.

Where was the other boat? I couldn't see any lights. Meanwhile, wild ducks were everywhere in the water, taking off in droves that sounded like concert hall applause as *Alliance* carved through their midst. A tanker roared past as I nervously kept out of the way.

I went under the Golden Gate against a foul tide, and the beautiful bay opened up in a myriad of colours in front of me. I crept into the shore to cheat the tide and crossed the finish line as a cheer went up from ashore.

I thought I recognised Bud's voice. 'Is that you, Bud?' I asked.

'Yes,' I heard.

'Who else is in?' I asked nervously.

'Just you and me, and two Peters,' he said.

I couldn't figure that out, but it turned out that Bud, hallucinating, had thought I'd tried to swim to his boat and crawl on board, so he'd yelled, 'Over here, over here', but when he'd put his spreader lights on, he'd seen I was an elephant seal. For a long time he'd thought someone was on board with him. Presumably, my alter ego had already crossed the line in his boat …

'How long have you been in?' I asked.

'Only about 5 minutes!'

What a race! – 5 minutes' difference after 94 hours? In fact it was more like an hour; Bud had sailed a great race, with virtually no sleep and pushing his boat as hard as he could.

I have occasionally been asked: as you're on your own, how do people know you don't cheat? My answer to that is that it's out of the question that anyone would, because it would be so unsatisfying. Plus, singlehanders are a close-knit group, so it would be hard to face your friends/rivals afterwards. You *could* cheat on the Fastnet, or any number of around-the-buoys races, but people hardly ever do, for the same reasons. Finally, if anyone were to raise any doubts the burden of proof would lie with the skipper, hence the sunshots and LORAN photos we took.

Alone in mid-Pacific

0205, 24 June 1986: The alarm goes off rudely. I roll over to switch on the SSB radio and sit up to see if any satellites have been over while I was asleep, but the next good one is not due until 0326. The wind has dropped since our last few days of violent surfing, and I have a feeling that I've lost my lead in the monohull division to Dan Newland. But I'm pleased with my boat's progress, considering that at 18,000 lb she is the heaviest in the fleet, and also the oldest, now in her tenth year of racing.

Now that we have travelled 1,700 miles the radio signal from San Francisco is only just audible: 'High 1030 millibars 38 north 140 west … 1020 isobar 49 north 125 west 28 north 133 west 25 north 145 west …'. I replay the tape-recording several times to get all the numbers right, and then I plot it up. As I fear, the Pacific High is moving south, and I'm facing the risk of every TransPac racer's nightmare: getting

Helming Alliance in the North Pacific

stuck in the high. This is especially bad for me, as I've taken a flyer further north than the rest of the fleet. I know they're all hoping that the high will sit on me.

The moon is full. *Alliance* rolls dead downwind under poled-out blooper, reacher and double-reefed main. Jupiter has risen and I take a sighting on it with my sextant. Earlier on in the evening, before the moon rose, Venus had been so bright that she'd lit up the sky and cast a dazzling glitter path, defining the horizon and enabling me to get a shot of the Pole Star. I draw the lines of position: I am at 26°34'N, 146°36'W. There are only 780 miles to go.

I go down to get a wine cooler. I don't have to do any soul-searching to ask why I'm here – it's very pure, very peaceful, and I'm lucky to have the experience. For ten days I haven't seen a ship or a plane, or even a vapour trail.

The blooper collapses, and I trim the sheet. The knot meter goes up a tenth of a knot. I look back over the trip so far. It hasn't always been easy.

The Singlehanded TransPacific start

The hard part was leaving the dock before the start. It was cold, grey and overcast. Bonnie[13] and Jim Parrett, my support team, had been up most of the night fixing rigging problems, provisioning and loading dry ice. They were on the dock with a TV crew and other friends when I waved goodbye, setting out solo from San Francisco to Hawaii.

The good news was that I could not incur any more expenses, or pay any more bills, for at least the next couple of weeks. The wind was out of the west, promising a beat, which suited me, as my competition were mostly ultralight.

The 18 boats at the start displayed a lot of hi-tech equipment. Dan Newland had Kevlar spinnakers. Most of the favourite boats had commercial sponsors, including the Australian Crowther 40 trimaran *Bullfrog Sunblock,*

---

13 Bonnie and I were to marry soon after, in 1989.

co-owned by Ian Johnson and Cathy Hawkins. Hank Dekker, who had impaired vision, was doing his first race and his third Pacific crossing. Linda, née Webber-Rettie, who had recently married Dan Newland, was the only woman in the race, and this Pacific crossing, in *Predator*, a 28-foot Hawkfarm, was her fourth. Favourite Mark Rudiger had done six TransPac races, and this was his third singlehanded. 1984 winner Peter Hogg, from New Zealand, was sailing his Newick 40 Catamaran *Tainui* with a new cabin; his previous one had been destroyed by waves during the last race. *Alliance*, like a lot of IOR designs, was a real handful downwind for a crew of nine. I had been developing spinnaker and self-steering techniques to be able to surf her singlehanded. The race would put this to the test.

My race got off to a good start, as I stayed offshore and caught more wind so that by the evening I was in the lead, ahead of even the three big multihulls. Having studied the weather statistics, I'd decided that the way to win was to sail rhumb line rather than the more popular dive south into the Trades, and that I was going to concentrate on sustainable speeds rather than bursts of surfing. This strategy put a lot of emphasis on avoiding fatigue. The history of any singlehanded race points out the drastic consequences of the sail-handling disasters, navigational errors and equipment malfunctions caused by fatigue.

1228, 16 June 1986. I take a gamble and tack on to 230 degrees magnetic, taking a flyer to the north of the High as it spins an eastern lobe off straight at my competition. I beat towards a trough into a rough northwesterly swell and drizzle all night. I awake when the wind shifts north-west in the morning. I tack back to starboard as a line squall sweeps through, then hoist the chute as the wind frees. The plan is working!

1500, 16 June. I am in despair. There is a bang and a tearing noise. The ½ oz chute has ripped beyond repair from luff to luff. I put up the ¾ oz but the wind is dying, and worse still, the barometer is rising. The second High is moving in to camp on me. I dive south to try to put myself between the finish line and the rest of the fleet.

The life of a singlehander on the ocean

I soon settled into a routine. My days started with a shower and a big breakfast, then I spent my waking hours sail-changing and trimming, and optimising the self-steering, avoiding manual steering unless there was too much wind or too little for self-steering. Upwind I could adjust the sail area very easily with slab reefs and a furler. But downwind was another story, and then as the wind rose I would go from ½ oz chute to ¾ oz chute, to 1½ oz chute, then a reef in the main, then one or two headsails (either reacher, drifter or blooper poled out), then to double-reefed main, then no main. Above 30 knots I would either drop one headsail (on a loose luff) or furl the other one until the boat tracked under control.

I ate well every evening, with fresh vegetables from net hammocks swinging around, and initially frozen meat in dry ice. Bonnie had prepared all the provisioning, and had also packed a string of presents, some of which would cause me to burst out laughing, such as a singlehanded table tennis game. The best was a mouth organ with a book

Taking a sun-shot with the sextant

called *Learning the Harmonica for the Musically Hopeless*. For most of the trip, I was over 200 miles from the nearest competitor so I didn't have to worry about upsetting anyone as I practised. The evening often ended with a couple of beers and *Chariots of Fire* or African R&B at sunset. I was up many times each night to trim or change sails, catching sleep only in short spells.

The first few days I had an overwhelming desire to talk to someone, either another racer or my support team. A huge number of people had helped prepare the boat, and I felt like an astronaut representing a team effort. One night I had a hilarious conversation with the marine radio operator onshore on long-distance SSB. Apparently, he was being called by another ship, the *Pacific Alliance*, at the same time, but could not be heard by it, and was getting most frustrated and confused.

He asked me, '*Alliance*, how many radio operators do you have on board? Over.'

'Only one, over.' I replied

'Roger – is this a personal call? Over.'

'Roger.'

'Is it for the captain? Over.'

'Roger,' I replied, trying not to laugh.

As the days wore on, I began to enjoy the solitude, the porpoises by my side, the blue-black swells, and the stars and planets. There was often an albatross circling me.

The Trade Wind sleigh ride

Now I was in the Trades, and flying fish fluttered from wave to wave, sometimes landing in the boat for breakfast. At night, I surfed at 11 knots with the main vanged out on one side and the reacher poled out on the other. As my new equipment and ideas began to prove themselves I soon developed enough confidence to sleep through all the crashing and banging without fear of a gybe. I could balance the rig with the furler, and I could reef going downwind. I vanged the main out with a light line to the foredeck rail, designed to break in a heavy-air gybe, and replaced the vang with a boom brake, which did a wonderful job during a gybe as both a cockpit-controlled vang and a brake.

My self-steering design was working well for upwind work as I had a windvane, and for light air an autopilot – but the big problem was how to self-steer this monohull in heavy air downwind, as my electronic devices were too slow and my vane devices reacted too violently to changes in the apparent wind direction. A combination would, I thought, be the right approach, so I set up a system where a tiller-type autopilot drove a vane, allowing compass course control, and a very powerful response from the servo-pendulum in the water. The result was highly satisfactory; although *Alliance* would yaw a bit she never gybed accidentally in thousands of miles downwind. The other racers behind me were, however, having a terrible time – broaching, gybing, losing halyards up the mast, losing things overboard and sailing over their spinnakers – generally because their self-steering would not work with the chute up, so they were getting fatigued from hours at the helm.

12 noon, 20 June: I pluck up enough courage to set the 1½ oz small chute in the fresh conditions, and have a ghastly time of it. It takes two hours to do a ten-minute job, and I have big reservations about the snuffer system afterwards. I wear a hardhat, kneepads and harness for the foredeck work, and even so I take a battering as the boat rolls me from the port lifelines to starboard and back. Standing would be suicidal, and each round trip to the cockpit takes several minutes. The sock wraps around the forestay, the spreaders, and any running rigging it can get hold of. When I finally raise the spinnaker, it has a monstrous hourglass in it.

I crawl back to trim the guy. The pole-end fitting has come loose. Reattaching it is a nightmare, and I use my head as a third hand to wedge the pole against the pulpit.

Self-steering in the Trade Winds

The lazy sheet is wrapped around the pole such that I cannot let the spinnaker fly for a heavy-air take down. I must not have a wrap. This is where I need my other eight crew members. I have a net up, but it is possible for the spinnaker to get between the net and the furled jib, furling everything into an almighty mess. To my horror, I notice it is doing just this. 'Okay, don't panic', I shout at myself as a squall descends. I put a bolt on the furler to prevent it rotating. I untie the knot on the end of the pole with a 20-foot boathook, as we roll in a series of near-broaches, then I rush back to take the helm.

Surfing big waves

The next two hours were a pure adrenaline rush, as nasty squalls sped overhead and with the spinnaker up *Alliance* surfed down 10–15-foot waves in roaring sheets of spray.

'How am I going to get this monster down?' I asked myself out loud.

'Let's break it down into 20 steps, and do 3 steps at a time,' I replied.

I waited for the lighter wind immediately following a squall, engaged the self-steering, and released the guy and the lazy sheet. I prayed hard, and then went forward and hauled the snuffer down. A few more trips back to the cockpit and then I waited for a roll to weather and dropped the whole shooting match on the deck. I gasped a quiet 'Thank God!'

I discovered that piling on the sail area didn't add to the day's run, even though we had longer bursts of surfing. This was because the extra sail made the boat follow an S-shaped, hence much longer, course through the ocean.

The other racers were having a hard time of it. Mark Rudiger had been up the mast three times to retrieve halyards, and on the last occasion the boat had gybed and broached, with the boom hard over on the runner, and the boat two-thirds under water. He coolly told me on the SSB, 'I had to slide down the mainsail to release the runner.' Mark was a superb sailor but was running into a lot of bad luck with his boat and the weather on the southerly course he had pursued. He was the Pied Piper of Singlehanded TransPacs; much of the fleet appeared to follow him around, which made things easier for me, as my rhumb line approach was paying off. Bud Fraze was having trouble too; he said, 'It's impossible to sleep in this fibreglass coffin, and whatever I do I can't stop this boat from surfing.'

For me, though, it was now turning into a race to get there before everything wore out. The rudder was creaking ominously, and now the whole cockpit was coming loose from the hull, making loud cracking noises every time it moved, preventing me from getting any sleep in the quarter berth. I bolted it all up with teak and epoxy. I had blown a hole in my blooper and torn up the drifter on the self-steering oar when I lost it overboard in a douse. The spinnaker halyards were fraying badly, and the mainsheet traveller had sheared in a squall, requiring me to cannibalise the baby stay for parts.

Approaching Hawaii

On the approach to Hawaii the weather became unpleasant; big squalls hit at night, descending pitch-black down to sea level. In the day the sun rose to 89 degrees, almost vertical, and the heat was intense. I tried to avoid sail-changing in the heat of the day, and I found that even in good conditions I would need to drink a gallon of water, along with several salt pills, just to set and douse the spinnaker. I realised I could only do that a limited amount of times before I drank all my water supplies.

I was also having a lot of trouble with my snuffer, and it was only giving me 50 per cent success, mainly because the rolling of the boat made a cat's cradle out of all the halyards and rigging.

1215 p.m., 25 June. The snuffer jams as I try to drop the big ¾ oz in a rising squall. I resort to an untried experiment in shorthanded spinnaker drops, as follows: The first problem is that the boat will not self-steer in its overpowered condition and I have to steer all over the ocean trying to avoid a crash or gybe. I bring the pole forward and down, and trim the clew on the lazy guy, which makes the chute lower and more stable, but the wind is still rising, and I cannot leave the helm to go to the foredeck. I let the lazy sheet and guy go, and drop the pole and go forward. Normally at this point it takes a three-strong crew to drag the chute in under the boom, and one more on the halyard. To do it singlehanded requires replacing two of the crew with a winch, and have me hauling in the sail from right by the winch near the companionway. Finally, I cannot risk being dragged overboard if the chute fills or goes for a swim, as even with a harness on I would never get back on board at 7–8 knots.

I take the sheet's snatch block off the leeward rail, and attach it with the sheet still inside it to the weather rail opposite the cockpit, and then grind the chute in under the boom and across the cockpit, slacking only enough halyard to achieve this. When the clew reaches the snatch block, I lash myself into the companionway and let the rest of the chute drop, pulling it in conventionally. The advantage of this method is that the chute can be brought halfway down under total control, and if anything goes wrong with the second half, I can let everything go and still have half the chute in.

1014 a.m., 27 June. I notice that the vane is about to tear loose from the transom. It is coming off its mountings. I go over the stern to work on it as we reach along at 7 knots. In the middle of the job a squall descends and the boat broaches. I clamber back on board, using the stern light as a foothold until it shears off and I fall. My life

PC at the Singlehanded finish line in Kauai

harness works! The tragedy is that I am wearing my only pair of pyjamas at the time (to keep the tropic sun off), and they get torn and written off in the process. I repair the tears with Spinnaker Ripstop tape.

1130 a.m., 28 June. My autopilot fails, and I am unable to self-steer in anything except the lightest breeze with the chute up. Two hundred miles out from Kauai, my radar detector alarms, and I see a battleship hull down on the horizon. Radar detectors are a great invention, but the majority of commercial vessels do not use their radars in clear weather, even at night.

0800 a.m., 29 June. I am looking out for Kauai, as I have only a few miles left. Sure enough, there is a grey shape behind the squall clouds on my port bow, and soon the weather clears to reveal the most beautiful landfall imaginable: rugged jungly pinnacles, cane fields and the sheer 3,000ft drop of the Na Pali Coast. I feel in better shape than ever before: well exercised physically and mentally. The horn blows, and then Bonnie steps aboard with a lei garland, cold wine coolers and champagne. The race is over! Porpoises escort me to my anchorage.

Recovering on Kauai

I came in second in the monohulls, behind Dan Newland, and was second in class. Dan had nearly been dismasted when his lower shrouds broke, and to carry out repairs he had crawled up his mast with an electric drill running off a 110-volt generator on deck through some 12-volt light wire. He had also lost a lot of gear overboard during some spreader-in-the-water knockdowns. Towards the end he described his boat as a prison cell. He had missed the monohull record by just four hours – but Ian Johnson in *Bullfrog* had broken the overall record by nine hours, a tremendous achievement. Peter Hogg had limped in with a broken mast step rotator the day before I arrived.

Two days later, most of the rest of the pack arrived. Dee Alcorn came in to win Division II of the monohulls, and then proceeded to liven up our Fourth of July party by demonstrating his technique for waking up ships' sleepy watchkeepers: catapulting a stick of dynamite at the bridge. The sticks had four-second fuses, and we played chicken by counting to three slowly before releasing them from our fingers.

Last to arrive was Peter Cameron, in a Freedom 25 under 'damage control' (Peter was ex-US Army). When he was closing the Kauai coast on a pitch-black night, he called me on VHF, saying, 'There's something very large out here, breathing very deeply, and it's bigger than your boat and mine combined. Its head's on my starboard side, and its tail's on my port!'

Cathy and Ian sailed *Bullfrog* back to Australia, and Mark Rudiger sailed *Shadowfox* to New Zealand with his wife Kay. Most of the others shipped their boats back, but Bonnie and I decided to sail back to San Francisco.

Back to California

On the return journey we took a truck driver charter client with us, so that he could learn how to cross oceans. We had a spectacular run down the wild and precipitous Na Pali coast, then headed north towards Alaska. We had a rough trip of it, with three weeks of continuous 30 knot-type heavy weather, mostly beating; there were only six hours when it was dry enough to sit in the cockpit without getting drenched. The heavy air was largely caused by a 30-millibar pressure gradient between the Pacific High and the lows. We had three gales, 20-foot seas, and one 65-knot hurricane-force blow – but even that did not stop Bonnie from baking a loaf of bread. But then the boat was knocked over and pinned down on its side for so long that the bread rose diagonally – and our client, in the head at the time, could not get out as the door was now above him. When the worst of the wind abated, he emerged, saying, 'I know what an astronaut feels like in a NASA simulator. It was dark, cold, I was half-upside down, there was water backing up from the head and pouring in through the deck, and there was a terrible shaking and vibration. Never again.' Ever afterwards, he would eye the head door suspiciously for several minutes before plucking up the courage to go in.

For two and a half weeks we didn't see a ship or plane, or talk on the radio, but we did eat some large flying fish that came aboard. We broke the headstay fitting with a very loud bang as we hit a wave, which detached the forestay, and we almost lost the mast. We then did 2,600 miles under a jury rig. We blew out the No. 3 jib twice, and broke a halyard and the baby stay, but we got back without losing the rig by stringing our remaining running rigging as standing rigging. We did almost the whole trip under storm jib and double-reefed main, spending three weeks down below reading books and caulking leaks. The race out had certainly been more enjoyable.

Bonnie helming down the Na Pali coast

Flying fish which flew aboard

The navigation station

Bonnie cooking for Alliance charterers

Professional sailing

I got back to San Francisco only to face financial crisis. My oil industry work had cratered, as the international oil price had collapsed. So I decided to convert my part-time charter and yacht skipper work into a full-time business. It was launched with a stroke of luck. A good friend in the restaurant business had started a new concept, providing luxury meals and evenings on yachts while sailing around San Francisco Bay. The breakthrough came when a TV crew from a major US network filmed this gourmet sailing from *Alliance* and broadcast it on prime time. Then my restaurant friend decided to leave San Francisco and offered me the business. While I was still sailing back from Hawaii, the TV programme aired and 450 bookings came in. I was saved from bankruptcy. We quickly cleaned up *Alliance* and converted her from a singlehanded racer to a luxury yacht. Bonnie organised all the catering and formed a company: Meals on Keels. We added more yachts for larger groups. It was a great success.

Other nautical business avenues I explored included yacht deliveries up and down the West Coast, a sailing and navigation school, yacht maintenance, and – via the all-new video technology available at the time – a learn-to-sail video called 'The Sixty- Minute Sailor', in which I used my venerable Wayfarer, *Calypso*. The video was still doing business 30 years later, having helped thousands of people learn to sail. Some time later I dropped into a rental store and found the video in the 'adult film' section, in a plain cover, hiding its contents. I pointed out to management that it should be in the sports section, but they wanted to keep it where it was – rentals were doing great, since customers apparently thought they were getting the late-night activities of a sailor in a dockside red light district! I often think of the lives I might have changed when they discovered what they were actually getting was sailing tips.!

I remember one particular offshore sailing course I ran. I took *Alliance* out through the Golden Gate as usual, but this time it was different, in a winter force 10 storm. As the ebb tide ripped into the Pacific seas we found huge waves were breaking all around us, so I quickly dropped all sails and ran back under bare poles. As we went under the Golden Gate Bridge, a thunderbolt slammed into the north tower. We were the only boat out. At least my two crew got a credit for the 'heavy weather' section of the training programme – both of them, however, unaware of how dangerous it had been.

One of my better delivery contracts was to skipper a former maxi-racer, *Kialoa II*, with a crew of 15 down to the Mexican border. The aluminium hull sprang a leak, and we only just managed to save the yacht from sinking. We also had an interesting experience when a rocket was launched from a military site, and we had a great light show, followed by an investigation by a US warship.

The delivery business picked up during the winter, as owners didn't want to sail their yachts to Mexico in the darkness (15 hours a day) and face the storms of an unruly North Pacific.

A 14,000-mile delivery from San Francisco to the Mediterranean

Then another stroke of luck. I met up with a graduate from my father's International Politics class at Exeter University. She introduced me to her brother, who wanted to buy a luxury Swan 65 in San Francisco and deliver it to the Mediterranean. It was too big to truck across the USA, so I offered to sail it there. I got the contract.

The boat had just been sailed across the Pacific so the first task was to organise surveys of the vessel, her 16 sails, engine, rigging and electronics. I took her out for a sail, along with a crew of eight. She was pure magic, a powerful sea-going vessel weighing 32 tonnes and displaying quality everywhere. She punched through waves effortlessly. A sister ship had won the Whitbread Round the World race in the Roaring Forties, round Cape Horn. This voyage would satisfy my lifetime ambition of sailing a long voyage – and better still, I would be paid by the mile, even while off watch and asleep!

The yacht was a dream: ketch-rigged with spinnakers, teak deck, three cabins, fresh water maker, four electrical systems, weatherfax, radar, SSB and VHF radios, sat nav/LORAN, Autopilot – altogether $1.4 million replacement value. I would add a generator, gimballed microwave, scuba gear, windsurfers, waterski dinghy and other items for both the transocean delivery and the later conversion to luxury charters. The boat was renamed *Beija Flor*, Portuguese for hummingbird.

Each of the five surveys was completed by a specialist. They were very thorough; the engine survey alone ran to 19 pages of checklists and defects. I soon had hundreds of items to fix, modify or install, and we had teams working on it round the clock. I had to make sure that nothing would fail, as we'd be away from repair facilities for much of the voyage, especially going down the remote west coast of Central America and, later, across the Atlantic.

We also had to bring with us everything we would need for several months and 14,000 miles. We brought spare parts for a year. The boat was very complex, with, like a spacecraft, everything that an isolated community needs generated on board: fresh water maker, navigation systems, electricity generation with 12v, 24v, 110v and 240v power systems, medical facilities and, below the floorboards, a huge truck engine. I drew up maintenance procedures for the crew, daily, weekly and monthly. The stowage list ran over 1,000 items, including 85 charts. We couldn't get everything done in San Francisco in time, so we planned to stop twice for rebuilds, first in Fort Lauderdale, Florida, where we would also repair major items that had failed on the delivery, and second on the Hamble in the UK, where we would modify the boat for racing and its later conversion to charter. These improvements would cost over $100,000.

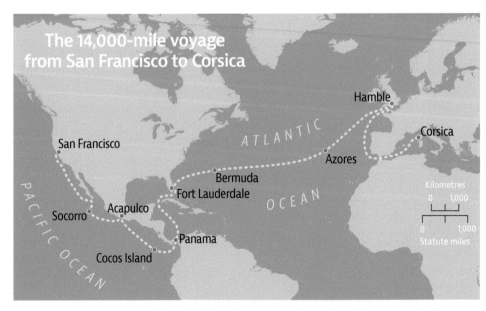

The 14,000 mile voyage from San Francisco to Corsica

The Swan 65 ketch Beija Flor

Part of the voyage was through seas infested with pirates, most of them smuggling drugs across the Caribbean. These gangs would board yachts at gunpoint, kill the crew, transport the drugs, then sink the yacht, so I sought advice from the US Coast Guard and from Control Risks, the security firm my father had co-founded. We were advised to carry weapons, and to demonstrate to any pirate vessels that we had them and were ready to use them. One of my favourite weapons was a repeating gun loaded with small cannonballs, which we could fire 20 of in a few seconds. It was intended for firing below the waterline of vessels trying to board us, thus sinking the pirates' boat before they reached us. I also had a Winchester 1200 Defender.

This was not a joyride; it was a serious business with a lot of admin, including contracts, milestones, timetables, budgets, accounts and other management aspects. IBM had just brought out its first personal computer, and we made good use of this. In addition, while we were in international waters we were outside any country's jurisdiction, and as captain I had the power to arrest and lock up troublemakers in the crew, then deliver them for imprisonment at the next port. This power was to prove handy at one point during the voyage.

I put together a professional crew of 6 from a shortlist of 25: Bonnie as cook/medical officer, for which she was ideally qualified, having crossed the Pacific with me, run her own marine catering and provisioning service for charters and deliveries, and having gone to medical college. The others were Hamish Murray, a Canadian meteorologist and skipper as first mate; a Hawaiian chief engineer; and two Australian deckhands, one a 6'5" strongman called Hunter Drinan. I tried to get a good mix of experience along with dependable personalities.

We loaded up with four truckloads of food, costing $4,000. A lot more work was in involved in even this than you might think; for example, knowing that when the labels on the thousands of food cans got wet they would fall off, we removed them and relabelled the cans with marker pens.

Bonnie and Hamish running before the gale

Bonnie on Beija Flor in Force 9 gale

Leaving San Francisco in a force 9 gale

When we were ready to leave a storm came down, and we looked at the weatherfax before deciding to leave on the storm's tail. On 23 March 1987 we sailed out into a 40-knot force 9 gale, running under bare poles at 10 knots, and then doing 17 knots when we got some sail up. Smaller yachts would have been overwhelmed, but *Beija Flor* took the 15-foot waves in her stride. We overtook a large ship, which was intermittently disappearing from view behind the big seas. We clipped onto our lifelines at all times. When we got knocked down by a big wave and Hunter was hurled right across the cabin into a bookshelf, which he destroyed with his skull, saying 'No brain, no pain' (apparently a common Australian expression); but dinner was lost and Bonnie, in the galley, was burnt.

What follows is Bonnie's version of the story, which shows a completely different perspective:

It was a cold windy morning in March as we sailed under the Golden Gate Bridge. I was bundled up to my eyeballs, hanging over the rail. How was I going to survive the next three months crossing two oceans; and better yet, how were the other five going to live, since I was the cook and food was the last thing on my mind?

No words could describe the feelings I felt as we entered the Pacific in the teeth of a gale, its cold powerful waves crashing against the boat, causing it to roll back and forth and back and forth.

I stood watch bent over the rail for the next four hours while my watch partner chewed on beef jerky and sung colourful songs. He was happy as a lark just sitting there steering the boat, and excited that he was off on an adventure at sea. The only way that one can describe the motion of a boat sailing off the coast of California during these high seas is by imagining what it would be like to be loosely strapped to a rabid bull standing under a salty waterfall, whose only aim in life is to get you off his back.

No sooner was I off watch than someone asked the dreaded question: 'What's for dinner?' Food was not of utmost importance in my life at this time but I knew I had to prepare something for these iron-stomached individuals. It was cold and wet so there was no way they would have let me get by with sandwiches so I strapped my body into the galley, to prevent myself from being thrown about, and began digging into the fridge for the necessary items. Somehow, I was successful at getting hot food onto the table only to watch it fly across the cabin as the boat gybed violently. Needless to say the crew ate sandwiches that night.

That was it; I'd had enough for one day. If I could just lie still and close my eyes and maybe get some sleep, I would have a fighting chance to beat this motion sickness. What I didn't realise is that sleeping is an art on a boat, especially on one that is heeled over 30 degrees and rocking violently back and forth. After a heroic effort of propping, stuffing and angling I was able to get into a reasonably comfortable position and, yes, my eyes closed and I drifted off to sleep. I was not out 10 minutes when the cry GYBE HO rang out and I found myself flung to the other side of the bunk and hanging on for dear life as the boat went crashing through the waves.

After four days we reached San Diego and my last chance for freedom. Back on board the whole thing started again for about five days, then it was gone, no sickness, no headaches, no high seas. Sweet calm, something I had dreamed about for days. What

I didn't dream about was the heat and when it was calm it was hot. I began praying for the wind to return and it did, and we sailed on and I hung over the side, because we were being escorted by a school of dolphins. Such beautiful creatures, so graceful and trusting.

Down the Pacific Coast

We stopped in San Diego, where we posed by the America's Cup, and at Cabo San Lucas, where we were unable to check into Mexico because I did not have notarised proof that I had not stolen the yacht. So we pushed on to a remote, uninhabited island volcano, Isla San Benedicto, and tried to anchor off it. But it had changed shape with recent eruptions since it had been charted – and it was also charted in the wrong place, as our satnav put us in the middle of the volcano! The island was also a lot bigger than the chart showed. Not only that, but the surf was too heavy, and we ran the risk of the anchor dragging and being wrecked on the lava cliffs, so at sunset we sailed on and stopped in the dark at another beautiful Mexican island, Socorro, where we were able to scuba dive.

On this leg, we caught a 10-foot sailfish, leaping majestically out of the water, which we put back. This was quite a saga, trying to avoid getting speared by its long spike. We ate fresh fish every day, usually tuna, dorado and wahoo. On to Acapulco, where we had a clifftop dinner watching men diving from 115 feet up into just 12 feet of water.

Fabulous uninhabited Cocos Island

We sailed on for a week, to Cocos Island, an uninhabited, undiscovered jewel with 1,000-foot waterfalls in the jungle. It had been an English pirates' base when they had plundered the conquistadores' gold galleons, and *Treasure Island* had been based on legendary stories from this island. It was very wet, due to 25 feet of rain falling annually, feeding hundreds of waterfalls that cascaded down cliffs into the jungle. The waters around it were crystal clear, with 100-foot visibility. Although there was a big swell running we braved the surf to land and explore a jungle stream, crossing it by swinging from vines. At anchor overnight we switched on our floodlights and saw hundreds of hammerhead sharks circling below. We threw in some meat, and a small fish ate it – whereupon a larger fish ate the small one and a hammerhead ate the lot.

It was here that I had to deal with a mutinous situation. One of the crew thought he was more experienced and more suitable to skipper than I. He'd been belligerently refusing to do what I asked, so I knew that I'd have to establish my alpha male status rapidly. I saw my chance. He was walking along the deck towards me, next to the lifelines, which were just 2 feet high. We could both see the hammerheads below. I leaned against him so that he was on the point of falling overboard, and said, 'I understand you're not happy with me. I will not tolerate this –do you understand? I am the skipper, not you.' He was no trouble the rest of the trip.

We sailed on, to Panama. The weather became thundery, with light winds. We amused ourselves by being dunked overboard in the bosun's chair and dragged in the water, slung from the masthead. Our starter motor failed, so we sailed all the way into our anchorage. In the huge locks, lead balls were thrown down to us, attached to mooring ropes. We went up three locks, through the Culebra Cut across the mountains, across Gatun Lake, and down three more locks. Torrential rain poured down many times and lightning put on great displays at night. We ate out at a restaurant that advertised 'petrified animals, birds and fishes, which are serving some as fountains'.

The Panama Canal was an experience, if only to see the engineering that went into constructing it. Because of the curve of the isthmus our journey through it did not run west to east as one might expect, but from southeast, the Pacific entrance, to north-west at its exit in the Caribbean. The statistics are amazing: 25,000 workers died to make it, and for years 400 trains a day were hauling dirt out of the Culebra Cut.

Approaching Cocos Island

Bonnie: We were in Panama for five days, repairing the starter, before crossing the continent, which was an exciting experience. The next day we were in the Atlantic after overnighting on a freshwater lake. We were sailing fine but still worried about the starter motor.

On towards Florida, then when 15 miles off Cuba, boarded by the US Coastguard for a search. They weren't interested in our semi-automatic short-barrelled shotguns or slug shot ammunition for repelling unwelcome boarders, but I was impressed by their system.

Bonnie: It looked like something from a Rambo movie. Armed and wearing helmets and bulletproof vests, the squad boarded us. That was in no way a safety check. They took apart everything from toilets to freezer and bilges and cushions.

Hunter in the Caribbean

Practicing against pirates

They stopped a tanker after us. They had diplomatic connections to be able to board any nationality of vessel in international waters.

We stopped at Fort Lauderdale, close to Bonnie's family home, for a few days for a rebuild at a shipyard. I got little rest, as the loudspeakers kept calling 'Captain Clutterbuck, please report to the office.'

Across the Atlantic

On the way to Bermuda we were hit by the edge of a small hurricane, but we nevertheless had a wonderful landfall at night on this Atlantic island, talked in by Bermuda Harbour Radio. We then had a good passage running under spinnaker before westerlies, which built to near-gale force, to Horta in the Azores, which were wonderful islands, rather like a Portuguese-speaking combination of Ireland and Hawaii – and yet another largely undiscovered paradise. There was a tradition of painting an arriving vessel's name on the harbour wall, which we did, decorating it with a swan and a hummingbird.

Another fast passage under spinnaker got us to the UK. My parents came down to meet us on the dock, and I felt very proud to have completed the passage and the Atlantic crossing. Bonnie

Bonnie approaching the Azores

went ashore to provision, and asked the supermarket staff if they 'grew their own vegetables on the island', as we had found on all the previous islands. Then – an innocent American – she asked, 'Where can we buy drugs?' and was reported to the police. A few days later, I was apprehended and asked to hand over my weapons. The police told me they would be destroyed. I objected and asked why, and was told, 'Because they are heavily modified and very dangerous.' 'That's what they're supposed to be' I replied. That didn't help, and it was goodbye to my guns.

Bonnie: The rest of the trip was smooth and easy, and we made it to England on time. I benefited from the experience, not only by becoming stronger and learning a little about survival but I also went home tanned and 20lb lighter. The only sad thing that happened during the trip was that my father died a couple days after we landed in England, but my mother says he followed my progress every step of the way, and that he died feeling proud of what I had achieved. So am I.

Then came a week of racing in the Channel Islands with a 15-man race charter crew. We won the main race; we happened to have a *Times* reporter on board, who complained that we were so far ahead of the other 40 yachts that he couldn't cover the main pack. We ended up winning the European Championship.

Next, we had a fast run down the 'Coast of Death' off Spain and Portugal, then a dramatic entry into the Mediterranean, with Europe on our left side and Africa on our right. Then into Gibraltar, followed by the Balearic Islands, Sardinia and Corsica, to do some chartering.

Our first charter was part of a two-yacht group with, on the other yacht, the King of Spain, Prince Charles and Lady Diana; we had to keep 100 metres from them. We often anchored in deep water, and on one occasion my crew let the anchor chain go out too fast and it broke at its end, dropping 120 feet into the sea. We had a spare anchor, but no more chain. I couldn't find any ashore, so I hired a diver, and we went back to the spot where we'd taken detailed bearings for our return. I put on scuba gear, never having been trained, nor indeed dived below 20 feet. I went down to 120 feet with the diver, but he had to come up. I felt I had no option but to go on down alone – in retrospect, very dangerous. I went down a vertical line from our boat, and found the pile of chain in the inky murk. It was being guarded by an angry moray eel. I avoided it and its sharp teeth, and attached my rope. Suddenly, I was gasping for air. I looked at my pressure gauge – it was on empty. I had no option but to rush to the surface, risking the bends and other physical damage. When I got back on board the crew winched up the chain – but the rope broke on the last foot and it all fell again. We never did get it back. And as I'd been down there for only a very few minutes I was, as it turned out, fine.

After 23,000 miles of mostly professional sailing in a year, I was glad to get back on to dry land and start up new oil exploration with several geologist friends of mine from the early seventies. However, it wasn't that simple – I ended up flying 40,000 miles a month, working mostly on opportunities in the Middle East, offshore Europe and Latin America, living in Dubai, then in a country manor in England, and then in Bogotá.

In England Bonnie was still my business partner, doing the geology and much of the admin. And we had Jason, our Alaskan timber wolf; he lived on the tennis court, which worked fine until he dug through its hard surface to bury a bone.

6   Sailing on the edge in mid-Atlantic

We were in the lead on the 1998 Round Britain and Ireland race in my 43-foot Grand Prix trimaran, *Spirit of England*. The leg to Barra up the west coast of Ireland promised a force 8 gale on the nose, and our primary concern was not to break the boat.

As night fell I was unable to keep any food down and was steadily getting colder. It was very unfriendly down below and quite impossible to consider sleeping in the bow cabin on account of violent motion and crash-bang pounding. Going below to navigate was out also – everything was pre-programmed on deck. We stayed on deck and under the jet aircraft cockpit canopy.

At dawn, the big black seas and the rocks and cliffs off Ireland loomed, menacing and forbidding. The wind moderated and backed, allowing us to fetch the Hebrides. The decks were covered in seaweed from the green water we had taken. It was now getting very cold and we used fur-lined underwater diving gloves. Would we survive this open ocean passage? I prayed for no more gales.

While living in England in the 1990s, I continued windsurfing year-round to keep job stress and fitness under control, using three layers of neoprene and one of titanium to survive the snow and hail that so often batter these waters.

I also continued multihull sailing, racing an F-27 with Olympic gold medallist Rodney Pattisson, an idol of mine, and a 40-foot trimaran, *MTC*, with David Scully.

During the summer of 1994 I also sailed on the 92-foot catamaran *Enza*[14] *New Zealand*, the fastest boat ever around the world (75 days non-stop). Video footage showed 30-knot bursts, huge waves, seas strewn with growlers, and weeks sailing at an average of 17 knots. The circumnavigation averaged 14 knots. I also had a sail on Steve Fossett's *Lakota*, an American 60-foot trimaran and holder of the Round Britain record. Both boats had clocked well over 30 knots and were among the fastest offshore boats ever.

Spirit of England

That same summer I bought my dream boat, a 40-foot Grand Prix offshore racing trimaran called *Spirit of England*. Although she was part-built and had never been raced, I could see that with some rebuilding she could

---

14 Eat New Zealand Apples

Spirit of England beating. Photo credit Beken of Cowes

win. She had previously been owned by Mike Golding, who had set a new record of some 160 days for a non-stop solo round the world against the Roaring Forties in *Group 4,* a British Steel boat.

There was a lot of work to do on *Spirit* to finish the construction and get everything working. It was an experience to get to know her. With 1,236 square feet of upwind sail area and 2,493 square feet downwind (similar to that of a 60-foot racing monohull), plus a rotating 62-foot wing mast on a 2.4 tonne displacement, the boat had a phenomenal power-to-weight ratio, further amplified by her own apparent wind, which could be almost double the true wind at times, similar to that of an ice boat. As she had a beam of 35 feet, she could take on a big sail area without capsizing.

I'll never forget the thrill of sailing her. Starting from an underpowered, stalled position, it would take just a twitch on the tiller for the power to come on. The lee hull would part-bury and we'd be up to 25 knots in a matter of seconds, weather hull in the air, main hull skipping over the waves, and lee hull throwing up a big plume of spray. Then we'd trim the sails, adjust the mast rotation, and focus our 15 instruments to maximise speed and VMG. To depower for reefing, foredeck work or helm changes, we would only need to free the mainsheet slightly, and we'd be back to a safe 10–15 knots.

But as in a dinghy we had to always be careful to avoid a capsize, which could easily happen if we heeled more than 30 degrees. Luffing up would make the heel worse due to centrifugal effects on the mast. Another, bigger, risk was pitchpoling, especially in the 'death zone' on a beam reach, when bearing away would dramatically increase both the apparent wind speed and the boat speed, burying the lee hull thus twisting the boat downwind even further.

Due to the significant risk of capsize to 180 degrees, from which we could not recover, in the bow cabin we had an escape hatch which, if the boat was inverted, would be above the nets. We could also retreat to the bunks, which would be above the water which would then be swishing about in the cabin. Then we would set off the EPIRB emergency radio beacon and await rescue.

Spirit on Round the Island Race

Another challenge was structural. Every year we would push the boat harder, and under the ever-increasing loads fittings would break – often at the top of the mast, 66 feet above water.

We were always pushing the envelope – we had to be a step ahead of the competition – so we needed a professional team for design, construction, crewing and shore support. Managing all this, consisting of typically 40 items per day, was a full-time job.

Spirit beating. Photo credit Beken of Cowes

Spirit specifications

The construction material was strip cedar, carbon fibre, Kevlar and Nomex aluminium honeycomb. There were three berths in the bow cabin and a bucket for the toilet. The main cabin had a simple galley and navigation area. There was also a doghouse – a repurposed canopy from a jet fighter aircraft.

Spirit had a Proctor rotating wing mast, a bowsprit for downwind sails, both spinnakers and furling reachers. Her sails were controlled by 4 winches and 36 rope clutches.

The electrical supply was from four solar panels, a wind generator and petrol generators. Navigation equipment included eight wind and other displays on deck, with repeaters down below. We could operate the self-steering on deck or from down below. We also had two GPSs (one on deck, one below), with digital charting and radar.

Communications were with SSB, weatherfax and VHF. Auxiliary power was from a 10 hp outboard. Emergency equipment included an 18-foot para-anchor sea anchor and a 30-inch Galerider drogue.

The Round the Island race was our first in *Spirit*. It is held over the same course as the inaugural America's Cup (during which Queen Victoria was horrified to see the schooner *America* round first), and today, Round the Island has the world's biggest start, with 1,200–1,600 vessels. But unfortunately, when we opened up the throttle for the first time we blew a whole bunch of gear.

Our second race was more successful; we won the Doublehanded Round the Island race, setting a new record of some six hours. It was quite satisfying to be greeted by the boom of the cannon in Cowes instead of a foghorn or shotgun. We were the only multihull against 130 monohulls, the first of which finished three hours behind us. We also won the Nab Tower race, our first test against the UK multihull fleet of 17 starters. Then we took *Spirit* out in a 40-knot gale under bare poles to prepare her for ocean races starting next year.

In October 1994 I sailed *Spirit* across the Channel for sea trials with Bill Bullimore in a force 6/7 near-gale on the beam, to Cherbourg in four hours – faster than the ferries. In an incredibly wet passage, we sliced off the crests of the waves with water boiling over the decks, doing 15–20 knots with three reefs in the main and furled jib. At one time the entire boat was submerged as a big wave broke over. Bill taught me how to work the waves on the beam, bearing off sharply on the crest and inducing a strong centrifugal force that pushed the weather hull down and took the pressure off the lee hull, which was always threatening to bury. This was against all instincts, as it risked catastrophe in the death zone on a beam reach. But it worked. The key was to keep bearing away and not chicken out. It was rather like a surfer's manoeuvre, curling along and down on the crest. I believe this could have been the fastest-ever cross-Channel time to Cherbourg by sail.

The Azores and Back race

The Azores, about the same distance from North America as from Britain, are the focus of the Azores and Back race (AZAB) – 1,170 nautical miles each way from the UK. Held every four years, it is one of the world's greatest ocean yacht races.

Spirit leading at the start

Race day, 3 June 1995, dawned grey, rainy and windy, heralding a typical Atlantic day's sailing. We checked and rechecked the hundreds of items on our punch list, then we were pushed to the start area to join 69 other boats, including four more racing trimarans – the biggest turnout ever for an AZAB. The tris represented the fastest offshore boats in Britain: *Severalles Challenge*, co-skippered by John Chaundy, winner of Three Peaks and class winner in Round Britain, with a Singlehanded Transatlantic race behind her as well; *Shockwave*, another Three Peaks winner and record holder; and *Mollymawk*, at 40 feet the same rating as *Spirit*, and previously, as *MTC*, winner and record holder in both Singlehanded and Doublehanded Transatlantics.

In the monohulls the favourite was Mark Gatehouse, sailing *Queen Anne's Battery*, formerly a BOC Challenge winner as *Credit Agricole*. Mark had also won the last AZAB in a Formula 40 cat. On the return leg, he was sunk by whales while in the lead.

This was to be *Spirit's* first ocean race. Sailing with me was Brian Thompson, in my view Britain's top offshore multihull sailor. He'd completed five Transatlantics, including the Singlehanded race, in which he won his class, and in the last Round Britain had taken *Severalles* to a dramatic second place overall behind the 60-foot tri *Lakota*. I had met Brian while he was sailing *Lakota* in 1994. He then sailed on *Lakota* again, to break three of the 12 internationally recognised speed records, and later delivered her to California and a record win in the TransPac, in place of a planned Route du Rhum, which was abandoned after *Severalles* had been rammed and dismasted by a French trawler at an impact speed of 22 knots during the qualifier. Brian struck me as an enormously capable sailor: competitive and athletic, yet with a calm disposition.

Sir Robin Knox-Johnson, Yachtsman of the Year, fired the cannon on Pendennis Castle near Falmouth, Cornwall, discharging flame and smoke (reportedly from condoms full of petrol) from its 6-inch bore. Sir Robin held the Jules Verne Trophy, and I had sailed briefly on his catamaran *Enza*, which had given me some good ideas for *Spirit*, one of which contributed to our being able to save the boat from destruction on our return leg.

Seconds before the gun we depowered by heading up a touch, then won the start,[15] leaving our 200 hp chase boat behind. *Severalles Challenge* was hot on our heels. We bore away a touch to power up, and instantly throttled up to 22 knots in the fresh nor'westerly with two reefs in the main. It was a tremendous feeling of power: the wind hard on the sails driving the three hulls, the leeward one diving into the waves in sheets of spray. We had 1,250 miles to go.

In the Channel chop, the top of the mast was bending and pumping alarmingly, as the head of the main, reefed down to below the hounds, was not stabilising it. So we furled the genoa and set the staysail, which was better for the mast but allowed *Severalles* to close the gap. As a grey dusk fell, we bore off to lose her in the Channel – little did we know that *Severalles* would never be seen again.

I wore my white-water canoeing hard hat and visor which, in the sheets of spray hitting us at 25 knots, was much better than ski or motorcycle goggles. The going was so hard that below, we could not sleep in our two-hour off watches for two days due to the loud banging and crashing, but by focusing on de-stressing rather than sleeping, we achieved some fatigue recovery. It was easy to keep track of the situation from down below, as *Spirit* had duplicate instruments and an Autopilot above the bow bunk, plus a mainsheet quick release running the length of the cabins.

In the Atlantic

Past Ushant on the westernmost tip of France, the weatherfaxes indicated a veer, and the next day we were able to set our small fractional kite. That evening we dared to set the big Doyle 1,700-square-foot ¾-oz masthead asymmetric spinnaker, an immensely powerful sail, which soon had us back over 20 knots on the GPS. The night was absolutely black under thick cloud, and I was always looking for low spots in the phosphorescent white horses to break through, as the waves were only travelling at 15 knots. The lee hull was shrouded in a huge plume of phosphorescent spray. I could follow the lines on deck by tapping them, causing them to sparkle. Then

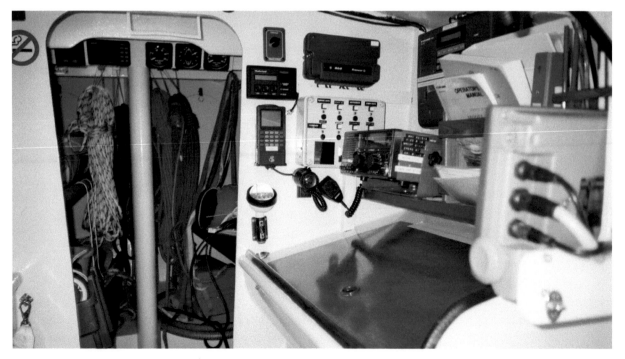

The navigation area

15 The start of a yacht or dinghy race involves envisaging a line across the water between two markers, and crossing it at maximum speed immediately after the starting gun. If you cross it too soon you have to sail in a circle, putting you well behind the other boats.

I noticed something very strange: vertical green shafts of light, rather like the loom of a lighthouse but close by. When a huge luminous shape dived under the boat, I realised that the glowing shafts had been whales, spouting as they breathed. Rather eerie.

We put in a day's run of 320 miles point to point and reached the halfway mark at 49 hours. We were hoping to complete the race in under four days, thus knocking two days off the record. By this time we were very wet in spite of wearing drysuit tops under our oilskins and replacing drenched thermals daily. The entire boat was wet below. It was too bouncy to cook, and we survived for four days on snacks and fruit juice, preferring to drive the boat rather than use the autopilots, for better speed.

The wind came aft and at last the noise below was a loud swish-swish rather than crash-bang. At last we could get some sleep. While down below and watching the instruments, I marvelled at Brian's driving skills: first the angle of heel building up, then bearing away on the compass course, then true wind going aft as he bore away on a wave, then the boat speed breaking through 20 knots, the apparent wind building all the time as he weaved back and forth optimising wind and wave, keeping the knot meter as high as possible as long as possible.

A near-disaster

At dawn on the 6th we were broad reaching with full main and genoa at 15–20 knots in 8–10-foot seas in a force 6. The main was hauled out on a preventer run from the bow, the genoa on a barber hauler. Brian was on the foredeck untangling the furler line, which had come loose due to Allen screws breaking free of their Loctite seal in the Profurl.

We came over a wave – and there below us was a line of orange buoys connected by a cable. The wire would take off our daggerboard and rudder like a guillotine. A fishing boat, the only vessel other than *Severalles* that we saw in those four days, was a mile off, flashing a red light and shining a searchlight at

Brian Thompson in the galley

us. 'Gybing,' I bellowed, gesticulating at Brian, but he obviously couldn't hear me as he carried on working. I gybed over all standing and came beam onto the wind, the boat heeling alarmingly at 30 degrees, two hulls out of the water with the boom high up in the sky, unable to crash across due to the preventer run from the bow.

'We're going over!' I yelled.

'Not sure,' shouted Brian. 'Maybe … maybe not … nothing we can do anyway.'

We got away with it, and gybed back. The fishing boat came by, pounding away into the big seas towards the end of its drift net.

One night Brian put up the 1½ oz in a force 6, but *Spirit* shot down a big wave and buried all three hulls. 'Not good,' I said. 'Have you ever pitchpoled?'

'No,' Brian said, 'but there's always a first time.'

'Well this is pitchpole country.'

'Agreed.' We got the 1½ oz off.

Next morning, I was having great fun driving the lee bow under at 18 knots when Brian surfaced. 'You're crazy,' he said, 'you're going to pitchpole.' We were even.

We had been keeping well high of the course to stay clear of the notorious Cape Finisterre and the Coast of Death, where strong northerly gales up to 200 miles offshore pass between the Atlantic high and the Spanish low, funnelling past the high cordillera. Now that we were clear of it, we started looking for more wind, homing in on the closest isobars.[16] We switched between the two kites as the wind went back and forth between force 4 and 5,

---

16 The closer the isobars the stronger the wind.

getting up to 22 knots on the big swells coming off the Finisterre gale, gybing on the wind shifts. 'This has been a continuous sprint rather than an ocean race,' Brian commented.

Breakage up the mast

There was a loud bang, and the boat shuddered as the big Doyle masthead kite dropped a few feet. Something had blown off the top of the mast. Brian awoke from a deep sleep and tried to get the spinnaker down, but it was jammed solid. I hauled him up the shroud, whereupon he got wrapped around it ten times in the big seas. He was getting badly beaten up, but when I loosened the halyard he couldn't slide down. An interesting situation for me, with a crew stuck 50 feet up, and our main chute stuck 66 feet up there too.

Brian spun round back again a few times and dropped down. We snuffed the chute and he went up the mast, tying the chute to it in several places. He found that the U-bolt at the masthead had sheared off and the spinnaker halyard had jammed where the cover had stripped in the exit block. This was a major blow, because

Brian driving Spirit at over 20 knots

we had lighter following winds now but no capability to set our light-air sails. We had visions of *Severalles* and the rest of the fleet catching us.

The options were to repair the U-bolt, rely on the smaller sails or set the big sails from the hounds. The first option was out due to the wild motion at the top of the mast, even if we tried a simple shackled-up jury system. The second meant we'd lose a day in the race, so we went for the third, and set the big kite, dragging it along in the water and only losing a knot.

Another problem arose – we were out of electric power. There had been not a glimpse of the sun in the four days since the start of the race, so no power from our two solar panels. The following wind didn't power our small wind generator fast enough, and the Tanaka generator, which put out 20 amps from a 15-lb machine, had run hot and unreliably. We had no engine. Now we were out of fuel, and had to sail without much of our electronics. It was time to get to the finish line.

Winning the race

On our last day at sea the sun came out, we cooked our one and only meal of the race, and we saw the cloud over São Miguel island. Porpoises played among the hulls, and while I was up on the bow filming them Brian told me, 'You missed the ones back here with the beach balls.'

It was to take us 18 hours to finish in the lee of this high volcanic island. Lots of boats came out to greet us, alongside TV crews, press photographers and race officials. Our SSB had not been operational, so we didn't know how we'd been placed, and asked the club naval on the VHF. 'You're the first,' was the reply.

With Bonnie and Mike in the Azores

At the dock we were greeted with champagne and a radio interview. We'd broken the record by 28 hours. We also learned that *Severalles* had pitchpoled 100 miles off Finisterre and was lost. John Chaundy and Dick Skipworth were recovered by helicopter three hours after setting off the EPIRB, but for Brian it was a sad moment, as he'd spent so much time on *Severalles*. They'd spent the three hours below and got out through the escape hatch. 'Could have spent a couple of weeks like that,' John told me later. I later found out that it appeared that a leak in the bow might have contributed to the pitchpole.

The first boats started arriving the following night, two days after us, thus ensuring that we had won on corrected time as well.

Back from the Azores

I had originally planned on singlehanding back, as a qualifier for the Singlehanded Transatlantic, but with the national press coverage focused on *Severalles* plus the failure of our SSB radio my family had got overly worried that we had disappeared in the Finisterre gale, and convinced me to doublehand back. John Chaundy agreed to join me. He had an enormous amount of ocean experience, and had done an OSTAR in *Severalles*, finishing with a bow broken off in sheets of spray. He'd also won the Three Peaks yacht race many times.

We started on a hot, sunny day, with a game plan to beat *Shockwave* on the way back, as she was the only boat that could beat us on corrected time. *Spirit* had won the outward leg on both corrected and elapsed time, but *Shockwave* was just a day and a half behind on the outward leg, and had the capability of winning it back on corrected time on the return leg. So we started behind her, in among all the keelboats and water-ballasted monohulls, and watched to see which way round the 30-mile-long island she would go. She went east, so we followed her out, launched our masthead reacher, and overtook. A school of pilot whales played around us. It looked like a good trip home. To win the race back, which would ensure winning the round trip, we didn't need to push the boat; all we had to do was avoid busting anything major.

The first night there was a thunderstorm. In a squall, the spinnaker tack unclipped and the snuffer jammed in the hounds. A thunderclap rolled overhead. We dropped the kite in a hurry all over the nets under a deluge of rain. We got the kite up again later that night. I was recovering in the doghouse when John yelled 'Whoa, whoa, losing it … Peter … quick, on deck … lost it … let something *go*!' We had two hulls flying under the kite in a pitch-black night, and the rudder was grabbing air rather than water. It was time to let the mainsheet off and get the main hull back into the water – I didn't want to go like *Severalles*. It was a busy night, with the reacher up and down three times and the spinnaker twice.

The next night I saw a most beautiful sight, looking like a huge floodlit spinnaker on the horizon. Then it started rising slowly above the horizon. It was the moon, quarter full! Then John saw something even more spectacular: a meteorite hitting the sea in a shower of blue sparks. When the moon hid behind clouds, I lay on the nets on the weather side while the boat steered on autopilot, marvelling at the phosphorescence around the main hull, the daggerboard and the rudder, all neatly slicing through in a bright green glow – a sight that leaded monohull sailors could never see.

Our SSB was working now, and we learned from the AZAB headquarters that *Queen Anne's Battery* was 150 miles behind us, becalmed, so it appeared that we had chosen the right side of the course, close-hauled up the east side of the high. We were travelling 30 per cent faster than the rest of the fleet. I went up the mast to take some film and video, and to check the rig. It was a big mast, 62 feet high, with a 15-inch chord, and with the rigging and sails it weighed a half ton. We had adjusted the rigging to reduce the wobbling, and as we creamed

Beating back, all going smoothly...

along at 12 knots close-hauled it looked solid. I rigged a trapeze, and hiked out for a while off the port hull to stretch my legs and enjoy the view of the hulls slicing the water.

At sundown the wind came up and we put a reef in. An hour later we decided to put in a second reef, furl the genoa and hoist the staysail. This dropped our speed to a safe 7–8 knots. I looked up the mast with our searchlight. It looked straight and steady. We had reefed early, at 20 knots true, as against 25 in our reefing schedule. I then collapsed in the doghouse, exhausted from all the deck work. It was 11 p.m., and it was raining as the wind rose. It was pitch-black again. We were now in the middle of the Atlantic.

Dismasted in the Atlantic

There was a deafening crash in the bow cabin. We must have hit something. '*The mast has gone!*' John yelled. I thought it had broken the compression tube below the heel, and gone right through the bottom of the hull, judging by all the splintering wood noises from the bow cabin. I switched on our powerful aft deck floodlight. The mast and sails were laid over the side. I clipped on my harness and underwater headlight to slide down the forward cross beam and inspect the damage on the starboard hull, which was rising up 6 feet with every wave, and crashing down. The mast was broken just outside the starboard hull, the top 40 feet pointing straight down. One of the bottom spreaders was broken off, and the other was busy grinding holes in the hull.

The seas were now beam on and rising. There were two holes in the starboard hull, three in the main hull: one where the mast base had ripped out, a big one where the mast rotation spanner bracket had broken through above the starboard bunk, and one where the forestay had ripped through the foredeck and torn off the pulpit. All appeared to be taking water. The broken mast was grinding pieces off the outer hull with big booming noises, hanging off a mass of halyards, reef lines, wire and so on. John narrowly escaped being guillotined by the port shroud, which knifed across the cockpit as the mast came down, but he had been leaning forward at the time, checking the instruments

Visibility closed in. It was now raining hard. The seas were rising. This was not forecast. The barometer was falling. The 'Coast of Death', on the west coast of Spain, was busy accelerating the northerlies again. After the shock of no longer being in the race, we set about saving the boat. There was now a wild motion without the mast in the steep cross seas. It was impossible to stand or kneel. We slithered around on the end of our harness tethers. We started cutting loose what we could with bolt cutters, and an emergency saw knife. There were over 60 points of attachment between mast and boat. We both got seasick, and weakened rapidly, unable to hold any food down, grinding down to an exhausted stalemate, then having another go, wielding havoc with our tool chest and emergency gear. We could not pull the masthead up to the deck, as it would have been 20 feet aft of the transoms. The gear over the side weighed half a ton, and would need daylight and a calm to retrieve. Daylight was five hours away, and now that the northerlies had set in, they could blow half a gale for weeks. We decided to try to salvage the staysail, boom and bottom 18 feet of mast.

None of the sails would come off, even after releasing and cutting the halyards. Their heads were 20–40 feet underwater. We slashed most of the running rigging with the saw knife and the smaller wires with the bolt cutters, but the three main wires were holding the mast and were too big for the bolt cutters. The starboard one was under the mainsail and could not be reached. The port one had bent the chainplate and jammed the split pin, but could be released further up. The bar tight headstay with its furled genoa was causing the broken mast sections to grind away at the hull, and it needed releasing immediately. The furling drum was sunk into a tiny recess below the deck and even

Dismasted in Mid-Atlantic

in port was very hard to access. At sea, at night, in what looked like a rising gale, seasick in the violent motion, it was almost impossible, to do so. But was essential to save the boat from destruction.

I tried for two hours to get the split pin out. First I tried from the deck. Then I went through the bomb-bay doors and crawled forward in the 2-foot-high sail locker to undo eight screws and release the access hatch. There was room to get an arm through.

Waves rolled in every few seconds as I attacked the system with hammers, vice grips, hacksaws, bolt cutter and Allen keys. The pin would not budge, even though we were destroying it in the process. The Allen screws were solid with red Loctite. We took the load off the distorted forestay plates by grabbing the furled genoa with two lines and winching up hard round snatch blocks.

Everything was still jammed solid. We couldn't cut the wire as it was inside several layers of heavy Kevlar and the furler foil. It would take two hours and many hacksaw blades. We attacked the split pin again. It was amazing to think that we would lose the boat if we didn't get it out soon. The Allen key wrench exploded into several pieces. My underwater headlight failed.

We gave up, exhausted.

Cutting the mast loose

Miraculously, the other spreader had sheared off and the mast was now grinding the topsides rather than the waterline. We decided to take a two-hour break till dawn, and abandon ship if it broke up in the meantime. We were too fatigued, and were now having trouble just clipping and unclipping our harnesses as we slithered around. risked making the situation a real emergency; if we got the mast partly off, it could pound holes in the bottom, and one of us could easily go overboard in our fatigued state.

The wind was strengthening and the seas getting bigger all the time, we collapsed below in our oilskins. The bow cabin was soaked with all the water pouring in through the leaks, all over the bunks, but we slept through the crashes and bangs of the mast grinding the hull. I was lacerated and bruised, and had damaged my right elbow. John had put his back out.

At dawn, we continued methodically detaching lines and salvaging what we could. John got the rotating mast base and the boom gooseneck off. We decided to leave the mast rotation spanner where it had impaled the deck, so as to prevent the mast sliding around any more.

We used the saw knife to cut the heavy Kevlar mainsail off, and threw it over the side. We cut the inner forestay with the bolt cutters, and I was able to pull the staysail back as its halyard had not jammed in the mast – the other four were all jammed where the mast must have bent further up. With the sails off the nets, it was now less slippery and hazardous to work on the starboard side. I was able to detach the starboard cap shroud. There was a slight lull in the weather but it was still grey, windy and raining.

The bottom section of the broken mast

We attacked the forestay for another two hours. First, we took the load off the clevis pin by tightening a portable vice over the bent stem head chainplates. Then we worked feverishly with three vice grips and a hammer to release the split pin and clevis pin as the waves poured in through the furler hatch. After that, we had the masthead held by the genoa sheets round temporary blocks in the bows, the port side diamond and the Spectra halyards. I sawed through the halyards, which were very tough, even for my special saw knife, designed for the US Coast Guard for cutting ropes under tension.

To reach the halyards I had to put my hand over the side between the two sections of mast as they ground and crashed like Tyrannosaurus teeth. With each wave, I quickly withdrew my hand to prevent it being amputated. John cut through the genoa sheets and the remaining lines.

Then my worst fear came true: the mast dropped 2 feet and started hammering the bottom of the hull. Something was still holding it.

'Quick, the diamonds!' I shouted. John chopped them off with the bolt cutters, and I scrambled clear as the whole lot sank rapidly into 16,000 feet of water.

The following lists the items freed to jettison the mast, and the tools used:

1 × 10 mm forestay – 2 winches, 3 vice grips, hammer, screwdriver, saw

2 × 12 mm cap shrouds – vice grips

2 × 7 mm diamonds – bolt cutters

2 × 8mm runners – bolt cutters

2 × 6mm check stays: bolt cutters

1 × inner forestay – vice grips

10 × lazy jack attachments – undone/cut with saw knife

2 × spinnaker halyards top section – cut Spectra with saw knife

2 × spinnaker halyards bottom – cut Spectra with saw knife

1 × main and 1 genoa halyard – cut Spectra with saw knife

1 × staysail halyard – undone and pulled through (only halyard saved)

4 × reef lines – pulled through

5 × electrical cables – bolt cutters

6 × sail slides – saw knife through multiple Kevlar layers

1 × Cunningham – undone

1 × outhaul – undone

1 × mainsail clew shackle – vice grips

2 × genoa sheets – one cut, one undone

11 × staysail hanks – unclipped

1 × furler line – undone

1 × reef safety strop – undone.

Total 59 points of attachment, 31 of them requiring tools such as bolt cutters, saw knife or vice grips.

I had climbed the mast mere hours before it crashed down. Had I still been up there when it collapsed I would have been either killed on impact or drowned 40 feet down.

Setting the emergency parachute anchor

Now free of its mainsail sea anchor, *Spirit* started rolling and crashing from hull to hull in the big beam seas, the outer hulls slamming badly and causing the carbon cross beams to shake the whole boat at a 4 cycle/second frequency. We urgently needed rest so we could clean up the remaining wreckage, seal the holes and get a jury rig up. It was now force 6 and time to get the para-anchor deployed.

First we set a 130-foot partially buoyant trip line with a small retrieve fender on one end and a larger fender on the other to buoy up the parachute and pull its ripcord. We streamed it from a bridle and swivel off the bows on 200 feet of 20mm braided nylon. It was all fed out in careful sequence to weather, and under the starboard hull. I attached the bridle lines, which were the spinnaker sheets, to the two lines from the bows already reeved for this purpose before we had left the Azores; it wouldn't have been possible to reeve these offshore on the bouncing bows of the outer hulls. When the system went taut, the weight of the swivel pulled the para-anchor out of its bag; it opened up to its full 18-foot diameter and pulled the bows head to wind, with about a quarter of a knot sternway.

The GPS indicated we were on a west-going 1-knot current. We jammed rags into the holes. The wind howled through the generator, allowing us to run the SSB and organise shore support, which was being superbly coordinated by my wife Bonnie and Bill Bullimore, the manager of the Doyle sail loft.

I now understood how Chris Dickson felt when winning the Whitbread Round the World race, and also Isabelle Autissier in the last singlehanded BOC race around the world; both had been dismasted. *British Steel II* was another boat dismasted, while leading the British Steel Challenge, so all the leading boats in the last three Round the World races had suffered our ill fortune. We had done everything to get the rig professionally checked – yet fate had still got the better of us. Mark Gatehouse had been winning the last AZAB, but was holed and abandoned his boat.

As John put it, 'You win some, you lose some.' In this type of sailing you've got to be able to take the knocks as well as the smooth sailing. We later determined that the likely cause of the mast break was the top of the starboard diamond most probably ripping the tang out of the mast wall due to wave-induced G-forces. Maybe due to a manufacturing or design defect.

We lay to this for the best part of three days as the wind blew from NNE at force 6 and the seas got up to 15 feet. It was too rough for us to raise a jury rig. Thankfully, the work we'd done in the Azores to fix the SSB paid off now, and we were able to inform everyone ashore that we were safe but would be a week or two late. Our shore contacts researched a tow, but it was fraught with problems, as the only vessels that would do it were ocean tugs, which would cost over $100,000 together with a likely salvage claim risk – in other words, we'd have to buy our own boat back off the tug company! It was strange for me to be negotiating coolly with hard-nosed Norwegians in Portugal over the radio as the seas crashed and banged at us; it was as though I was back at work at a conference table. The only other option was to declare an emergency, either by radio or with one of our EPIRBs, but we didn't want to put the rescue services into action, as we weren't in a life-threatening situation. So we decided to get back to shore – either the UK or Spain or Portugal – without assistance.

We learned that Trevor Leek in *Mollymawk*, the second-fastest boat in the fleet, had been rescued by a Russian ship en route to Venezuela. I later heard that his daggerboard had ripped a 12-square-foot hole in the bottom of the main hull, through which a whole lot of gear had been lost, including his drinking water, meaning he was forced to give up the race. He was lucky not to have been crushed. The ship lifted both Trevor and *Mollymawk* on board.

Now, we saw that going east would involve sailing into worsening weather with the damaged float on the lee side, so we elected to sail west towards Canada and into an Atlantic high, so that we could dry out and repair the damage. For a temporary fix I sawed up a hatch cover and bedded it in over the biggest hole.

Building a jury rig

There was too much spray over the decks to do any epoxy work, so we decided to put a rig together and accept that we would be taking on water in two hulls. We hoped to get into the high, then be hit by the forecast westerlies to get home. Getting the para-anchor in was a problem, as the wind was still force 6 and the waves some 12 feet high, preventing us going onto the outrigger bows to release the bridle. John winched in one half of the para-anchor, allowing me to grab the other, slack, half with a long boathook off the bows and clip it through a bow snatch block. Then John winched it in until I could reach the trip line, whereupon I tripped it and we sailed off under bare poles without poles: 'bare hulls'.

John skilfully masterminded the jury rig, consisting of the boom as mast, nine rope stays and three halyards. We waited for the seas to subside, but they never did, so John said, 'About time we went for a sail again', and much to our own amazement we got the boom up in 10-foot seas, carefully winching it up into a hole I had chiselled into the deck. It was still impossible for us to stand up, so there was lots of crawling around with lines and snatch blocks. The base was held by four ropes going to clutches and winches, and half of our bolt cutters as an anti-rotation device. In place of instruments we tied tell-tales on.

Jury rig and storm jib in Force 6

We set a tiny trysail upside down, then our staysail upside down with a knot tied in the last 10 feet. Whereas my morale had been some 10 feet below rock bottom, now suddenly it took a lift as we reached off to Canada. We split our one and only beer on this weight-conscious ship to celebrate that we had a rig again, rather than saving it as planned for the finish line.

The wind dropped, and we set the 1½-oz chute on its side, with three knots tied at positions 10–25 feet from the head to allow it to be sheeted in and out and reefed. It could be set 45 degrees to the apparent wind or a close reach. It was balanced, and proved to be our workhorse for over 1,000 miles. However, the remaining mast section had jagged edges that threatened to tear it, and if we lost the kite we expected to run out of food before we hit land.

We gybed in the high to do the epoxy and glasswork as the sun dried the damaged, sodden wood. I pumped out a half ton of water from the starboard hull. We tossed the last section of mast overboard and watched it torpedo down at an angle towards its grave 3 miles below. John put together an emergency VHF aerial, designed by the Portishead radio engineers, over the SSB, which I hoisted up on a spare mainsail batten, using my jumars to climb up a halyard in a wild jerking motion. We hoped a ship would come by, and we rigged slings round the cross beams; Rupert Kidd in *Fiery Cross* had been lifted aboard a ship in mid-Atlantic after his boat had broken up in the TWOSTAR. His comment: 'Broken cross beams make pretty good fenders'.

Persistent light north winds allowed us to make only 130 miles towards the UK in a week, clawing every inch we could up to weather. On the outward leg we had covered the same distance in five hours, and I avoided looking at the chart, with its amazing outward-leg progress. Costs to tow to port or deck cargo out of Lisbon would be prohibitively high, so we decided to head for La Coruña, on the north-west corner of the Iberian peninsula. There we could build a better jury rig to get back to the UK. We had to keep high to avoid being swept down the Portuguese coast.

We had provisioned for a five-day race, but now realised we would be out for 14 days, so imposed rationing. John refused to eat our hard-boiled eggs, which had gone green and sludgy, but I reminded myself of the Chinese 100-year-old eggs and took a chance. We had an emergency hand-held water maker, so were not worried about dying of thirst. We conserved fuel by optimising the electricity drain, rewiring the GPS sets so that we could switch off the other instruments, and optimising our boat speed on the GPS. We got advice from Autohelm over the SSB on reprogramming the unit with a non-standard procedure to reduce sensitivity and current drain.

Then we were becalmed. John whistled for the wind: 'It usually works within two or three days.' After a few hours my patience was at an end – my business, working on oil fields in Arctic Russia, was falling apart, and I had to get out of the Atlantic – so I tried my way, slapping the water with a line with knots tied in the end, one for each ten knots of wind requested. 'Usually works within two or three hours,' I said. John on the other hand was very pragmatic about it, seeming to enjoy 'pottering about the ocean experimenting with jury rigs'.

The Coast of Death

After two weeks we saw a ship going our way, but they declined our offer of negotiating a contract for a lift, even though they had nice-looking derricks and lots of deck space. 'Nice cold Budweisers on that,' I said. 'Probably chilled lobster as well,' said John.

Eventually we approached the Coast of Death, and hit two large pieces of driftwood. It would have been different at 20 knots, but this time the maximum speed we'd managed was half that. A search plane flew over, then a lifeboat came out to check we were okay. We sailed into La Coruña harbour, surprising a local yacht by outsailing it with our quarter-height rig and sideways kite.

My brother Julian drove down from England with a 26-foot jury half-mast on top of a Range Rover, John Beharrel, who had delivered *Spirit* to the start line, had previously had an experience similar to ours when his 40-foot tri had been abandoned after a dismasting on the Route du Rhum. He'd built a jury rig, which had also been driven down to Spain, and offered it – a mast and two sails – to us. While I went back to the UK with Julian, the two Johns sailed *Spirit* back, hitting 16 knots with this tiny rig, again with the small, knotted kite on its side. All told, *Spirit* completed 1,200 miles under her jury rig.

I learned a lot from this experience, and was asked to sit on a committee for the Royal Ocean Racing Club to draw up regulations for multihulls, derived from Offshore Racing Council Special regulations. This set the rules internationally.

Arrival in La Corunna with the boom as a jury mast

The Scottish Islands Peaks race

This annual event, held in the Highlands and Islands of Scotland, is a sailing and fell-running adventure race that has been described as 'one of the toughest endurance events on the Scottish calendar'. The race, usually with over 60 teams of five each, has a higher entry list than the classic Three Peaks yacht race. The military and police regularly field several

Testing the rowing gear

teams. Only muscle power can be used, and the use of engines, even in neutral, is prohibited when runners are on the boat. The scenery is magnificent and the sailing challenging, with rock-strewn passages and tides up to 8–9 knots spewing forth into the Atlantic. The mountain running is largely off-road: over 60 miles across five mountains on three islands, with 11,500 feet of vertical ascent, the same height as from Everest Base Camp to the top of Everest – and down again. The winning boats are usually multihulls crewed by sailors with extensive local experience gained in previous races.

Fell runners are a toughened, wiry breed. They are able to complete two and a half marathons incorporating that challenging ascent and descent, much of it in darkness, cloud, fog, ice and snow, and climbing boulder fields and sometimes cliffs – in 11 hours. Recovery time between runs is as little as 4 hours, and a whole new technology has been developed to help with recovery, focusing on special cocktails of electrolytes and carbohydrates taken mixed with water from the mountain burns, to be consumed in the bow cabin, often in head seas and 20-knot speeds while the sailing crew yell at each other in a less than relaxing environment. Packs containing sleeping bags, survival bags, first aid and emergency rations have to be carried, meaning weight-reduction becomes an obsession – there is even cutting of fingernails just before the start! Proof of reaching each summit is demonstrated by a card-punch system.

With me and *Spirit of England* would be Paul Jeffes, a naval architect and marine surveyor who had skippered one of the British Steel vessels in the Round the World Challenge, known as the 'world's toughest sailing race'. He'd also skippered the winning vessel in the previous Scottish Peaks race. He had prepared an 11-page route plan to optimise tactics in differing conditions of weather and tide.

There would also be John Chaundy, who had won the race in 1989 and 1990, and had in the last year survived both a pitchpole and (as you will have read) a dismasting, in two separate boats in the Atlantic – yet his appetite for winning races in multihulls never waned! John's runners from previous Scottish and Three Peaks races – Ken Taylor and Jack Holt, rugged veterans from the north of England – joined us. Both took the sport very seriously, with a disciplined training programme, immense experience, detailed local knowledge and thorough medical research.

In the May 1996 race 59 yachts had entered, including 11 multihulls. Not all had made it to the start, as many had to get up there from the south coast of the UK, which involved a 600-mile delivery mostly in headwinds in the coldest May on record. Our own delivery had been extremely cold; the night temperatures had got down to 1°C (33.8°F) and we had sailed past fresh snow on Dartmoor. We had found that seven layers of clothing and three-season mountaineering sleeping bags had been inadequate, so for the race we had five-season (whatever that is) foam on the pipe cots, and an additional four-season mountain sleeping bag.

Most of the competitive boats were now rigged with four oars on racks, like Sydney Harbour 18-foot skiffs. We, however, had opted for two carbon rowing boxes with sliding seats, mountable in a choice of four positions on the outer hulls, and a pedal-powered propeller on the stern driven in reverse from the main hull. In trials we had managed about 1 knot per person. The Farriers were serious competition, as although they are slower under sail, they can be rowed at 5 knots and are more manoeuvrable in the anchorages, able to get right into the shoreline; there are eight drop-offs and pickups in the race, so a saving of five minutes on each one means 40 minutes overall. Rigged with long bowsprits, screachers and square-top mainsails, they could be driven hard. Robin Herbert's F27 *Naga* had two international-level fell runners on board in Alec Keith and Colin Donnelly, and would be the boat to beat in a light-air race, when the running time is around half the sailing time.

A bad mountain accident

A piper played from the bows of a yacht as the fleet circled in what has been described as a boating bumper car event, or a marine Le Mans start. Our fell runners, Ken and Jack, had decided to take it easy on the initial 6-mile run around Oban so as to preserve energy for the first mountain run on Mull. Paul rowed them back in the middle of the pack. Just after we hauled them aboard, a yacht crossed our bows and we collided with a crunch. We had right of way on two counts. Then a dinghy underestimated our speed under wing mast only, and we ran over them. When they popped out from under our rear cross beam, there were mutterings of protests and

Spirit leading the first leg of the Scottish Peaks Race

Spirit on a reach on Scottish Peaks Race

720s. We powered up, and soon got into the lead across the Firth of Lorne, hotly pursued by the press in RIBs, who had now decided we were favourites.

We beat down the Sound of Mull and, with a six-minute lead, dropped the runners off on the rocks at Salen. Three hours later we were circling anxiously, but as five boats got away there was still no sign of our runners. When they eventually returned I was shocked by Ken's appearance – he looked as if he'd run across Mike Tyson and then fallen down a cliff. He had a stitched head injury that looked like half a cricket ball, and blood spattered all over him. The two of them had been first up Ben More, and were completing the 24-mile run when Ken tripped and fell among rocks, splitting his head open and injuring his leg muscles in addition to gaining numerous bruises and lacerations. Jack had bandaged him up and they'd been able to run 7 miles to find a doctor, who'd put in six stitches as the seconds rolled by. Apparently the villagers had been both terrified and amazed at the sight of this apparition. Paul had been instructed to observe Ken for shock and concussion (he appeared to have both), and pull out if he got any worse, to prevent the risk of a fall on the Paps of Jura, the most dangerous mountain section.

The leading boats had got away from us as the wind reversed, so we did our 720 and then had to beat back again down the sound as night fell. John pedalled for additional power assist as we strived hard to catch the leaders before the tide turned foul in the gate at Fladda around midnight. This gate is the most critical of the race; streams run at up to 7 knots in the 400-yard gap between the rocks. But fortune was smiling on us; a puff of wind took us down the Firth of Lorne at 16 knots and we caught the stern lights of the two leaders right in the gate.

Light winds took us past the notorious Corryvreckan, and we were

Scottish Peaks sunset

Sunset and still in the lead

Whirlpools in the Corryvreckan tide race

careful not to get swept out sideways in the flood tide known as the Great Race which sweeps out into the Atlantic at up to 9 knots. The Pilot warned us that standing waves of up to 26 feet can form in a swell. The roar can be heard 10 miles away. Here, eddies form both vertically and horizontally. A research team once threw a mannequin fitted with a depth recorder into the race. It was dragged down to 282 metres, and finally resurfaced a long way down tide. An early Pilot described it as 'the most dangerous stream in all Europe ... a deep whirlpool wherein if ships do enter, there is no refuge but death only'. The U-shaped track plot kept me glued to the GPS map.

When we arrived on Jura, Ken was unable to bend his leg, which he'd crushed on a rock when he fell, and he wasn't sure if he could stand on it either. He looked, and obviously felt, awful. His leg must have caused him intense pain, even relative to his head wound, which he referred to as 'just a scratch'. It was a good thing we didn't have a mirror ...

The runners cross a pain threshold on each run, so the mental side of the race was not a factor. However, the Paps were unmarked, very steep and rocky, and the race instructions warned of the hazards of the cliffs. Descending these three peaks at speed requires great skill and the agility of a world-class mountain goat. Jack was reluctant to put Ken at risk and to incur possibly permanent injury, while Ken estimated it would take six weeks for his current injuries to heal. Courageously, however, they decided to give it a go.

We had a three-hour lead on the fleet, so the pressure was off. Paul got them to the landing stage at the Isle of Jura Distillery at Craighouse, whereupon the race marshals refused to allow the pair to continue due to an assessment that their jackets were 'water resistant' and not 'waterproof'. We resupplied them with lightweight foul weather gear from the boat, delaying them half an hour. They took the GPS, and we agreed that in an emergency Jack would mark Ken's position, pack him inside the emergency gear and come back to get us all for a rescue. Paul refilled our water bottles from the whisky distillery, as I'd underestimated the amount of fluids the runners use on their recovery schedules. Amazingly, the two of them returned within 45 minutes of a top performance time!

The next leg saw us rowing and pedalling against the tide in the Sound of Jura, then we gybed round the Mull of Kintyre under spinnaker. John was driving *Spirit* at up to 18 knots.

The end of the Scottish Peaks race

We arrived at Lamlash on the Isle of Arran at dusk, with *Naga* 45 minutes behind. Violent squalls hit us from all directions in the lee of Holy Island. Since we'd expected Ken's injuries to set him back 30–45 minutes, this made for an exciting finish. The rest of the fleet had caught up in more favourable tide and wind, and *Naga* had been driven at 22 knots. Lamlash was described in the Pilot as 'more suitable for a fleet of warships than a yacht. There are at least a dozen large ship moorings, painted yellow, but none of them lit.' So we moored 200 yards offshore in order to reduce the risk of hitting something on our getaway in a rising north-easterly, which was now sending a swell into the bay. Even though Goat Fell was in cloud and the climb would be through the night, Ken and Jack had left the GPS behind to save 9 oz in wright, relying instead on their senses and their experience.

Naga was being held waist-deep by two crewmen in drysuits, ready for a lightning getaway; apparently their dinghy had blown away during a gust, but had landed up further down the beach. Our carefully rehearsed getaway would be much more complex and would take 10–15 minutes longer. Whose runners would be first back?

John rigged the mooring off the port hull so we were already 45 degrees to the wind. He recognised Ken and Jack's torch movements. They signalled from the dinghy, Paul rowed as if in the Olympics, and soon we hauled them aboard.

'We pulled out all the stops, but they're right on our tail. Now it's up to you,' Ken told me.

The wind was gusting 25 knots, a force 7 was forecast, and the adrenaline was pumping. Other vessels arrived later, including an Oyster 68 maxi monohull, which was knocked onto its beam ends by what they called 'a katabatic downdraft, a white squall from hell', until their crew was standing on the mast.

We half-unfurled the headsail and backed it to allow us to drop behind the nearest hazards, and hoisted a triple-reefed main to beat out. The swells had thrown the halyard round the top spreader and the reef lines around the antennae, delaying the hoist. We went right up to Holy Island, which we couldn't see, as we'd lost our night vision, and since the bottom sloped up at 45 degrees we were totally reliant on the GPS map. As soon as the depth sounder dropped below 10 metres, we would have less than five seconds before we hit the rocks. Paul knew the area well, and as the depth dropped to 9 metres we listened to the breakers as we skirted the northern end. We unreefed to one reef for the last two-hour close-hauled sprint to the finish, with the Scottish mainland lights in view underneath the weather hull as it heaved up and down in the gusts and swells.

We arrived at 0400 in a total time of 39:49:15. We had won the race, and it was only then that I realised Ken had pushed himself into the highest echelons as we followed a piper and the press ashore, and he slowly climbed the steps to the bar backwards, having lost function in his legs. *Naga* came in 20 minutes later with 40:11:26, and one of their crew with a bandaged head due to a boom-induced gash over his eyebrow. Next day, the newspaper headline said it all: 'Bloody Victory in Jura Race'. The rest of the fleet had had a rougher time, with reports of hail and snow on the mountains, and St Elmo's fire in the rigging. All in all, in the best British tradition, 'a good time was had by all'.

Three Peaks yacht race

The 389-mile Gelert Three Peaks yacht race was first staged in 1977 under the presidency of the late mountaineer, Arctic explorer and sailor Bill Tilman. It's the original adventure race: 73 miles (approximately three marathons)

Spirit leads after the start of Three Peaks Race

set over 11,000 vertical feet up (and down!) on the three highest mountains in England, Wales and Scotland, with recovery times between mountains of as little as five hours, combined with just over five days of sailing monohulls for 389 miles in Britain's coastal waters. Teams compete for various trophies, including the coveted King of the Mountains, or Mountain Aggregate.

In the early days of the race the runners had scaled the mountains in oilskins, plus-fours and boots, taking around eight hours to climb each mountain in what can now be run in three. Today's fell runners wear nothing but shorts and T-shirts, even when it's below freezing at night, burning up like nuclear power plants at an estimated 6,000 calories per mountain (power plants that need to be refuelled with liquefied carbohydrates on each sailing leg). Running at night and in thick visibility has also since become an art in itself, with headlamps, hand torches, pre-programmed 9-oz GPS, marker lights and fluorescent tape attached to rocks on the way up to hasten the scree-ride back. Many runners also represent their countries in international events, and compete in road marathons as well as fell events – some have even reportedly trained in the Andes to improve fitness, and in Florida for possible heatwave conditions.

In the same period, the development of multihulls and water-ballasted monohulls has seen a similar improvement in sailing boat performance, including a doubling of boat speed, to the point that some elite runners purposely choose slow monohulls in order to get more recovery time between runs.

The Three Peaks concept was such a success that it has now been duplicated through the Scottish Peaks, English Universal 500, the Australian Three Peaks and a Norwegian Three Peaks. At the time of writing similar events are being planned in the USA and Japan.

In 1996, the year we raced, there were 15 starters including three multihulls, a low turnout that reflected the recession, injuries and conflicting events. *Kaos*, Ian Loffhagen's F27 multihull, had three support vehicles. F27s had won three of the last four Three Peaks races, reflecting good moderate-air performance, shallow draft manoeuvrability, rowing speed (as mentioned above), most Farriers now had four oars in the Peaks races, and *Kaos* had reached 5.6 knots under full-length carbon oars off a rowing eight, and relative comfort below. Next in size up was *PDA Janette*, a brilliantly designed 35-foot catamaran conceived, built by and campaigned by David Southward.

Spirit of England, the largest tri at 40 feet, was described in the race brochure as follows: 'doubt whether any bookmakers would take bets on this team, but as many have found out before, there are a number of uncertainties en route'. Making up the sailing contingent of the *Spirit* team were John Chaundy and Brian Thompson. John had been on the winning boats in three previous Three Peaks races, and Brian was fresh back from setting new transpacific records on *Lakota*. Our runners were once again our rugged fell runners from the north, Ken Taylor and Jack Holt. They'd been on *Severalles* in two previous Three Peaks wins. Ken had broken the Mountain

Aggregate record in 1985 at an amazing 10.32 hours, which although attempted some 600 times since had never been bettered. Ken was still sporting a scar on his port side temple from his serious fall in the Scottish Peaks, but had returned to 'go for a matching pair' on the starboard side. His leg injuries were still evident but fortunately almost healed.

The race administration was very efficient and had the support of the army, who had set up eight radio/telex stations in ports and at mountain summits for race reporting. The day before the start, Steve Isles (TV cameraman) and Robert Howard (press photographer and journalist) requested a trip on *Spirit* to get some action shots. However, they were a bit disappointed at the light, sunny weather, which conflicted with the race description of 'gruelling', 'arduous', 'serious' and 'extreme'. We were politely asked if the helmsman could dress in foul weather gear and one of us chuck buckets of water over him, apparently a technique employed in previous events. Fortunately, a puff of wind came along and we were able to generate some genuine spray off the bows at 19 knots without getting the cameras wet. The publicity for the race was organised very professionally by Ron Isles, who had hooked into Trans World Sport and Reuters, and secured TV coverage via Channel 4, CNN, ESPN and WTN in 77 countries, and potentially some 2.5 billion households.

The Three Peaks race start

The race started from Barmouth in north Wales. *Kaos* got to the start first at the pin end, leaving a gap just wide enough for *Spirit* to power through to weather. Across to Hell's Mouth, past Devil's Ridge and Devil's Tail, then Bardsey Sound. This was the first of seven tidal gates on the race, which unfortunately did not suit fast passages, in general penalising the leading boats. Bardsey was no exception, and after catching an eddy in the lee of the island, Brian short tacked *Spirit* a few feet from the rocks against the foul tide. This was hard work with a rotating mast, but could be optimised to a few metres using a GPS map in the cockpit area. Since the cliffs went down at 45 degrees, a good rule of thumb was to tack on the 10-metre line, indicating that the rocks were either 10 metres down or 10 metres in front of the depth sounder (in other words, 5 metres from the bows), or a combination. We were lucky that the winds were light, as the Pilot described the area as 'a continuous race' with 'an evil reputation' and 'hell itself'.

A spinnaker run got *Spirit* over the Caernarfon bar at low water, and to the drop-off point at the bottom of a fearsome-looking ship's steel docking tower – a tricky operation at night in the strong tide. Again we were lucky it was light, as the bar is impassable in heavy seas, and the Pilot advised crossing it only above half tide. *PDA* came in 1 hour 41 minutes later, and *Kaos* after another hour, having suffered the foul tides. Ken and Jack put in a blistering Snowdon (3,560 feet) night run time of 3 hours 54 minutes, and opened up *Spirit*'s lead to nearly 3 hours. But we then lost 2 hours anchored in the Menai Straits in the dawn, waiting for the tide.

The most interesting part of the Menai Straits is between Brunel's Britannia Bridge and Telford's Suspension Bridge, each of them revolutionary 19th-century engineering masterpieces. It was even more interesting that day in particular, as there was a pipelaying barge with cables strung across the straits at the Britannia Bridge. Between the two bridges are the notorious Swellies – drying rocks with a 30-metre gap through which spring currents reach

John Chaundy and Brian Thompson reefing down

7 knots. During the previous winter My brother Julian (who was heading up the shore support teams), John and I had been up there reconnoitring (standard practice for Three Peaks planning), and had noticed people white-water rafting in the rapids, even at neaps. After hearing stories of bust rudders and oars, we'd come fully prepared with our two oars, which could be set inwards off the outer hulls to reduce the beam, and a pedal-powered propeller set off the stern.

Julian also carried a spare rudder and oar in his van. We tied up to a barge's anchor buoys to wait for the foul tide to drop below 2 knots, then set off at low tide through the Swellies, with Brian working on oar repairs, and on to the Suspension Bridge, where our light Doyle reacher took over from muscle power. Again, the weather was kind – had the headwind had been significant our route would not have been possible at low tide, as the channel was too narrow for short tacking. The Pilot recommends doing this passage only at high water, advice that the competitors in this race have to ignore.

Through the Irish Sea

The new fair tide slung us back into the Irish Sea, where we caught a fresh cold nor'westerly in bright sun, and tucked a reef in. Four of us had crashed to catch up on sleep, confident of an uneventful passage to Ravenglass – when half an hour later *Spirit* sailed into a hole, slopping around in choppy seas generated by a fresh wind that must have been immediately upwind. The Irish Sea is strange, with winds and tides in lots of different directions as a result of its topography and thermals, so it can get exasperating. We tried rowing and pedalling but generally just got splashed without forward progress, and so had to wait it out. Eventually the wind came back just as before, and we reached into Ravenglass near high water, which was fortunate as at low water the onshore wind would have made it very tricky or, as the Pilot warned, 'dangerous and difficult'.

As the entrance is mostly drying and unmarked, most competitors chart out the area at low water before the race, with compass, GPS, cameras and videos. We had done this in March and found it invaluable. We were particularly keen to avoid an unmarked pyramid-shaped rock in the middle of the channel, which we had named Chaundy's Rock on the waypoint list. In the winter we had also picked out a little pool in the estuary, which we planned to anchor in so as to avoid getting stranded at low water, meaning delayed refloating. After dropping the runners, we carefully found this spot with GPS, rangefinder and compass.

We told Ken and Jack not to hurry, as we couldn't get out until 90 minutes after low water – but they had their own agenda, and again put in a winning night run for 32 miles to Scafell

Ken pedalling off the stern

Spirit leading in the Menai Straits

(3,210 feet) and back. The other multis were on the putty. As soon as there was a half-metre of water in the shallowest area we were off, nudging the bottom then following the channel with the aid of our nightscope and GPS, which was now proven accurate to 20 yards. The monohulls, meanwhile, were all outside the bar, waiting to come in on the tide.

Light winds were fine for exiting at low water, but not good for boat speed in the slop, and at dawn, with *PDA* a mile behind *Spirit*, the race started all over again. As we cleared the Isle of Man the wind came up, and in the lee of the Mull of Galloway it piped up to force 5 on the nose. We put a reef in and close-hauled at up to 16 knots of boat speed.

We found the wind often stronger in the lee of land, especially when heated up with thermals (known on board *Spirit* as the Chaundy effect). Sure enough, as we reached the Mull the wind lightened, and Brian predicted another Bardsey. He was right – we had to put in dozens of rock-defying short tacks, optimising the foul tidal streams on the GPS map – but it did allow us to finally escape from the rest of the fleet. Fortunately, the wind then allowed us to sail past the Mull of Kintyre into the relatively tideless Sound of Jura, but then it died, and we had to row and pedal for five hours through the night and dawn, attempting 'The Song of the Volga Boatmen'). The three of us were able to average 2.8 knots. Later in the morning, the gentlest breeze of 3 knots arrived on a glassy, mirror-like sea, and *Spirit* got up to 4–5 knots of boat speed under the light reacher – an extraordinary experience without a ripple on the water. John cooked up the last carbohydrate package for the runners.

Bad weather in the Scottish Islands

A long-awaited low was coming in, and soon a sou'westerly filled in, allowing us to set the big kite and get past two critical areas: Corryvreckan and Fladda. Once again, we were back to face the hazards of the Great Race.

Fortunately, we were spared rowing against this lot, and we got through the penultimate gate at Fladda just before the tide turned. The sou'westerly brought with it rain and thick visibility, down to 200–400 yards. We gybed back and forth at 10–14 knots under the kite, using a newly developed fast 'inside gybe' method, and the GPS map now really came into its own, completely replacing the radar, as misty headlands and ruined castles appeared and disappeared through the gloom. It was very Scottish.

Spirit in the lead in the Scottish lochs

Jack and Ken setting out for Ben Nevis

Jack and Ken returning from Ben Nevis

Spirit and the team, with Ben Nevis behind

We crossed the foul tide at the last gate, Corran Narrows, as our soaked shore team – my brother Julian, my wife Bonnie, and my son Mike – cheered us on from the ferry landing, and we dropped off the runners in the late evening near Fort William after a total sailing time of 2 days 18 hours 22 minutes. We had pulled out the stops to prevent Ken and Jack having to do their third mountain in the dark, and they shot off in pouring rain as if doing a four-minute mile. The top of Ben Nevis, at 4,406 feet, had pockets of snow and ice with thick cloud and gale winds. Ken also held the record for this run, and they were sprinting back, busting through an HM Forces finish tape in 3 hours 32 minutes to take all three running legs, the King of the Mountains Aggregate (against all boats including monohulls) and the overall race. Amazing results, considering that they had the minimum recovery times of any team, and that two runs had been at night, one in bad weather. They were as out of breath as the average sailor is after grinding the genoa in. Their fitness, at ages 47 and 49 (a combined age of 96), amazed us all.

We had won the race with a time of 3 days, 7 hours and 38 minutes. We had also won all three sailing legs and had the fastest running times. *PDA* arrived next morning, having been set back another four hours by the adverse tides at the Mulls.

The Three Peaks yacht race is a world classic, a fantastic race like no other, set in beautiful mountains with enthralling sailing. Every racing sailor should do it at least once.

The Fastnet race

The Fastnet rock, the southernmost point of Ireland, lies in the Atlantic off Ireland's south-west coast. In 1997 no less than 247 yachts from 15 nations entered the race, starting from Cowes, rounding 'the Rock' and finishing in Plymouth for a total course of 605 miles. For the first time since the original Fastnet race had been held in 1925, the Royal Ocean Racing Club allowed multihulls to enter: three 60-foot French Formula 1 trimarans and nine 30–50-foot multihulls in the S-Multihull class, representing the USA, the UK, France and Russia.

The race has a reputation for bad weather, which is common in the Atlantic in August, and roughly a quarter of all Fastnet races have faced severe force 8–9 gales, most often on the longest leg, some 180 miles between Land's End and Ireland. The sea has frequently removed chunks of the rock and the lighthouse itself, twisting steel at even 130 feet above sea level. The force 11 storm that devastated the 1979 race – the worst storm in Fastnet history – claimed 19 lives, 15 from the monohull fleet and 4 from an unofficial multihull entry. Only 85 of the 303 starters finished, and 24 boats were abandoned. A total of 136 sailors were rescued as a result of a huge air-sea rescue effort. A quarter of the fleet (all keelboats) were inverted 180–360 degrees. Search and rescue aircraft, which are equipped with radar that can measure wave height, reported 50–60-foot seas, and yachtsmen with experience of many Southern Ocean races reported that they had never seen seas as bad. The storm had been caused mainly by a 90-degree very sharp veer in a trough within a 135-degree veer over 12 hours, possibly also aggravated by shallow banks.

The race has had an enormous influence on yacht design. Winners in the first Fastnet races took 19–21 days to complete the course. About 70 years later, in 1997, Laurent Bourgnon's *Primagaz* broke the course record with a time of 45 hours, 45 minutes: ten times faster than those early racers. Few sports have seen such dramatic improvements over the years. *Gitana IV*, which broke the Fastnet record in the 1960s, had elaborate meals served by stewards below, and the crew were required to dress for dinner. But the boats nowadays rarely have even a table – dinner is freeze-dried, eaten out of mugs on deck. Few multihulls have any plumbing. After the 1979 débâcle safety standards worldwide were overhauled. Multihull safety has also improved since 1979, including principally stronger construction, more buoyant hulls, escape hatches, and drogues off the stern, or preferably parachute anchors off the bow, which allow survival in extreme conditions.

On the 40-foot Owen tri *Spirit of England*, we focused on two key areas in order to improve speed and safety prior to the race: weather research, and avoiding fatigue at night. Offshore sailing accidents occur most frequently between 2 a.m. and 4 a.m., which was also the worst time in the 1979 storm. The race that year had started in light airs, with a forecast of force 5–6 at the Fastnet, as a low was coming into the south-west of Ireland. For us in August 1997 there was a small high over the Channel at the start, a deepening low west of Ireland, and a forecast of force 5–6 in the west of the course – a classic Fastnet weather situation.

The early part of our race would be dominated by sea breezes and land breezes, which we studied in the days before the start. The key would be to keep inshore to optimise these and the tides, and offshore to catch the gradient wind in between, keeping both options open. While a gale was unlikely, the complex system of lows and fronts awaited us west of Ireland, so we took our drogue and para-anchor, partly because our skipper was wearing the MOCRA Safety Officer hat and wanted to set a good example. The key strategic issue on the Fastnet legs was which side of the rhumb line to go: we decided to edge south on each leg in order to hedge the expected troughs in the southerly airstream.

Our crew was a quiet one, with a collection of cool and logical minds and a broad wealth of multihull experience.

Spirit leading her class round Fastnet Rock

Brian Thompson joined us, fresh off another TransPac in Steve Fossett's 60-foot tri *Lakota*, and the 60-foot cat *Stars & Stripes* in the offshore Pacific. *Stars & Stripes* can sail at twice the true wind speed, flying a hull in a force 2, and had won the America's Cup in San Diego.

Brian was on his third season on *Spirit*, having previously been in the winning crew in the Falmouth–Azores and Three Peaks races. At the time, he was Britain's leading offshore multihull sailor, with a wealth of wins and world records. He had just completed delivering *Lakota* from Hawaii to San Francisco, flying to the UK the day before the race, so was functioning on Pacific time, which made it easy for him to stay awake on the night watches. We decided that to remain competitive in the future, we'd always send half the crew to the other side of the planet for a week or two prior to the race …

Richard Pocock and Digby Fox were rounding off a successful RORC season on *Spirit*. Richard was the A class national champion, and had extensive offshore experience dating from the 60-foot tri *Colt Cars*, which included surviving a pitchpole. Richard had also survived a 180-degree inversion in an OOD 34 in the 1979 Fastnet, the crew wondering whether the boat would ever come upright again. Digby raced Dart 15s and 18s, and like the others was an excellent multihull driver. He had a refreshingly positive outlook, and was our best line untangler, constantly sorting the snake pit of 32 lines in the cockpit area. Digby was also the production editor of *Yachts and Yachting* magazine, so we had to watch our language!

This year saw more fast boats and more rock stars than ever before in one race. There were races within races. It was the first time in history that the French Formula 1 60s, the Whitbread 60 fleet, the Ericsson 80/Grand Mistral fleet, Open 60 Vendée/BOC boats and the Admiral's Cup fleet had all been in one event. The crew list looked like a *Who's Who* of sailing. There were America's Cup drivers and Olympic medallists. It was a privilege just to be at the start line.

'Better look good. There's Beken, the famous yacht photographer,' Digby alerted us.

'Didn't know we had any. Got eggs as well?' came the inevitable reply.

The Fastnet start: Cowes

The monohulls started two and a half hours ahead of us, which gave them the chance to get the fair tide through the Needles and past Portland Bill. The faster boats, including all the trimarans and the W-60s, started at the back, with a two-hour gap to reduce congestion. Loick Peyron's *Fujicolor* was sparring with *Primagaz*, then it was our start, which went perfectly with a reach down the line on starboard, and a last-minute gybe onto port on the stronger fair tide on the island side. *Spirit* led the S-multis beating down the Solent, with Ralph Marx's American entry, the Shuttleworth 34 *Shockwave*, Richard Tolkien's Bailey 40 *FPC Greenaway* (*Mollymawk*), and Claude Develay's French Irens 50 *Nootka* snapping at our heels.

Spirit also led the W-60s out to the Needles, crossing tacks with Lawrie Smith, Chris Dickson, Paul Cayard, Grant Dalton and other 'rock star' sailors, surrounded by four helicopters. We used the sea breeze as far as Anvil Point, then positioned ourselves 5 miles offshore to catch the land breeze, as there was no gradient wind expected until 0300. We stealthily passed 200 kedged monohulls in 3 knots of wind off the Dorset coast in the foul tide, an amazing experience surrounded as we were by hundreds of red and green lights in a silence only interrupted by rattling anchor chains. The barometer dropped a touch, confirming that the high was drifting north, so we headed offshore to catch the expected easterly gradient, then gybed back in and went through the Portland Bill race to get maximum fair tide. As the race current reaches 9 knots in springs it is to be avoided in any kind of swell or foul weather.

We kept offshore, using the gradient and keeping clear of any interfering sea breeze, running close to *FPC Greenaway/Mollymawk* and *Nootka* down the Devon coast. After Land's End we had to drive very hard to get ahead of *Nootka*, with the light-air reacher up in a force 5 reach. We were now on the edge of the Atlantic low, feeling its southerly airstream. We blew out both of the reacher tell-tale windows (2 square feet, each reinforced with carbon and Kevlar).

Then during the night, while Brian and I were off watch below, there was a loud bang and Richard yelled, 'Need some help!' The reacher had blown the masthead shackle open and the sail had gone overboard – but we recovered it even though we were unable to drop below 10 knots boat speed.

We were driving the boat harder than ever before. I was reminded of someone who described living conditions in a racing multihull as being similar to trying to sleep inside a 5-foot diameter tube being towed at 30 mph along a bumpy dirt track. The three hulls were like racehorses galloping along. With the wind gusting to force 6, we hit 23–24 knots boat speed on a screaming reach overnight to the Rock, catching the W-60 fleet (which had got away from us in the light airs) in the process. Lawrie Smith's *Silk Cut* was the second W-60 to the Rock, having achieved a top speed of 22 knots.

Rounding the Fastnet Rock

Spirit was the first S-multi round the Rock, with *Nootka* 30 seconds behind, having just failed to establish an overlap – not a good place to call for water in some lumpy seas! Celebrations were in order, with a shot of whisky all round from Digby's silver flask, toasting the Rock, the race and Poseidon. We all recalled previous roundings, my last one in my Wayfarer dinghy, but Brian topped us all with a comment that in 1995 he had done three on *Lakota*: one as an unofficial Fastnet entry (breaking the record at 2 days 8 hours), one breaking the Round Ireland record, and one breaking the Round Britain and Ireland record.

After the celebrations, two mast rotator blocks and a barber hauler block blew up – replaced with spares. Next night a mainsheet block blew apart – also replaced with a spare. We put in a reef – and then there was yet another minor explosion as the first reef line blew inside the boom later in the night. We decided to unreef by default. There were some nasty black squalls in a cold front, looking like tornadoes in the night.

Nootka got away from us on the beat back to Bishop Rock. Jagged rocks jutted out of the sea at the southern end of the Scillies. We throttled up to 20 knots again to the Lizard, and I wore some excellent safety goggles which dealt admirably with the 30-knot spray.

'I'll go up the mast now,' Brian announced. We ran downwind so he could go up on the fractional spinnaker halyard with a boathook to grab the masthead spinnaker halyard. We then reset the reacher, complete with two large holes in it, and crossed the finish line in 3 days 46 minutes.

Heavy weather and the race crew

We were ahead of all the Admiral's Cup entries, and most of the maxis, too, in spite of their earlier start. It was fun to finish in among professionally sailed, sponsored entries twice our size with 50 times the budget. Although all of *Spirit*'s crew are or have been in the marine business, we were all treating the race as a fun event, on an amateur 'play hard' basis.

We won the class and the Crystal Trophy, and maintained our lead in the RORC 1997 Multihull series. We were 22 per cent faster than the fastest same-size monohulls. Our main multihull rivals, *FPC Greenaway/ Mollymawk* and *Shockwave*, arrived 9 and 16 hours later respectively.

In the launch with us was the crew from the wing-masted Open 60 *Aquitaine Innovations* (Eric Tabarly, Yves Parlier, Paul Vatine), and we were met on the dock by Isabelle Autissier off her Open 60 *PRB Poitou Charentes*. We were surrounded by legends! I had met Tabarly in Lequitio, northern Spain, after a RORC race in 1966, and he was still as modest and charming as he'd been back then. He also looked only slightly older – a lesson, perhaps, that the sea is good for you.

Round Britain and Ireland race

The Royal Western Yacht Club doublehanded Round Britain and Ireland race (RBI) is held every four years. The 2,000-mile course, starting and ending at Plymouth, leaves all the islands of the UK and Ireland to starboard, and takes the fleet out into the Atlantic to round remote uninhabited rocks north-west of the Outer Hebrides, and the stormy area west of the Shetlands. Gales are sometimes a feature on these first three western legs. There are four 48-hour stopovers, at Crosshaven (south-west Ireland), Barra (Outer Hebrides), Lerwick (Shetlands), and Lowestoft. The fourth leg, down the North Sea, threads its way through the oil and gas platforms, and is the most tactical, allowing the choice of the Scotland or Scandinavia side to optimise weather patterns. The final leg involves tidal planning through the Thames Estuary and the Channel. The race is generally regarded as more challenging than the Transatlantics as it's not possible to route around bad weather, and the coastlines present a lot of tactical work.

Past winners include Sir Robin Knox-Johnston, Sir Chay Blyth, Rob James, Tony Bullimore and Steve Fossett – all in sponsored multihulls. This year there was a 45-foot limit on multihulls, and 60-foot on monohulls, allowing monohull Open 60s a chance at line honours.

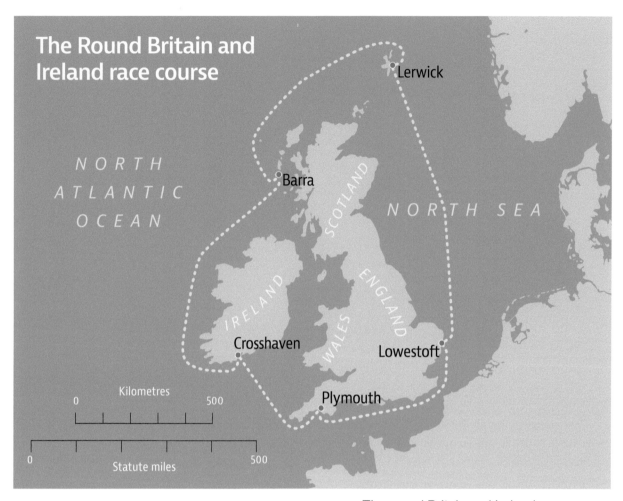

The round Britain and Ireland race course

Spirit of England was the race favourite in June 1998, on account of her prior performance against Open 60s and the other multihulls, involving 12 first place results to date. Weather research indicated a generally light-air race, with perhaps one force 6–8 blow – and that year the biggest ever El Niño was expected to cause slack pressure gradients in the Atlantic, based on prior El Niño year statistics. Accordingly, we optimised *Spirit* for light airs and downwind, with a bigger bowsprit and light air reachers. We also lengthened her from 40 to 43 feet by sharpening the bows and improving the stern exits.

Brian Thompson was co-skippering with me on his fourth season on *Spirit*, having previously been instrumental in our winning the Falmouth–Azores and the Three Peaks, and a class win in the Fastnet. The project team was managed by Merfyn Owen, Allen Clarke and Bill Bullimore. Brian had achieved an amazing second place in the previous RBI on *Severalles Challenge*.

At Queen Anne's Battery, Plymouth, we inspected the competition: 41 starters, including 15 multihulls, representing seven countries. Three other boats had the capability for line honours: Richard Tolkien on his fifth RBI in *FPC Greenaway*, well sorted with six Atlantic crossings behind her, but dismasted in her last RBI; Mark Gatehouse, also on his fifth RBI in *Victoria Docks*, Christoph Auguin's Open 60 which had won the BOC and been placed second in the Vendée Globe; and Nigel Musto (of the Musto clothing business) with BT Global Challenge skipper Andy Hindley sailing the Open 60 *Musto Performance Partners*, formerly Mike Plant's *Coyote*, a giant surfboard sailed by David Scully in the last BOC. Light airs would favour *Spirit*, upwind moderate conditions would suit *FPC Greenaway*, and heavy air would favour *Victoria Docks*, while *Musto* would be the boat to beat downwind in a blow. The three were sponsored entries, and very well sorted, with thousands of gale-hardened ocean miles behind them.

Spirit at the start of the 1998 Round Britain and Ireland Race

There were also two hot Open 50s, German Wolfgang's *Wolfie's Toy* and David Rowan/Ellen MacArthur in *Jeantex*.

The multihull fleet included two French tris: Patrick Coulombel's 40-foot tri *Somme Enterprises*, and the 35-foot *Acolyte*. Holland was represented by Trijnie Dijkhuis's beautiful Grainger 40-foot tri *Pandiono*. American Ralph Marx was sailing the high-tech Shuttleworth 34-foot tri *Shockwave* with Alistair Wood. The rest of the multihulls were British.

The Round Britain start

On start day, 7 June 1998, it was blowing force 6 off Plymouth, with a major gale expected as a 2,000-mile-wide winter-type depression headed our way across the Atlantic. The boats were reefed to two, three or four reefs. Our primary objective in the fresh conditions at the start was to avoid a collision, so we set off under-canvassed, with staysail and two reefs, beating past Eddystone to the Scillies.

Somme Enterprises broke her daggerboard before she even got to the Plymouth breakwater, and retired. *Fingers Crossed* blew out both genoa sheets while beating in Plymouth Sound, then had major mast problems, forcing an early retirement as well.

These upwind force 4–6 conditions were not good for *Spirit*. Unfortunately for us we had upwind force 4–6 for 60 per cent of the race, and all in all 80 per cent of the race was on the wind! We never once set the spinnaker, and in fact, after looking at the forecasts for each leg, left it ashore for most of the race.

At dusk we unreefed and took the lead near Bishop Rock; this was the last time we saw another competitor on the course until Selsey Bill, 2,000 miles later.

Bearing off onto a broad reach, we quickly put the two reefs back in as the wind freshened again. Soon we were hitting 22 knots going down some big, pale grey seas, keeping warm and dry behind Musto one-piece breathable HPX drysuits (which we lived in for the whole leg) and motorcycle goggles (which we wore for 80 per cent of the race). Food was our heavy weather onehanded variety, the other hand used for driving the boat or trimming lines. Roaring past the Kinsale gas rigs in thick visibility and force 6–7, we soon picked up the entrance to Cork harbour on the radar, and crossed the line at 20 knots, having averaged 17 knots since the Scillies and broken the class leg record in under 24 hours. *Spirit* was superb and just loved being driven off a reach straight down the waves on a big surf, burying all three bows in the back of the wave ahead, and often climbing over the back of it, without a hint of a pitchpole on account of the buoyancy in the main bow and the fine entry of the floats.

FPC Greenaway was 40 minutes behind, having stuffed the bows badly a couple of times, throwing the helmsman off the tiller. Two more multihulls and two monohulls retired in the rough conditions with mast, rudder and daggerboard problems. *Fiery Cross* ripped open her starboard float on a buoy in the dark at the finish and retired as well.

In Cork, we repaired the rudder, which was seizing up, and while we built up our 'sleep and food credits', expecting to deplete them severely on the next leg, the shore crew, Bill and Liam Dryden, knocked off the punchlist items.

Beating into an Atlantic gale

The leg up the west coast of Ireland to Barra promised a force 8 gale on the nose, and our primary concern was not to break the boat up. 'Are you ready for this?' Brian asked, referring to the expected 35-knot conditions 'I've got the weatherfax.' It looked horrendous. *Spirit* had been out in force 10 in the Solent, and force 7 reaching offshore, but never beating into an open ocean gale. We left with staysail and two reefs reaching down the Irish coast in some big gusts, climbing over huge green hills of water coming round the Fastnet, a warning of what the Atlantic had in store for us. Waves were breaking right over the 90-foot rock.

Brian driving on the Round Britain Race

It was a very bad night, beating into force 7–8 with three reefs, on 20-minute watches. Brian was doing most of the deck work and working hard on our VMG, tacking on the wind shifts. Tacking was tricky, as we'd stop dead on the wave faces, some up to 25 feet, then slide backwards down them, reversing the helm carefully to rotate the boat. Each tack, with runners and mast rotation, required nine line operations and was a handful singlehanded.

I was unable to keep any food down and was steadily getting colder. It was very unfriendly down below and quite impossible to consider sleeping in the bow cabin on account of violent motion and crash-bang pounding. Going below to navigate was out also – everything was pre-programmed on deck. We stayed on deck and in the doghouse.

We were able to beat at 9–10 knots, with 6–7 knots VMG, mainly because the bigger seas reduced the slamming that we often got in shorter inshore conditions. The big seas had lots of smaller ones on the front and back faces, which were actually more of a problem. Normally, we didn't like to clip on while driving in case of a capsize, but there were some big breakers coming green over the bow, and a short lifeline was essential to avoid getting swept over the stern.

At dawn, the big black seas and the rocks and cliffs off Ireland were menacing and forbidding. The wind moderated and backed, allowing us to fetch the Hebrides. The decks were covered in seaweed from the green waves we had taken. It was now getting very cold, but at least we were able to heat up some freeze-dried noodles for the first time. We were still living 24 hours a day in the Musto one-piece foul weather gear which we had only bought the day before the race and had been hand-delivered by Nigel, and we wore fur-lined diving gloves. We also had Guy Cotten TPS neoprene survival suits in case of emergency.

Nearly dismasted

We set the big reacher with a 1.25 tonne 'fuse' in the clew. After just a couple of hours it blew, so we doubled it up. While we were running downwind, Brian's jaw dropped as he noticed the 10-tonne-rated cap shroud toggle sheared on one side – our 62-foot carbon rotating mast was on the point of collapse. We quickly put on a Spectra lashing and two halyards as jury stays, then limped into Barra.

Greenaway arrived 5 hours later, having nosedived to 45 degrees and nearly pitchpoled in a 50-knot gust off Ireland. The Open 60s came in next, Nigel Musto and Andy Hindley describing the conditions as 'awful', 'horrendous' and 'hell', with the life raft and grab bag on deck on account of boat-breaking slamming in 20–25-foot seas. As *Musto* was a Roaring Forties downwind flyer, they had done admirably to punch through the gale at all. Andy was used to punching upwind due to his experience in the BT Challenge – but not in a carbon racehorse.

The fleet was now down to 32 boats. Others reported 45–50 knots (force 8–9) in the gale. *Paradox* had retired with rudder problems – we had noticed one of them badly delaminated in Crosshaven, and heard that the boat was hard to control on account of the float rudders swapping from one to the other. They had done amazingly well to get that far, given the extreme conditions. *A.R.S l'Albatross* retired, and *Pandiono* limped in with rudder problems.

We heard about the tragic loss of Éric Tabarly in the heavy conditions. As mentioned earlier, I had been talking to him after the Fastnet only the previous year. It just didn't seem fair that the sea should claim such a wonderful man. He had contributed enormously to multihull development, among all his other achievements.

It was now a race against time to get the new rigging built and sent up. We had beaten our shore crew to Barra, and they arrived on the ferry shortly after. Bill Bullimore had organised the entire project, but the problem was that it was a weekend, and we couldn't figure out how to get it transported to Barra. There were no flights in time, and anyhow the airport, on the beach, could only be used at low water during weekdays. The ferry was too slow, as would be a fishing vessel charter. We looked at a parachute drop into the bay, but it was illegal. Bill was frantically searching for a seaplane, but there were none in the area. So in case we couldn't get the parts delivered I bought some huge rusting trawler shackles to make up a Spectra jury rig.

Duncan Barr put two new sets together and Richard Laight brought the parts by driving to Heathrow, flying to Glasgow, then taking a train to Oban – and finally a high-speed RIB overnight in open water and force 5 headwinds with seasick crews. He arrived at 0230, looking as if he had come off a multihull in a gale – it was a fantastic 30-hour effort. As the hotel was full we hauled a bed up the fire escape so he could get some rest before returning. Meanwhile we struggled back and forth to the boat in our tiny beach dinghy, and rebuilt the rig.

Meanwhile, in Barra the town was out for some wild drinking, eightsome reels and bar fights. I noticed that the women mostly wore the same style of shoes, as there was only one type for sale on the island. The castle there was the property of some of my ancestors, the MacNeills, a Highland clan with the motto 'To conquer or die'. They would have had the right spirit for a Round Britain race crew. Their ancestors were Vikings.

Then there was yet another force 5 reefed-down beat out to the magnificent uninhabited St Kilda island. We left yet again with two reefs and staysail. It was light all night but bitterly cold – there was apparently frost ashore, and the sea temperature was a miserable 8°C (46°F), colder than the English Channel in midwinter. We wore four layers of thermals, insulated French seaboots and neoprene kidney belts. We carbo-loaded to keep the internal fires stoked. The wind chill off wet gear was gnawing; we would have been much warmer in a protected cockpit than steering from an exposed deck. The wind lightened up as we beat past the remote rocky islands of

Flannan and Sula Sgeir, famous for its gannet hunters. On our third day out we passed some very suspicious trawler activity, with strange groups of buoys being dropped off and picked up.

Rounding Muckle Flugga

The wind freshened as we approached Muckle Flugga, the 'Cape Horn' of the British Isles. It's at 61 degrees north – much nearer the Pole than Cape Horn at 55 degrees south – and is only 400 miles from the Arctic. It's at a similar latitude to the Antarctic regions that freeze over. Underneath us were iceberg scours in the sea bottom from years gone by. Brian overtook four killer whales travelling at high speed, then skilfully avoided a waterlogged telegraph pole right in front of us while reaching at 15 knots – his comment: 'Only the light from the midnight sun saved us'. We were now in waters where, 23 years earlier, I'd worked for BP over several winters; I'd experienced hurricane conditions and 80-foot seas for the best part of two months at a time. Now there was a north-easterly gale coming off Arctic Norway, sending big seas straight at us. We were completely airborne at times as we jumped over them at closing speeds of 35 knots. It was very bad for the boat, risking hull damage or losing the rig. Suddenly there was a loud bang. The genoa dropped – broken halyard shackle. Brian stuffed the wet sail below and hoisted the staysail. Black seas broke against cliffs.

The wind seemed much stronger than indicated, and we put this down to the very cold temperature, which makes the air denser. We nevertheless rounded the desolate spot, put in two reefs, then fast broad reached with the Arctic seas now coming from lee quarter, making for some unusual surfing. Brian hoisted our heavy reacher as we gybed and ran close by rocks off the Shetlands in tide rips and confused seas. We were rapidly losing control, so swapped the reacher for the staysail. We were both very fatigued.

At Lerwick we were met on the dock by the couple who'd hosted Brian on his previous Round Britain, and they took all our soaked and salty clothes, laundered them, bleached out some rusty stains and dried them in the fresh wind. We were interrogated by officials in connection with the strange trawler activity, and interviewed by

Brian Thompson and Spirit leading off St. Kilda

Off northwest Scotland

the BBC and the *Daily Telegraph*. After the race, the main news items was a drug bust involving several vessels in the area we'd sailed through. I hope we had helped bust them.

Richard repaired the port float, cracked from the Norwegian seas. We also replaced the inner forestay, which had stranded. The boat had taken a terrific pounding and we were constantly trying to assess loads and sail it to its structural limits.

The first four boats were all capable of line honours, and were being sailed flat out in a series of sprints. *Musto* was six hours behind us, then Mark Gatehouse in *Victoria Docks*, then *FPC Greenaway*, eight hours behind us. The Lerwick Boating Club and the mayor welcomed the fleet.

'The race begins again at Lerwick,' pronounced Mark. How right he was! The North Sea leg is the only one where you can go substantially off the rhumb line, and the lead can change. The wind was forecast southerly for the leg, so the choice of left or right would be crucial.

Beating down the North Sea

We had yet another beat, initially south-east, tacking on wind shifts down the rhumb line, aiming to cover both sides of the course. The wind built to force 5, and we were hammering into some swells coming from dead ahead. The aft mainsheet block blew, to be quickly replaced by a spare. A thick fog descended. Suddenly there was a bang as we slammed into a sea, and the main dropped – a blown halyard. With 200 miles to go on an upwind leg, this was a major setback. We rehoisted it on the masthead spinnaker halyard, with a half reef in the main. Then we sailed into a calm patch, and Brian spent an hour aloft trying to pull our reserve halyard through on the mouse lines, but it jammed. It looked like the end of our chance to win the event. He rigged a Spectra jury system, even though he was getting severely slammed by rolling seas. It was a fantastic effort – but then the Spectra parted and Brian went aloft again, rigging a block to the mast crane. It would only take a quarter of the normal load but it was the best we could do.

After we had been two hours becalmed a long-awaited front arrived, and with it a south-west wind. We were back in waters where I had worked in the 1970s, and we saw seismic ships, pipelay barges, crane barges, platforms and semi-submersibles, all bringing back memories. The wind freshened again and we close reached at 14 knots, nursing the main and constantly checking the leech tension when we should have been doing 18 knots. How many boats would be ahead of us? The deck cracked open by the genoa lead, drenching the bow cabin, including our dry clothing and sleeping bags. At least, now, in more southern latitudes, it was warmer.

At Lowestoft, our lead over the other three had dropped to 1–2 hours – not enough to ensure a win, but at least our jury system had started to blow the masthead block, so we had judged it just about right. *Greenaway* had been forced west by the wind shifts and a broken headsail furler, catching the front and its south-westerly early. 'We were incredibly lucky,' said Robert Wingate. They were doing 15 knots while we were drifting around making jury rigs in the (unforecast) calm on the east side of the front. *Victoria Docks* came in with the top half of her main totally shredded; Mark had kept going by relying on the wire leech line, as the top half of the sail had flogged like a huge flag. *Shockwave* had slipped back due to her mainsail track pulling out.

Our shore crew of Allen Clarke and Richard Laight repaired all the damage again, and in fact we ended up supporting four boats with our spares and tools: *Victoria Docks* was loaned our drill to bore holes in their backup Kevlar main and *Greenaway* used our epoxy kit to repair their daggerboard.

'I forgot to tell you it's a slow-setting type,' I told Robert as he lowered it into the case. 'Didn't want to have your board set up solid in the case.'

'Nice one, Peter,' Robert replied – all in jest.

The beautiful Dutch Grainger trimaran *Pandiono* had been dismasted as a result of the same fitting failure that had almost cost us our rig, and had put into Whitby. There were now only seven multihulls left in the race, none of them foreign.

Last leg to the finish

We were taking no chances on this crucial leg. We lashed all the halyard shackles with Spectra safeties and rigged a backup main halyard. We took off absolutely every non-essential item and everything not required in race rules, including heavy weather gear, cold weather clothing, spinnaker, warps and the outboard, which we replaced with a lighter, rented one. We ploughed through our stopover repair, which as usual was about 40 items.

The forecast for Leg 5 was yet another beat in southerlies until Dover, then fresh westerlies, which would suit *Greenaway* but not us or the 60s. We knew that *Greenaway* could point 2 degrees higher than us in moderate to heavy conditions – enough to overhaul us over 300 miles. We were faster in all other conditions: light or heavy, upwind or downwind – but not upwind in moderate force 5. A case of déjà vu! At South Foreland, our shore crew in the Range Rover reported *Greenaway* 1 hour 15 minutes behind. We saw her at dawn off Selsey. We both reefed and short tacked up the Isle of Wight coast, dodging the tide.

At St Catherine's[17] we both crashed through the ebb tide overfalls at 10–12 knots boat speed. We were neck and neck for 100 miles, going like smoke, covering each other in a thrilling match race. Across Lyme Bay the wind remained force 5, gusting 6 on the nose, with some very steep, rough seas on the ebb tide. The knot meter sometimes read 35 knots as the hull got airborne and we felt the wind under it. *Greenaway* was taking off on some of these steep waves, all three hulls airborne. Later, they told us that we were doing the same. How long could these boats take such punishment? Richard said afterwards that he'd thought his boat would break. I thought ours would too. The first reef pennant block exploded, whizzing past Brian's head. Fortunately the Spectra safety strop was rigged, so we kept the pressure on without any delay.

Our inner stay blew, and we rigged the staysail halyard as a jury. *Greenaway* pulled higher, utilising her larger genoa after we unreefed. We tacked in darkness off the Devon coast.

Approaching Plymouth, I couldn't get the GPS cartridge to work, and we were among rocks and unlit buoys in pitch-black, reaching off at breakneck speed. Brian was trying to locate the end of breakwater when suddenly

---

17 The southernmost point of the Isle of Wight.

a 20-foot-high rock flashed by a few feet off the starboard side. Then a 32-knot force 7 squall descended on us with driving rain and zero visibility – we hit 24 knots boat speed, sailing blind. How to get the main off? We couldn't round up as we would have pitchpoled, and getting it off downwind would be a hit-and-miss affair. We were a minute from piling up on the rocks. I managed to haul it down, and we finished under genoa, 36 minutes behind *Greenaway*.

We won our class, and came in ahead of all the boats in Classes 1, 2 and 3. The 60s came in several hours later.

It had been a thrilling end to the race. Richard said the conditions had been the toughest of any of the five RBIs he'd raced in. What an amazing experience – we'd had north-westerlies up the west coasts, southerlies in the North Sea and westerlies in the Channel. Interestingly, it was the first time in 13 years that British boats had dominated the fleet, and in fact all the foreign multihulls dropped out with damage. Upwind sailing seemed to be a British speciality.

Breaking the Cowes–St Malo race record

The best-known cross-Channel race is from Cowes to St Malo. It's a complex course in which tides play a big part: down the Solent, then west of the Channel Islands and on to France.

We were sailing in July 1999 for line honours and the course record (which looked achievable in the forecast conditions); the record for us to beat was held by the 85-foot maxi Longobarda at an average speed of 9.53 knots. With me were Digby Fox and Alastair Beardsall, and a last-minute addition in Dave Graham, resulting from Boris Webber dropping out at the eleventh hour. Dave had plenty of beach cat racing behind him, including this year's stormy Texel race, but he'd never been offshore and never used a winch, so – en route for the start! – we had a crash course on *Spirit*'s 37 Spinlock clutches.

Our race started with a series of gybes down the Solent on the mainland side with our VMG reacher up, leaving the rest of the 163 starters in a monohull pack along the Wight side, reminiscent of the Round the Island race – a mass of colourful spinnakers astern. Becalmed briefly, we were then funnelled by the wind through Hurst Narrows ahead of us, and in the Channel we set our light-air headsail as a fast reacher in the easterly gradient with, hot on our heels, the Whitbread 60 *Silk Cut* driven by Lawrie Smith. We decided to drop down to leeward, anticipating a shift to the south-west in the evening from a front ahead of a deep low off Ireland, and also to reduce the strain on the gear. This paid off, as we had some westing in when we got to Guernsey and the cold front came; this enabled us, with a couple of tacks, to clear Les Hanois in the dark. Then the exciting bit began. We were kitted up for a wild blast reach in the dark, and that's precisely what we got – we charged along in pitch-black at 20–22 knots (GPS and knot meter) with the boat completely shrouded in spray. Even better, the water was warm! Dave slotted right into it, noting later that it had been the wildest sail of his life.

We crossed the finish at 0250, with a time of 13 hours, 50 minutes and 20 seconds at an average speed of 10.83 knots – breaking the record by some 2 hours. *Silk Cut* came in 58 minutes later and broke the monohull record. The next boat in was 2 hours after that, and most of the monohulls took 30–45 hours. It turned out that *Spirit* had been 7 per cent quicker than *Silk Cut* in a mixture of winds from all directions, although mostly broad reaching, which suited both boats.

Racing results for *Spirit of England*

Race	Year	Place	Records/other notable achievements
Cowes–St Malo	1999	First	World Speed Sailing Council record
Round Britain and Ireland	1998	First in Class	Finished ahead of all boats in Classes 1, 2 & 3 Broke Leg 1 record, line honours on four legs
RORC Cowes–Ouistreham, Coupe Armand Esders	1998	First	
RORC season multihulls	1997	First	

Race	Year	Place	Records/other notable achievements
Fastnet S-multihulls	1997	First (corrected)	Broke S-multis record
RORC Morgan Cup	1997	First place (elapsed & corrected, and line honours)	
RORC Cowes–Alderney	1997	First (elapsed and line honours)	
RORC Cowes–St Quay	1997	First (tied-elapsed and corrected)	
Gelert Three Peaks race	1996	First	Record number of awards
Isle of Jura Scottish Peaks race	1996	First	
RORC Cowes–St Malo	1996	First (multihulls)	
Falmouth–Azores (Leg 1 of AZAB)	1995	First (elapsed and corrected)	Broke leg record
Nab Tower race	1995	First in Class (elapsed)	
Nab Tower race	1994	First (elapsed)	
Doublehanded Round the Island race	1994	First	Broke race record

Spirit of England was sold to Bill Foster, a captain with Delta Airlines and based in Westport, Connecticut. Bill, having been a professional skier and a US Navy fighter pilot, was, to put it mildly, familiar with speed. *Spirit* crossed the Atlantic, then was sold to a new owner and sailed across the Pacific to Australia. She was then sailed back across the Pacific.

How had our campaign performed? *Spirit* had been raced mostly with Brian Thompson (of the Steve Fossett *Lakota/Stars & Stripes* and *PlayStation* campaigns) as co-skipper with me. Brian was a truly world-class sailor: immensely experienced, a brilliant helm capable of driving hard all night without a break, innovative with repairs, highly competitive, but with a relaxed disposition. I had never known him get heated in a crisis. I once had the experience of joining the *PlayStation* crew for a passage with Brian skippering: everything going like clockwork at 25 knots with scarcely a raised voice anywhere – true professionalism.

PlayStation was 120 feet long and covered about one and a half times the area of a tennis court. She had the 24-hour record at 687.17 nautical miles, averaging 28.63 knots, and the transatlantic record at 4 days 17 hours, averaging 25.78 knots. These big multihulls had been clocked at over 39 knots, and were looking to break 800 miles in 24 hours.

How many other sports have seen speeds double inside two decades? I was closely involved with the *PlayStation* story, having arranged some key introductions and raced for years with and against many of the crew, including Peter Hogg, David Scully and several US West Coast sailors. *PlayStation*'s designer, Gino Morelli, also had some input into *Spirit*'s modifications, and most of her sails had substantial involvement of US lofts, so she was somewhat mid-Atlantic.

Spirit had made 15 race firsts. She'd set four international records which still stood 20 years later, including the Falmouth–Azores race and the RORC Cowes–St Malo; class records in the Fastnet, and the first leg of the RBI. Many of these records had come about due to reliability and the ability to sustain 20 knots for extended periods including at night, with bursts of over 25 knots – and, crucially important, a closely knit crew. We had also brought most of the navigation and off-watch activities to the cockpit, minimising the need to go below. *Spirit* completed all races she had entered except one: the Azores–Falmouth, as described earlier in this chapter.

Sailing Playstation, about the
size of a tennis court

Crewing winching coffee grinders on Playstation

Our Cowes–St Malo record was certified by the World Speed Sailing Record Council (WSSRC), alongside some well-known names such as *Windward Passage*, *Ticonderoga*, *Boomerang*, *Stars & Stripes*, *Group 4*, *Pen Duick VI*, *Lakota*, *Club Med*, *Fujicolor*, *Primagaz*, *PlayStation*, *Kingfisher*, *Yellow Pages Endeavour* and *Tokio*. *Spirit* was the only boat under 45 feet to hold an ocean race record ratified by the WSSRC, the others mostly being 60–80 feet. In the right conditions, she had been 7 per cent quicker than the quickest Whitbread (Volvo) 60s, yet had cost less than 7 per cent of the price – pretty good value in knots-per-dollar terms!

Our crew included Angus Buchanan and Ed Danby (ex-*Enza*), Graham Goff (ex-*Team Phillips*), Digby Fox, Alastair and Heather Beardsall, John Chaundy, Paul Jeffes and Richard Pocock. No other European multihull in this size range had ever come anywhere near giving *Spirit* any competition, and I believe the other similar multihulls in North America, Australia and elsewhere would have a hard time keeping up based on a comparison of sail area to displacement.

The boat had long been regarded as Britain's most successful offshore multihull of the 1990s, winning many RORC events, Peaks races and ocean races. For the Peaks races, as mentioned earlier, we'd had two long carbon oars and high-tech carbon sliding seats for four interchangeable positions, and a pedal-powered propeller on the transom. We found the runners the best of us on the pedals due to their strong legs and ability to keep going when muscles are screaming.

Although much of the racing had been doublehanded the boat was easily singlehanded, and could even be steered from the pipe cots in the bow cabin, where a mainsheet release could also be triggered. All the lines came to the cockpit, so very little foredeck work was in general needed in heavy conditions. In later years we replaced the spinnakers with furling headsails off the bowsprit, a delight for short-handed racing.

I put a lot of effort into safety, partly because as MOCRA's safety officer and the multihull rep on the RORC and ORC Special Regulations, I could not afford an accident. Accidents are also very expensive! Racing so much on a knife-edge was also useful for me in terms of being able to influence safety regulations without seriously compromising performance, although we had plenty of adrenaline rushes when we sometimes came close to pitchpoling or capsizing. Many races saw a lot of gear blowing up under the ever-increasing loads as we pushed the limits each season, hotly pursued by the ever more competitive British multihulls, but apart from the dismasting (which we had known was a risk given the poor design of the original mast), we never had a major failure.

We had some close shaves in the open ocean at high speed – as mentioned earlier, at 20 knots in a grey Atlantic dawn we avoided a taut fishing wire hawser that would have taken off daggerboard and rudder, and at 15 knots around midnight when 60 degrees north, thanks only to the light from the midnight sun, we avoided a telegraph pole. We had been out in force 10, 50-knot conditions (bare poles) and many offshore gales quite safely as long as throttled right back. I can vividly remember a big sea coming over on a beam reach, completely submerging all three hulls while Bill Bullimore was teaching me how to use the centrifugal force of the mast to keep the hulls in the water at high speed by bearing off hard on the wave crests like a surfer (another version of a multihull maxim to bear away when in trouble).

We had continuously upgraded the boat to keep her competitive, and it was clear that she had substantial potential for more horsepower to be added. Grand Prix racing generally sees competitors catching up on the lead within a year, so to keep ahead we rapidly formed some new ideas . This meant that *Spirit* led the way with many new concepts, including a loose-luffed headsail, later replicated by the Whitbread leaders as the famous 'Code Zero', and the downwind reacher, mentioned in the section on the Cowes–St Malo race, now known in the industry as a VMG reacher.

In addition she had been given a rotating carbon wing mast designed by Merfyn Owen and built by Duncan Barr. Merfyn did a fantastic job, building an immensely strong and robust structure that stood up to some colossal pounding, including beating into an Atlantic gale at 10 knots when we were opening up a big lead on the Round Britain fleet, later to see that much of the competition had dropped out with damage. The carbon beams were the *pièce de résistance*, and the rotating carbon wing mast was really bombproof – testament to Merfyn's experience in the Southern Ocean, skippering and managing many boats. Allen Clarke of Owen Clarke Design Group had managed much of the design and construction modifications.

We did a lot of work on the hydrodynamics as well, lengthening the bows to help them slice through waves when driving hard downwind, and adding new rudder and board shapes and extended transom exits to minimise drag. Bill Bullimore managed many of the design breakthroughs and race campaigns, and was responsible for the innovative sails.

It had been a privilege to work with so many top-quality people, who had focused on our challenges with passion. I learned so much from them and felt that we had initiated some technology firsts that were later picked up by the sailing world in order to improve performance and safety.

7 Dangers in Africa

We were halfway up the 9,400-foot Ol Doinyo Lengai volcano in Tanzania, climbing at night. And then at around 3 a.m. there was another earthquake. We found this unnerving, knowing that above us there were millions of tons of molten lava contained only by fragile walls. And then a bigger earthquake, triggering a rock slide down the gully to our right. It was even more unnerving hearing the rocks crashing down yet not being able to see them. … a major eruption could take place, and as we were downwind of the summit, ash would blow on top of us. Lava flows had recently come down either side of us. It was still pitch-black, and now, if possible, even blacker because cloud – or ash? – had obscured the stars.

Big game in Tanzania

While working in Tanzania from 2001 until 2011, I was able to visit some of the wild African bush country. I was managing the Songo Songo natural gas project, developing and supplying gas and power to the African people. This was the first natural gas project in East Africa, with a work force of 75 staff and a construction crew of some 1,500, funded by the World Bank to aid with poverty reduction. As a result, villagers gained access to electric power, clean water, medical facilities and energy for cooking, replacing charcoal, which had not only caused serious ill health but also deforestation. Our project, then, benefited the environment in several ways.

In 2002 I flew over the Rift Valley, past grey volcanoes, into the Serengeti to meet up with my guide and driver, Peter. We drove across the treeless beige plains, past lions mating in the grass, to Ndutu Lodge outside Serengeti National Park. The lodge was off the beaten track, partly because the nearest fresh water was over 50 km away, and the only water available for washing was a slippery alkaline brew derived from a salty lake.

Peter woke me in the pitch-black pre-dawn to listen to Africa waking up, and to watch as a red sky opened up over a nearby lake. 'Don't go in there,' he warned me, as I walked towards a scrubby area by the lake. 'You can't see what's in there – but they're watching you. You could get a surprise from something big and ferocious.'

We drove off with the sun on our left to a brow of a ridge, and were suddenly in herds of zebra barking away. There were hundreds of them, frolicking in the morning sun. Then, breakfast; we left our Land Rover and climbed through thick undergrowth to the top of a hill, encircled by the morning mist rising in a ring around it. There were rocks at the top.

'Isn't this the sort of place lions like to have breakfast?' I asked Peter.

'Yes, it is – but they'll be more scared of us than us of them.'

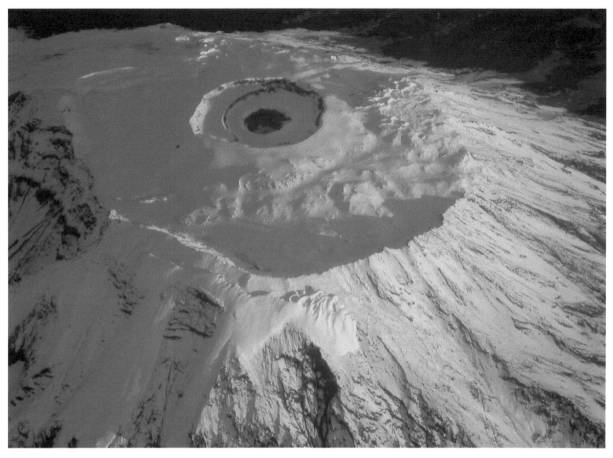

Mount Kilimanjaro summit

Storm clouds in Ngorongoro Crater

We had a great view, with thousands of dark specks around the horizon for 10 miles in every direction, about 400 square miles. 'Each one of those dots is an animal, a wildebeest,' said Peter.

'About how many?'

'Half a million or so, plus 200,000 zebra; and we're the only people here in this entire vista.'

The next several hours were spent driving off-road through wildebeest herds. Peter was looking for holes some 400 yards across in the herds, where the migrating animals would have diverted around lions or cheetahs. Sure enough, he located a pride of lions, and later a pride of cheetahs. We parked a few yards from each group, settling into the rhythm of the plains. A wildebeest carcass was close by, stripped to the bone the previous night by lions and currently being finished off by large, mean-looking vultures. On the inside of the circle were four individual wildebeest, each watching the lions in a taut, bolt-upright stance, while the rest of the herd behind them grazed and grunted peacefully. They knew that a cheetah's range was about 200 yards, after which the wildebeest could outrun them. The cheetahs looked frustrated with all this, as they knew well the game being played. The lions, meanwhile, were searching for old, sick or young wildebeest. They were unlikely to make a kill, though, until after dark. The cheetahs, over a mile from the lions, were alert with a hard gaze fixed on the herd, not only for an opportunity but also on the lookout for lions, which would kill them given a chance, to get rid of the competition.

Back to the lodge, with thousands of deer of different species leaping in front of our path, and ostriches, hyena and wild boar running across the plains. Next day we passed giraffes eating treetops; we were en route to Olduvai Gorge, where the oldest known remnants of humans – some 3 million years old – had been found in the volcanic ash strata that make up the plains. In a nearby hut we found several shelves of tools, including hand axes and round rocks for throwing, like shot putting. The people who'd used them had not been farmers or fish eaters: they had been carnivores, and they were a thousand times older than the pyramids. The origins of humankind.

Then a drive through the Ngorongoro crater, with each of the big five game animals packed into its 100 square kilometres. A thunderstorm sent shafts of light and dark into the green floor, dramatically lighting up the elephants and buffaloes.

Adventures in Selous

A year later I was thirsting for more adventure, so flew into the Selous Game Reserve[18] in southern Tanzania. A UNESCO World Heritage Site, this – at roughly the same size as Switzerland! – is the largest game reserve on the planet, and except for a few camps is now completely uninhabited, although this was not always the case. Most of the reserve is set aside for hunting, with only a few people coming in and setting up temporary camps.

Our pilot had a reputation for flying the tiny Cessna like a motorbike, and he got us there, complete with a heavy cargo of spares weighing the plane down. En route I saw lots of crocs big enough to be seen from the air.

Julietta, an Argentinean, met us on the rough airstrip and drove us to the camp by the Rufiji river, the biggest in East Africa, feeding the Indian Ocean. The sun set behind giraffes on a ridge, silhouetting them harshly against a bright red sky – the light in Africa is as magnificent as the scenery and the animals.

My lodging was a small thatched hut with three walls, the fourth open to the brown Rufiji swirling outside. Inside the hut, bats, mosquitoes and other insects buzzed around – a taste of African flying life. I remembered that malaria kills 300,000 people a year in Tanzania, and that the tsetse fly is the reason the Selous has never been populated by farmers – no domestic animal can survive its bites. A mosquito coil burned outside my mosquito net. I'd asked Julietta about malaria.

'No problems,' she'd said. 'Not likely to get it, but then again, our manager went down with it last month, so it's around. By the way, it's best to take a guard with you if you want to walk across the camp at night – often elephants, hippos, lions and other animals stray into the camp. Take a torch with you too, and if you're approached shine it in their eyes.'

I took my malaria pill anyway (I'd read that the Tanzanian type of malaria can kill in two days) and settled down for the night, keeping an ear open for wild animals. I sank into a fitful sleep, dreaming that there were

---

18 Now the Nyerere National Park.

crocodiles and hundreds of hippos grunting and roaring at the foot of my bed. I'd been warned that crocs kill hundreds of Tanzanians every year, and that hippos are one of the most dangerous animals in Africa, trampling natives to death and biting in half anything they feel is a threat, including boats, tourists and crocs – and these crocs, as I'd observed on flying in, were the world's biggest, some 20 feet long. The papers in Dar es Salaam were full of stories of people being eaten by crocs, or planes lost in the bush.

Angry hippo

Suddenly I woke up, expecting the dream to end, but it wasn't a dream: there were heavy breathing noises, splashing sounds, roaring, and low-frequency grunting just beyond the foot of my bed. The river was a mass of activity under a full moon as the heavy animals plotted, warred and schemed against each other. The roar of a lion up the riverbank added to the excitement. Crunching and rustling noises confirmed there were animals out of the water as well as in it and under it.

Before dawn, I was in an aluminium boat on a trip to Stiegler's Gorge with our boat driver, Carlos, and a couple from Zimbabwe who managed a large cane farm near Ruaha, in the centre of Tanzania. We passed hundreds of crocodiles, slithering off the sandbanks into the water as we approached; and hundreds of hippos, some floating, some sunk and walking on the bottom.[19] My fear was that a hippo could flip the boat (or, as it looked rather flimsy, bite it in two, or split it in two). If any of these scenarios were to play out, we'd be faced with a swim without lifejackets through all the crocs.

But we made it to a beautiful gorge, and up to rapids that prevented further progress. We saw a peregrine falcon, the world's fastest animal when it dives at 200 mph onto its prey. We stopped for breakfast on the rocks at the bottom of the gorge. Ours was the only boat on this huge river. Carlos pulled the boat up onto a nearby beach.

A croc leapt into the air in the rapids with a big fish in its jaws – I hadn't known that they could navigate rapids. Downstream were more crocs in the water. Behind us were lots of croc droppings. I decided to get my hat from the boat, as the sun was warming – and to my astonishment the boat had gone, swept away in the fast waters. I walked down the river bank, not relishing the thought of a night among leaping crocs – it would be hours before anyone knew we were missing. The SSB radio had gone down the river with the boat, and it would be impossible to walk.

Miraculously, we found the boat, caught up in an eddy further downstream, circling behind rocks near a group of crocs. I managed to catch it, and tied it to large boulder. I got a hero's welcome from the others.

After eating we went back down the river, past a magnificent croc who, lazing on a flat rock above the swirling waters, clearly just loved having his picture taken. He sometimes smiled, sometimes yawned.

In the afternoon, our guide, Dean, from Zimbabwe, took three of us to a place he called Adrenaline Alley. 'Haven't been there for over a year,' he said. 'It's a dried-up riverbed leg of the Rufiji, with thick jungly bush each side, so you're hemmed in. Big game comes out of the bushes onto the sandy riverbed. Got attacked by a bull elephant in there, and had to run for shelter up a hippo slide. The elephant wasn't the least bit fazed when I cocked the rifle, and I was on the point of pulling the trigger when he backed off … Three rules here: (1) look at my hand signals; (2) never run; and (3) don't get between me and the animal that's threatening us.' He had a pistol as well as the rifle.

---

19 They do this by deflating their lungs, reducing their buoyancy.

Cape buffalo – a dangerous animal

We found the lion that we had heard roaring: a lioness with a cub, lazing under a tree overlooking the river, not a care in the world, looking disdainfully at us. Then a hippo approached us with a firm, confident attitude.

'If he sinks the boat, would it be better to swim to the lion side of the river or the croc side?' I asked.

'I'd take the lion's side – at least we can *see* the animal.'

Then into the Alley: lots of elephant droppings and huge footprints; areas where elephants had dug up the sand looking for water. Croc droppings and trails by the ponds in the riverbed – areas where fights had happened, with grooves showing where the loser had been dragged off into the bush or the water.

Then we saw it: Black Death as Dean called it – a bull buffalo, the most angry and aggressive of all the African animals, taut, showing us his sides and tossing his head.[20]

'We'll run for cover in the roots of that tree over there if he charges. Anything could happen. He's full of adrenaline, scared and nervous.'

'So am I,' I thought. The tree in question had been uprooted by a flood and nested against the bank of the riverbed. It was the nearest thing to a cage we could find. Dean readied his gun. The buffalo backed off and went up the bank into the bush.

'Magnificent … it would've been a shame if I'd had to drop him,' Dean mused.

Shortly after, we heard some crunching noises and saw treetops wobbling. 'Two elephants fighting – there's a herd of them in there.'

---

20 Africa's most dangerous animal, with the temperament of a Jersey bull but 50 per cent bigger and with horns capable of going right though you.

It was like Jurassic Park. Soon, one of the bull elephants stumbled down the bank and was startled to see us. Again the posturing between us and the animal – neither giving ground, both trying to appear confident. The elephant gave up first, throwing his trunk up in the air, waving his ears and disappearing back into the bush.

That night was exciting, as a large bull elephant ransacked the camp, tearing up bushes and crushing several water containers. He had only one tusk, the other presumably lost in battle. Nothing was going to stop him, and we sheltered behind a wall. We all agreed that he would flatten the wall, or our three-walled huts, if he chose to lean on them. Thankfully, that wasn't to be.

Our pilot flew us out again. I heard that a week after I left Selous his Cessna had hit a giraffe on the airstrip, apparently taking the legs off the giraffe and the wing off the plane.

I then went to Saadani, on the coast, taking Dave Roberts and David Harper from work with me. We had a great time, walking more sandy riverbeds in search of big game and swimming nervously in the surf at midnight, wary of sharks and other predatory sea life. When something big rubbed against my legs I got back to land, fast.

We took a boat up a wide river and encountered herds of hippo, some bubbling air right under us, some charging along the shore in sheets of spray. I was remembering the stories I'd heard of hippos tipping boats over, and biting people in two. However, it seemed that the hippos were more scared of us than we were of them, which may or may not have been a good thing. Further up the river, we found a poacher's net strung across the water to ensnare crocs. We cut it loose, with the help of our guide, as the poachers watched from a distance. We were fairly sure they wouldn't shoot us; as Tanzanian park rangers shoot armed poachers on sight those poachers keep a low profile.

With Mike in Ruaha

After that trip, it was time to introduce my son Mike, then aged 11, to the game areas of Tanzania. We flew to Ruaha on a Cessna that was run like a bus, stopping every few minutes to drop off and pick up passengers. Ruaha was set in a beautiful mountain region in the Rift Valley area, and the camp was right on the Ruaha river. While we were there only three other visitors came to the camp, and the river was teeming with hippos and crocs.

During our three days there we saw cheetah, leopard, elephant, a herd of buffalo, and a huge variety of wildlife in general. We stopped the first morning to watch two male lions devouring a giraffe they had downed by a small river the night before. We returned each morning, until little more than a skeleton was left. The lions were exhausted from tearing it up. Vultures and jackals, covered in blood, waited their turn. Another time, we drove into a wooded area on the edge of a wide river, where a group of lions were observing the river plain below. Suddenly we noticed there were more lions around us – we were in the middle of a pride of 17. As we were against the riverbank we couldn't drive forwards, and the Land Rover had no sides or top – just a canvas

Mike looking for lions in Ruaha

Lion and giraffe kill

roof for shade. I felt quite exposed. A lioness got up and walked purposefully towards Mike. She looked a bit like business, so I gave her as fierce a stare as I could, in response to which she slinked off with a sloppy gait.

At night the experience was an audio one, and the drama could be heard for miles around as animals hunted and were in turn hunted. I heard lions roaring, gradually getting closer and closer until they were inside the camp. Three elephants slithered down the hill in the moonlight just a few inches from my bed. A leopard rasped just outside the wall by Mike's bed. I felt concerned about that; it was clearly hunting the young son of Peter and Sara Fox, who ran the camp. It had torn down the window netting and was crawling through to get him, but was chased out just in time. I learned that this leopard was only around when the little boy was there. And it was not around when the boy's father was in the camp.

The elephants too wandered through the camp. One had bust down a heavy door and ransacked the food store. And a hippo had charged one of the camp staff. Luckily, while running away she had fallen into a ditch, and the hippo had charged right over her and into the river.

This spot – right in the middle of the wildlife and with no fences – was a truly great place.

In the middle of Africa

After my fantastic experiences with big game and beautiful vistas in the Serengeti, Saadani, Selous and Ruaha reserves, I was intrigued to visit Katavi in the far west of Tanzania, an area which sees less than 100 visitors a year and where the only shelter is a tent. This in spite of the fact that Katavi extends to over 4,000 square kilometres!

I often wondered why there no fences around these wildlife reserves, and what kept the animals from escaping. In fact, most of them didn't seem to want to be anywhere near human habitation with all of its attendant dangers, and would turn back if they saw, heard or even smelled humans or their huts, fires and hunting parties. They were used to the game reserves and presumably felt reasonably safe there, even though in their natural habitat they were to all intents and purposes still wild. They would keep their distance from humans unless threatened, when the bigger animals, especially the herbivores such as buffalo, elephants and hippos, would respond with an attack.

I had planned to stay at a campsite on the edge of Lake Chada, a dry plain for most of the year, and a marsh in the wet season. The Katavi Plains are in the Rukwa Valley, part of the Great Western Rift. The plains were reputed to have the highest concentration of big game in Tanzania, and Tanzania was the best country in the world for big game.

There was only one camp open. After a year of trying to find a logical way to get to Katavi, I decided to fly to Tabora district and there meet up with a Cessna 206. But three days before my departure for Katavi, I was flying back from Songo Songo when I was dismayed to learn from my pilot that the Cessna had gone down, killing all on board.

'Dunno what happened, but the plane was fully loaded, and may have been caught in a thunderstorm downdraft in the mountains,' my pilot shouted to me above the roar of the engines.

My flight was rearranged for 21 October 2005, from Tabora to Kigoma on the shores of Lake Tanganyika. There I was to connect with a Cessna Caravan.[21] I would be the only passenger.

From my base in Dar it took nearly three hours to reach Tabora in a twin prop plane. Then I was asked to give my seat to former president Ali

Flying into a storm at Katavi after the plane cash

---

21 Also a single-engine plane, but more powerful than the 206.

Hassan Mwinyi, who was travelling with his entourage to a CCM[22] event a week before the elections. He and his wife were dressed in Islamic clothing, and several bodyguards with bulges under their jackets took over the front of the plane. I hoped they were not expecting a shoot-out on board.

On arrival at Kigoma there was a big ceremony on the red dirt airstrip, with lots of military and schoolchildren dressed in green CCM attire.

I saw my Cessna and walked across. 'Are you going to Katavi?' I asked.

'That's me,' said the pilot, a Ugandan called Eddie.

We flew into black and threatening thunderstorms, with bolts of lightning stabbing the evening sky. Big downdrafts threw us around like a rollercoaster. Double rainbows dropped away below us. Huge jungly mountains of the Mahale Range appeared and disappeared between the thunderstorms. Rain pelted the windscreen in a loud roar.

'Very wet at the Ikuu airstrip', Eddie said, pointing into a jet-black cloud to our left. 'We may not be able to make it. Too risky.'

'What other options, then?' I shouted.

'There's another airstrip 40 km away, but I think it's in the same storm. Big problem.'

Big indeed. It was sunset, and I'd learned that you couldn't land at Kigoma after dark.

We came out of the storm and into shafts of light and reddish hues. Eddie was descending over a big plain. There was some buffeting, then we lined up onto the airstrip on the edge of the bush.

After a bumpy landing the two of us trundled along in a Land Cruiser driven by Sylvanus, a Tanzanian, as night came down. Eddie told me some good stories. His main work was flying hunting groups around. He'd been out jogging on a dirt track near one of the camps and was being chased by a buffalo. It was catching up fast and Eddie thought he'd had it. Fortunately a vehicle came the other way and the driver, swiftly assessing the situation, opened the door for Eddie to jump in. 'Saved my life for sure,' Eddie told me. Unlike elephants, buffaloes don't attack vehicles – African animals, despite being shot from some vehicles, apparently feel they are not a threat – but millennia of conflict have ingrained in those animals a distrust and fear of any *Homo sapiens* on foot. I later heard that elephant attacks on people and cars tend to occur only when they are drunk on the fruit of the marula tree – a tale now considered a myth.

I remembered some of the people I'd met and stories I'd heard in Dar: men savaged by Tanzanian big game, faces torn up, buffalo horns piercing people right through from backside to stomach. Eddie told me a remarkable story. Two guides had taken a Japanese hunter on safari. All three were carrying loaded large-bore rifles. A lion attacked the lead guide and started mauling him. The Japanese hunter promptly dropped his gun and pulled a video camera from his pack to record the interesting event. The second guide caught up and shot the lion without injuring the first guide, who by then was very badly wounded – but he was so unutterably furious with his client that he staggered to his feet, put his gun to the man's head, and pulled the trigger – but he'd already fired his last shot. 'I wouldn't have believed it, but I've seen the video,' Eddie said. 'I heard the click of his rifle as well.'

I was met by the camp staff: Squok,[23] our guide; Howard, an American-Australian seconded from the Wildlife Conservation Department; and Sylvia, a Greek-Italian anthropologist. Howard showed me my tent; it was under a high canopy of acacia and tamarind trees in the miombo[24] woodland, and was set on the dirt, with a flysheet on top. It was about 100 yards from the next tent, so I would have plenty of peace and quiet. The bathroom was open-air: just a bamboo fence and a canvas bucket shower, with a long-drop toilet.

Howard gave me a torch with two LED lights, which looked like a wild animal. Just like at the Selous Game Reserve, night-time came with a warning: 'If you have to go to the bathroom at night, flash this around from side to side. We've had lions, hyenas and elephants in the camp at night. Be careful, as there could be a lion asleep on the path to your bathroom.'

---

22 The ruling political party.

23 That's how it sounded, but I don't know how it's spelt!

24 Hardwood trees that resemble oaks.

'Can I walk away from my site at night?' I asked.

'Definitely not. Stay in the tent, and go no further than the bathroom,' he instructed. 'If anything happens in the night, set off this foghorn.' He handed me the sort of device used by small vessels at sea.

Hyenas and lions outside my tent

After a wonderful candle-lit dinner and many bottles of wine while discussing the environmental issues facing the planet, I retired for the night, but was unable to sleep on account of a pack of hyenas somewhere outside my tent, howling all night with a huge range of calls. It sounded as if they were coordinating a hunt. I recalled that hyenas are reputed to try to eat you (or any other animal for that matter) while you sleep. While hyenas more usually scavenge a lion's kill packs of hyenas can kill a lion. Sometimes, though, the tables are turned, with the hyenas doing the killing of the prey and the lions the scavenging. I reminded myself that (unlike bears) African animals do not enter tents. I hoped they'd remember this important point of bush etiquette. In the early hours I drifted off into a light sleep, interrupted by nightmares caused by the anti-malaria drugs I was on, and was woken by a large crash on top of my tent, then a scampering across and sliding down it. I assumed it was a monkey dropping out of the trees.

I pulled on my hiking boots and walked across to the bathroom, startling a lizard on the way. I took a shower in the morning sun, avoiding several hornets, bees and tsetse flies trying to drink my shower water. However, one of them got me, turning a large patch of skin red and causing the area to swell up alarmingly. Various sting relief medications dulled the pain, and I was soon on safari with Sylvanus.

We found a wonderful area along a dried-up riverbed, full of hungry-looking buffalo, giraffe, topi, impala, waterbuck, zebra and mongoose, along with elephants digging for water. Lions were scattered around, hiding in the bushes. Hippos were submerged in the mud waiting for the merciless African sun to go down so they could do their nightly 20 km forage for food. They were packed together in a group of about 200, their backs like smooth, muddy rocks. Large groups of 14-foot crocodiles were piled several deep in caves along the riverbank, slithering over each other and writhing around. They were obviously being careful to avoid the hippos.

Walking amongst lions and hyenas hunting

Lion near my tent in Katavi

Most of the animals were preoccupied in the search for the last remaining water at the end of the dry season, and then at night a different stage would unroll, with the hunters and the hunted playing out their chess game. Thousands of tsetse flies swarmed around us all day, and I covered up to avoid the bites as well as the sun. The tsetse flies are the local wildlife's saviour, since they cause fatal diseases in cattle and other domestic livestock, which is why this lush area remains devoid of farmers.

In the evening, Squok and another armed guide took us for a walk in the bush. A herd of impala and groups of birds in the trees before us were in alarm mode.

'There's a lion ahead somewhere,' Squok whispered. 'Keep very quiet. Move slowly. Keep behind me. Don't get between my gun and an animal. And above all do *not* run unless I tell you to, and then only where I tell you to run to.'

We walked stealthily, our guides taut with anticipation, but the bush was thick and we could have been within 10 feet of a predator without seeing it. Squok heard a rumble and a low grunt, then a crackling of leaves underfoot. 'I think he's gone,' he said.

He told me more about the Cessna crash that had killed the pilot and passengers, but it was clear that the staff didn't want to discuss it too much. 'Could have been a bird strike or engine failure or a downdraft or something else. We just don't know, and don't want to have too many false rumours floating about until we know what happened.'

I asked Squok if he could take me on a walk along the riverbed.

'No way,' he stated. 'It'd be suicide. The sort of thing that can happen is that you come round a bend and startle a buffalo, which charges. Then a herd of elephants behind you stampedes in panic. This alarms a hippo,

150

Thirsty hippos in Katavi

A cave full of crocodiles

which rushes past you to crash into the water. This causes some of the crocs to jump out and scurry around. So you're compromised on all four sides and everything's out of control.'

The night sky bristled with stars, startlingly bright in the clear southern hemisphere. We were also some 3,000 feet above sea level, so the air was clearer still. The candlelight attracted many insects and we would often be picking them out of our food – at one point I was just about to eat a piece of meat when it crawled off my plate.

Next morning, we went on a fantastic walk along the edge of a plain, again with two armed guides. Five lionesses were chasing a herd of zebra, but when they detected us approaching they hid in the bushes. Giraffes lazily walked across the plains, confident that a well-placed kick would deter any lions. Warthogs scampered about. A hyena approached the area where the lionesses had been and started eating a carcass. Elephants and buffalo congregated around a waterhole. Vultures circled overhead. It was amazing to be walking among so much big game without any sense of fear on account of the wide views in the open plain.

Squok came down with suspected tick fever, so Sylvanus took me back to the riverbed, where we saw a python in a tree. Sylvanus was also delighted to find a leopard dozing on a branch, looking out through a gap in the foliage.

I slept my best night, as the hyenas had gone. I woke to the sound of small flowers falling off the trees onto the tent like a continuous rain, and I looked outside it to see a giraffe, a zebra and a topi grazing on the plains.

Sylvanus took me on a wonderful drive to the east through wide-open plains and palm forests, and across deep ditches in the plain, which were full of crocodiles in the rains. He was a great driver, negotiating rough terrain where there was no sign of previous vehicles. In the distance volcanoes shimmered in the heat.

Stuck in a dangerous place

Sadly, it was time to say farewell to this most majestic of places. The Cessna Caravan flew us to Mahale, where we picked up Zoe, who had been working at the camp.

She was still distraught over the air crash. 'It's hard to come to terms with the fact that it's the nature of the business we're in,' she said. There were now lots of government officials sorting through the charred wreckage and clearing it up.

At Kigoma, I had three hours to kill before transferring to the twin-engine plane to fly back to Tabora, and on to Dar with the ex-president and his entourage. I went to the spot at nearby Ujiji where the Victorian journalist Henry Stanley had found Dr David Livingstone and uttered his immortal phrase. There was a small dusty museum there, with papier-mâché sculptures of the two famous men, and paintings of Livingstone wielding a big saw to cut slaves free from their yokes and shackles. A page from Livingstone's diary showed how he had been on the point of death due to tropical diseases when Stanley arrived and helped him back to recovery. I was amazed that Livingstone had survived all those years here, without proper medicine or any contact with the outside world. Being a doctor and being religious must have helped. But he eventually died of malaria, as had his wife previously. I was the only person in the museum. The curator asked where I was from, then exclaimed: 'England! You must know Michael Palin. He was here ten years ago.'

After six attempts to start the plane in the heat of the African sun the pilot told us to get off. After hours in the dilapidated airport shack trying to find out what was going on, it appeared that we were waiting for spare parts from Mwanza to be flown in, along with two mechanics from Tabora. It seemed the battery had gone flat, and there was no charging system in Kigoma. When it became clear we would not be leaving before dark, I went off into this incredibly poor and dirty town in search of a bed for the night. Clothes for sale were scattered on the red earth streets. Men were cutting up rusted corrugated iron roofs to make pots and pans in a sort of open-air factory. Insects buzzed.

I found a bed, as did the rest of the passengers in a hotel that won the prize for worst I've ever stayed in, jointly with a Soviet hostel in Hanoi. It certainly wasn't worth the $15 charged. There was a better hotel but the ex-president's entourage, and a large group of Belgian soldiers fighting the civil war in Congo, on the other side of the lake, had occupied all its beds.

Stranded with me were two other *mzungus* (Europeans): a Sicilian American called John Biera, who was building medical facilities; and a Catholic priest called William Crombie, who had been in Congo and Tanzania for 23 years. He'd come from Aberdeen 'a very long time ago' to teach English and religion.

I asked if he'd taught at a Catholic school in Congo.

'There are schools, and much more than that – there's a Catholic university.'

In John's group was a Sikh gentleman who'd spent three years building the dirt road into Katavi: 'A very desperate time, always tormented by insects, often watched by lions, always dangerous.'

I asked Father Crombie if there was a bus to Dar.

'It'd take two or three days, with a high chance of a breakdown and being overnighted under the stars. Plus the risk of bandits, who'd steal everything, including all the clothes you're wearing. They'd leave you naked in the bush, and drive the bus off. And there's plenty of wildlife too.'

I could imagine the torment of being naked under the brutal African sun, tormented by insects, watched by waiting carnivores. So, 'How about the train?' I asked.

'Same problem,' he said. 'Bandits. They'll stop the train and strip you naked.'

I hoped the *fundis* (mechanics) would be able to fix the plane. Meanwhile, as a UN four-prop cargo plane had just flown in with supplies for 400,000 refugees from the wars in neighbouring Rwanda, Burundi and Congo, I asked if I could take a lift out with them. But they weren't due to leave for several days. We were just 40 miles from Burundi, and about the same from Congo, across the other side of this huge lake.

Lake Tanganyika is interesting. It's part of the Western Great Rift Valley, and on the western side of it glaciated peaks rise to nearly 17,000 feet. The lake is the longest in the world, holding around 16 per cent of the planet's fresh water, and its surface is currently 2,434 feet above sea level. Millennia ago it had flowed into Lake Victoria, but its path got blocked by a volcano; the result was that when the lake was discovered by Burton and Speke in 1858 it was endorheic. Since then, however, its waters have risen, and it now has an outflow into the Congo Basin and to the Atlantic. But it's dropping again.

We were just a few miles from what some consider the true source of the Nile: the Ruvyironza river, which feeds into Lake Victoria, then on to the Mediterranean, making it the world's longest river. The Lake Tanganyika ferry has been running for 85 years, except for a period in the First World War when its sole vessel[25] was scuttled by the Germans.

We were in the heart of Africa. Our hotel rooms were awful. Flickering lights, leaking plumbing, torn mosquito nets too short to reach the ground, no air conditioning or even ceiling fans, no breeze in the hot night, pools of water in the bathroom, rusted hardware, broken windows. Locals were clearly using my bedroom wall as a toilet. Disease seemed to be lurking everywhere. The food looked dangerous, and I avoided it. Hornets buzzed around. Mosquito bites appeared. The bathroom looked infected and I only went into it with my hiking boots on. Father Crombie's tap stuck open and water gushed out of it all night. He was concerned that if he tried too hard to close it, it would break right off. I went everywhere with a large bottle of water to avoid using the hotel's bottles.

In the night, I was struck by an intense fever that came on suddenly and almost rendered me unconscious. I tried to imagine how I'd get out to a proper hospital, but couldn't think of a solution in my incapacitated state. I'd have to call for a plane medevac – but the runway had no lights. Would I still be conscious by daybreak? I remembered how meningitis and cerebral malaria can kill in hours. I took some drugs and the fever subsided just as suddenly, leaving me recovering in a dazed state. Eventually I succumbed to hunger and ate the safest food that Father Crombie could recommend: chicken. But it was more like a used leather shoe, and what little meat there was attached to the bone so strongly that it was only possible to get part of it off – rather like trying to eat tightly wrapped rubber bands.

To go back to the airport we piled into an overcrowded, overloaded, dusty, dirty *dala dala* minibus which rolled precariously from side to side. After a couple of hours in the airport shack, we were off, the pilot apologising for the late departure due to 'technical problems'.

---

25 MV *Riemba*, formerly *Graf von Götzen*, the inspiration for C.S. Forester's *African Queen*.

Apart from the flying and the squalid hotel, it had been a good trip. The open countryside was just magnificent, and more than made up for the difficulty getting there, which is why it's still pristine. Africa is said to be a continent where beauty and death are never far apart – so true.

Zanzibar

When I had the chance in my heavy work schedules, between meetings with ministers, CEOs, presidents and management of many organisations to make the Songo Songo development happen, I spent a few weekends on the island of Zanzibar.

My first trip there, in 2005, was a disaster. There was a security alert advising people not to visit it on account of political riots, so I thought it would be a good time to go because the hotels would be practically empty and there would be hardly any tourists around. When I'd flown in I took a cab from the airport and the driver appeared to be both drunk and suicidal. Bicycles loaded with merchandise leapt off the narrow road rather than be mown down, and eggs, charcoal, water cans and the like were scattered to the ground as in an all-action movie.

The hotel I booked had closed, as I was the only guest. So I needed to find alternative accommodation, but by then it was dark and my driver crashed his taxi. Fortunately I found a place on the beach, and having checked in went for a walk along the sea wall under the light of scattered lamps in the palm trees. Suddenly I fell down a gap, having mistaken the darkness for the shadow of a palm tree. I lacerated and bruised my leg, and used my first aid supplies to patch myself up rather than risk infection from a local doctor's clinic, or worse still, a witch doctor using local plant materials (widely practised on Zanzibar).

Next morning, I hobbled and limped along the beach, looking at men building large sea-going dhows in a manner unchanged for thousands of years. They used two types of local tree and only four tools: a large double-handled saw for making the planks (as in Europe in days gone by), a drill powered by rope-pull, a hammer and an adze. I imagine that were there to be a global catastrophe all shipbuilding around the world would cease due to a lack of specialist materials, except for the industry happening right on this beach. Here, everything was locally available; in the past even iron has been smelted in Tanzania.

On returning to the mainland I took the ferry, surrounded by 200 locals, many of them seasick – not exactly luxury travel. I was worried about my wound becoming infected from all the vomit.

My next trips to Zanzibar were better, and I got some super snorkelling in, marvelling at the beautiful reefs, and swimming with dolphins just inches away from me.

With Richard in Tanzania

I bought two sailing dinghies, a 13-foot Laser and a 14-foot Hobie Turbo. Both were singlehanded boats, and I enjoyed the fun of sailing for its own sake without the complexities of organising crew or dealing with maintenance problems. I employed a boatman called Seif (Swahili for 'sword'), who got everything ready for me before each trip and afterwards repaired whatever had broken. I usually sailed out to Bongoyo and Mbudya, two small uninhabited islands. There was always wind, usually just the right amount, and the water was warm. When the wind was strong, I took the Laser, capsizing it sometimes in very rough conditions in the big seas. On quieter days, I took the Hobie, which was a real handful, with two sails and trapeze. It was a very bouncy boat, and I often lost my footing while horizontal on the wire.

If the seas were calm enough, I would sail outside the islands into the open Indian Ocean. Here, my only company was the occasional sailing dhow en route to or from its fishing grounds, plus jellyfish, flying fish and sometimes even whales. I knew that sharks – tiger, mako and whitetip – would be swimming below, thankfully out of my sight. This did, unsurprisingly, encourage me to avoid capsizing, and when I did, I got the boat back upright as fast as I could. After a few years I sold the Hobie Turbo and got a more modern Hobie Dragoon, so that my younger son Richard, then aged 10, could sail it with me on a visit. This was a super boat, and everything worked reliably as we shot off at speeds of over 15 knots. Richard went on the trapeze, and we would have wild rides in the strong south-east trade winds.

PC sailing at Bongoyo Island offshore Tanzania

PC sailing a fishing dhow

Richard and I went to Ruaha, and had some great times. We would rent a *banda* (hut) on the edge of the river. One night I had to join a conference call for an Orca Exploration Board Meeting. I hated doing this in such a pristine wilderness but it was unavoidable. I had borrowed a sat phone from the office, and as this needed a direct line of sight to the Iridium satellites above, I had to walk outside the banda in the night towards the river – not a great idea with all the wildlife around. I left Richard on watch in the banda, armed with a night vision scope to let me know if anything big approached me.

I got on the phone and joined the meeting. The others were phoning in from the UK, Canada and France. I didn't want to let on that I was out in the bush, but suddenly there was a commotion and a hippo charged past me and jumped into the river. More people in Africa are killed by big game in these circumstances than any other. The hippo simply panics in its dash for safety to the water and runs you over without stopping to check that you're not a lion. Behind this particular hippo was a Maasai *askari* (guard), chasing it with a spear and trying to ensure that its line to the river was deflected away from me.

Suddenly David Lyons, our chairman, said, 'What's all that background noise?'

'Not sure,' I promptly replied, 'but I should be able to tell you later.'

I was by now leading a social development programme in Tanzania, aimed at improving the lives of the poorest in a sustainable way, and focused on health, education and rural solar power among other things. We installed solar power for computers and projectors that screened animated songs in the English language on the classroom wall; the children were brought up speaking Swahili but the university entrance exams were in English.

The main intention of our programme was to enable village children to get to university, and we started on Mafia Island, where no one had ever made it. A crash course in English was the answer, using traditional song, dance and storytelling with an IT enabler. The children were bright and hard-working, but they lacked opportunity, which is what we gave them. This programme involved visits to remote villages and the worst slums in Africa – in Kenya. Walking inside those slums was the only way to truly understand the appalling living conditions: dangerous, lawless, overcrowded and filthy, with no sanitation. Our initial work was taken on board by bigger organisations, with a plan to put 450,000 children a year through the programme.

By this time, I had really fallen in love with Africa, especially Tanzania. Walking along deserted beaches, getting within inches of lions, watching the dhows sailing along the coasts with their cargoes, soaking up the smells of cooking on wood-fuelled fires, listening to the sound of big animals hunting at night. The wide-open views and clear air were magical.

Large offshore cargo sailing dhow

Lions having a look at Rich

But it was also dangerous. Malaria and unknown tropical diseases were rampant. People often came down with a fever and could be dead within two days. One of my colleagues contracted malaria and was immersed in a bath of ice to try to bring down his temperature. I was nearly killed three times within a month, including being dragged along by my catamaran at high speed after a capsize, a near-miss in a bush plane, and a near head-on vehicle collision – it was the other vehicle that turned over. The wildlife was unlikely to kill you. The real killers were malaria and car accidents.

Rich and a Maasai warrior
sheltering in a tree trunk

Scuba diving

At the weekends I took up scuba diving. I'd done it before: in Abu Dhabi in the 1970s, where I'd been a co-owner of the only compressor in the country, so had won several commercial contracts to salvage sunken equipment and so on; and in the 1980s while skippering the Swan 65 yacht *Beija Flor* in the Mediterranean, which, as mentioned in Chapter 5, had involved an emergency ascent while trying to recover an anchor and chain lost overboard. But I'd never had any formal training, and by 2009 it wasn't possible to join a diving operation and get access to compressed air without a certificate. So I enrolled on a PADI training programme. After five pool dives and four open water dives, I took a series of exams and got my Open Water Diver certificate. I was then able to dive off Tanzania and Zanzibar.

All the diving was over coral reefs, among Moray eels with their fearsome teeth, poisonous lionfish and scorpionfish, and all kinds of colourful marine life. The best was a wall off an island near Zanzibar, where I

Diving in big swells in the Indian Ocean

Oceanic white tipped shark – the most dangerous

could go down to 100 feet. We saw some large green turtles sheltering from the strong current behind coral heads, and were able to get to within inches of them. We always did drift dives, as the currents were usually strong; the dive boat would follow a marker buoy on a line attached to our dive master. The currents had to be treated with respect: a group of five divers had recently disappeared without trace in strong currents off the Pemba Island. I had a fantastic dive off the wall at Pemba, which dropped to 1,800 feet. I nearly didn't get back, though, as I was hit by a very powerful down current that pushed me into the depths faster than I could fin up. I managed to grab a coral head, then slowly pull myself back to the surface.

PC in Indian Ocean

I also had some wonderful diving in the Seychelles, probably the only granite islands in the middle of an ocean, all other islands formed either from much younger volcanic rock or from coral. The huge rocks and canyons underwater are majestic in these clear waters under the big ocean swells. In one place there was a natural amphitheatre which had 20 sharks swimming in circles inside it. I was taking their photos when I realised I'd lost sight of my colleagues. They were all hiding behind me! Some of the sharks were large whitetip oceanic sharks, the world's most dangerous in terms of people killed. They were gliding effortlessly over a granite ridge into the amphitheatre, and then with a flick of the tail they became supercharged. I stayed stock still and watched in awe.

Another time, while I was working on the Mafia Island school project, I went swimming with whale sharks, gentle giants over 30 feet long, and within touching distance. And I once swam inside a school of dolphins in the open ocean, one of them leaping right over my head. They were very playful, obviously indulging in a marine form of hide-and-seek, swimming behind me so I couldn't see where they were.

White water on the Zambezi river

In July 2009 I travelled to Zambia and the Victoria Falls. There was a global recession, meaning the falls were pretty low on tourists. The Zambezi is truly mighty; although it's only the fourth longest river in Africa it has much higher volumes than the Nile. It is also a dangerous river, claiming on average one human life per day, mostly through crocodile attack and rapids.

The falls are absolutely magnificent; standing on the edge of the cliff opposite in clouds of spray high above the canyon I found the spectacle utterly enthralling. In terms of width (over a mile/1.6 km) combined with height (330 feet/100 metres), the Victoria Falls are the biggest on the planet.

That year the Zambezi had its strongest water flow in 40 years, some 5,000 tons per second. However, by the time I'd arrived there the dry season had progressed and the water volume had declined to about half its peak. This was a good thing, as in peak flow the falls are not visible from the ground, and barely so from the air, due to the huge volumes of spray being lifted thousands of feet, giving rise to its name: Mosi-oa-Tunya, or the Smoke that Thunders. When Livingstone travelled here in 1855 he knew the falls by this name when he, being the first known European to see them – from upstream, stopping at the island now named after him.

I went to Livingstone Island by boat, somewhat concerned that we could be swept over the edge, but there was a large anchor ready to throw over if the engines failed. On the island I was able to stand right on the lip of the falls, above the 300-foot drop, with the water thundering down on each side of me. A bright double rainbow shone

Over the Victoria Falls on a Microlight

On the Zambezi below the Victoria Falls

in the morning sun. I noticed it was not a distant rainbow, as in rain showers, but was right by my side, and even in front of a rock just 5 feet from me, the heavy spray allowing me to see these stunning prismatic effects close up.

I went back to the riverbank, then went around to the gorge and scrambled down it to the first rapid, the Boiling Pot. It was getting dark and the setting was just magnificent. The canyon walls were shiny black basalt and the water was swirling black too, with areas of boiling white. There was a deep roar, which shook the ground beneath my feet. It was amazing to think that all the water cascading over the mile-wide falls just above was compressed into this chasm 100 metres wide, with the river running 80–90 metres (250–300 feet) deep. Then the water hit a cliff on a 90-degree turn and formed a huge eddy with frothing edges. Spray from the falls drifted through the canyon in vertical sheets. This was a primeval place.

Downstream, the river continued in a series of 90-degree turns, some near 180 degrees, in a chasm about 400 feet deep cut though hard, shiny black basalt. The falls are unusual in that below the falls the plateau is the same elevation as it is above them; the mighty Zambezi has simply cut the channel in areas of weakness caused by the rock fracturing. As you go downstream in the gorge you find the sites of previous falls, each one about 100,000 years older than the last and roughly parallel with each other, as the river carved its zigzag way northwards. When I was there a new angle was just beginning to be carved on the Zimbabwe side.

I walked over to that side of the falls, clearing customs and immigration overland on foot for the first time since my student days. Zimbabwe was a total mess due to Robert Mugabe's dictatorship, and unemployment was over 90 per cent, with basic commodities unavailable. I exchanged a single US dollar for a 100 trillion Zimbabwe dollar note, apparently the largest denomination note ever printed in any country in history.

Next day, I tried white-water rafting down Batoka Gorge, below the falls. It has the reputation of being the most extreme 'commercial' white-water rafting in the world, with many Class 5 rapids: 'Very difficult. Extremely tough, long and very violent rapids, following each other almost without interruption. Riverbed extremely obstructed. Big drops, violent current, very steep gradient.' Class 6 is unrunnable. The top few rapids were off limits due to the very high river flow, an order of magnitude higher than the Colorado in the Grand Canyon.

We had a safety briefing above the gorge and signed indemnity release forms. I was instructed on how to grab a throw line and be towed back to our raft on my back. Some of the rapids were dangerous for swimming due to violent whirlpools mixed in with the big waves, and we had to get back on board the raft, assuming it was still upright. If not, we might have to brave the rapids. The whirlpools could apparently suck you down 100 feet. 'Don't get caught on a rock, as you'll probably drown,' was one of the messages. 'If you can't get out of a whirlpool, one of the kayakers will try to reach you. If you grab his paddle, you might drown him, so he'll fight you off. Try to grab the stern of his kayak.' I'd seen videos of rafts going headlong into huge waves and being flipped backwards, bow over stern, with everyone dropping 15–20 feet, some hitting the back of the raft and risking injury on the steel framework. Another video showed oars being broken like matchsticks. There were stories of broken limbs and fatalities.

On the edge of the Victoria Falls

A group of rafters clambered into the bottom of the gorge down a ladder made of tree branches to the start of the first runnable rapid, Number 10: Gnashing Jaws of Death. The ladder was very makeshift, held together with single large nails at each rung, many of which were broken. There were 12 more rapids to be run, with names like the Washing Machine, Terminator and Oblivion; three were Class 4, five were Class 5. In our group there were five rafts, each with seven rafters. The last raft carried a stretcher. There were three kayakers whose job it was to rescue rafters who had been swept away from the rafts, and try to help them get back on a raft again, before they were smashed on rocks or sucked under. We all wore helmets, wetsuit tops and high-buoyancy lifejackets, which would hopefully enable us to pop out of whirlpools. We carried nothing with us on the raft, as it would be swept overboard: no sunglasses, no water bottles, no cameras.

We practised being swept overboard and clambering back on. The technique for getting a crew back on board was to grab their lifejacket shoulder straps, push them under, and let the buoyant rebound help push them up and over the tube. Capsizes were talked through, the main things being to avoid getting trapped and to try to hang on the raft so as to avoid being sucked under by a whirlpool. The rafts had large self-draining holes in the bottom.

We were ready. Our guide, Monde, tightened all our lifejackets until they were more like straitjackets. She took to the oars, battered though they were, with chunks missing off the blades. She was the first – and so far the only – woman river guide in Zambia.

We drifted down on the swirling black water. There was a silence of anticipation. Ahead was an ominous deep roaring noise, as the river dropped from view. As we went into the rapids, we came up against the famous continuously curling wave with a tunnel inside it, like classic beach surf but never travelling, never subsiding. Our team was (apart from me, aged 59) made up of strong athletic men in their 30s. We had a good crew.

We paddled hard on Monde's commands and when in white water we dropped into the bottom of the raft, hanging onto the ropes along the raft. She warned us of the huge whirlpools in the next rapid, so we needed to take particular care not to get separated from the raft. Paddling was difficult, often in thin air or froth so the

White water rafting in Batoka Gorge down the Zambezi

blade couldn't grip. It was utterly exhilarating, sometimes terrifying, and we shot past black walls of basalt at 12–15 knots, being tossed up, sucked down, spun around, until we were thrown out of the maelstrom into the calm section at the bottom of each rapid.

Sometimes we were sent backwards up the river on a big frothy wave, or in a big whirlpool. Our boat would often point skywards, be tipped on its edge, or crash under several feet of breaking wave. Before each wave, Monde shouted commands to us to get us in the right place, so as to avoid rocks, holes and whirlpools. Once in the rapids we no longer had control, and Monde's oars were often wrenched from her hands. She also had to let go of them so as to grab the steel rowing frame she was sitting on, as we all disappeared into frothing water. The key was to avoid rocks, and especially holes or whirlpools, which we'd been advised were hard to get out of. We avoided the big Seven Day Eddy; we understood that getting out of it takes a week.

On Number 13, the Mother, one of the rafts flipped, tossing the rafters into the rapids. Another raft got ripped and needed pumping up in the calm sections between each rapid. In Number 15, the Washing Machine, we had to avoid a huge crashing hole that we might get stuck in. Monde shouted, 'Hard forward, team, harder, harder!' as we struggled to avoid a frothing whirlpool with a huge wave behind it, and then 'Get down, get down – *now*!' We grabbed the ropes and dropped into the bottom of the raft.

Then lots more wave trains, including Number 18, Oblivion, apparently responsible for more raft flips than any other rapid on the planet. This was the toughest rapid on the mighty Zambezi. We shot down a smooth green chute and hit a wall of churning white water 10 feet high, a cliff of rock flashing by our starboard side. Only a quarter of the rafts get through this the right way up. Ours was one of the fortunate ones.

After this, the rapids got a lot easier, and I swam down one of them, later passing a crocodile, much to my surprise. 'The crocs prefer white meat,' Monde told me. It mystified me how it could have got there; from upstream it would have had to survive the falls (unlikely), from downstream it would have had to beat the rapids (impossible, surely), and the gorge was too steep, mostly cliffs. A plausible theory is that crocs may come down a tributary to the Zambezi. When we got to the take-out point, the gorge had deepened to 750 feet and broadened, allowing more sun in, and seeming friendlier than the black, dark, steep and narrow rift further up.

On my final morning of the trip I went for a flight in a microlight above the falls. This was basically a combination of a motorbike and a hang-glider, with a propeller on the back. Sitting astride it, 2,000 feet above the falls, was another adrenaline rush and a wonderful way to enjoy the view. And the feeling of sitting on a motorbike half a mile up in the air is quite something. On the way back, we flew over crocs, hippos and a white rhino.

The Mountain of God

I first heard about the Ol Doinyo Lengai volcano while reading up on Tanzania's geology. In the Maa language of the Maasai, the name means Mountain of God. The Maasai fear it, and I read an account when it erupted and the villagers all paraded in a long line to its base, dressed in their best clothing, in the hope of appeasing it. But the volcano was not appeased, and they fled. It is a fascinating phenomenon: the only carbonate volcano in the world and the only active volcano in Tanzania. It erupts natrocarbonatite lava at a relatively cool 520°C (970°F), which glows red in low light but looks black in daylight, turning white a day later.

In 2007 I decided to climb the volcano out of sheer curiosity, but also to get into shape for some climbing I was planning to do in Antarctica. My company was also just about to start exploring for oil in the Western Rift Valley in Uganda, and I wanted to understand more about how all this worked, because the interactions of faulting, volcanoes, lavas, ash falls, sandy deposits, ancient swamps and salty lake beds would determine whether or not there was oil or gas to be found. Several geologists and volcanologists had been up Lengai. Some had camped on top and been burned by the lava. One had had his sleeping bag burnt, and another his tent. There were stories of armed bandits at the bottom, putting planks spiked with nails across the track to stop 4×4s. There was also a leopard roaming the mountain, although very elusive. Its presence was only known due to its glinting eyes at night, its rasping roar (like a wood saw) and its footprints. On the top of the mountain, there were cobras and pythons. There was even a story of a raven dropping a rock onto a geologist.

The climb up was known to be very demanding, ascending from 3,700 to 9,400 feet, an altitude gain of 5,700 feet and mostly up a very steep, slippery slope of lava and loose ash. This was over five times the height of the Eiffel Tower, to be climbed in pitch dark, with packs on. People who had also climbed Mount Kilimanjaro told me that Ol Doinyo Lengai was much harder; it was steeper, more dangerous and ascending at four times the rate of climb.

The volcano has been building for the last 350,000 years and now its mass is around 60 cubic kilometres (about double the amount of material ejected from Krakatoa in 1883). It stands on the western edge of the eastern arm of the Great Rift Valley, which extends the 6,000 miles/9,500 km from Syria to Mozambique, and, still spreading and dropping, is forecast to eventually split Africa in two. Ol Doinyo Lengai has two craters; while the southern one is inactive, the northern one erupts approximately every five to ten years: sometimes explosively, as in 1917, when the forests in the region were destroyed; and sometimes in the form of very large lava flows, extending to the bottom of the mountain, as in March 2006, when it ignited the vegetation at its base. Its ash is often carried hundreds of miles. A century ago the volcano's northern crater was 600 feet deep but it has since filled up, and now lava frequently overflows down the sides of the mountain. It is in a very remote part of Africa, just a few kilometres south of Lake Natron, 58 miles long and only 50 cm deep, with water of up to 60°C (140°F);[26] it's the most caustic lake in the world.

Having been on several active volcanoes before, I was intrigued by Ol Doinyo Lengai. As mentioned in Chapter 3, I'd climbed Anak Krakatoa some 18 years earlier, when it had been about 400 feet high. Since then it has grown about 300 feet higher. Its 1883 eruption had fascinated me since childhood. The sound waves went round the world seven times, as recorded on Victorian barographs. Its earlier eruption, in 532 CE, was the likely

26 While 50°C (122°F) is enough to burn you.

Lava flows at the summit caldera

Approaching Oldoinyo Lengai

Oldoinyo Lengai re-
cent lava flows

In the Rift Valley

cause of the demise of most of the world's civilisations, and the onset of 100 years of what some call the Dark Ages. Many civilisations took 1,000 years to return to their standards prior to the Dark Ages.

Volcanoes shape our history. When will there be another giant eruption?

Also as mentioned in Chapter 3, I'd been to the erupting volcano of Mauna Loa, flying over the crater in a helicopter with Bonnie and Mike, and Carl, a USGS geologist keen to take lava and gas samples.

I'd seen another rift valley, in Iceland, where the island cracks in half for miles from time to time, spilling out lava in long sheets and creating *jökulhlaups*.[27] I'd been to Pompeii, which is still mostly buried; and to Santorini, where a Minoan town has recently been dug out, buried in 1630 BCE by an eruption four times bigger than Krakatoa's 1883 eruption. After that eruption the Minoan civilisation disappeared, and it was 1,500 years before its sophistication was matched – by the Romans.

I had started training for the climb on the stairs machine at the gym, getting my heart rate doubled to 145 beats per minute, and doing the equivalent of the Eiffel Tower in 13 minutes.

In 2007 I flew to Dar, then Arusha (under Kilimanjaro), and went overland with a Tanzanian driver, Fabian, to Lake Natron; I told him that he was named after an early Roman pope, which delighted him. There was no public transport along these dirt tracks, so a hired Land Cruiser was the way to go. As we left Arusha, Fabian pointed to a place where 22 people had been killed in a bus crash the week before. The dusty track led through parched areas inhabited only by the Maasai tribe. Here there were no buses, only the occasional 4×4.

The Maasai

The Maasai are in many ways truly impressive, living as Iron Age people did around 3,000 years ago. The Maasai building design, their use of iron tools and their lifestyle is very much of that culture. During the European colonial era they earned a fierce reputation, and they still hang on to their traditions. Maasai *askari* (warriors) used to have to spear a lion to earn the right to marry. They still have the right to an unlimited number of wives, each with their own house, or *inkajijik*. The women have few rights.

The language of the Maasai is their own, not the Swahili national language of Tanzania. I once asked a Maasai how they can kill a lion with a spear, and he said, 'We can predict what the lion is going to do better than it can tell what we will do.' A Maasai askari is quick to identify the personality of the lion being hunted, be it aggressive, cowardly or arrogant, and plan accordingly. One of them told me what to do if I encountered a lion while out walking: 'Do not move at all, and fix the lion with a calm, strong stare. The lion will eventually walk away.'

I often think that the wealthy western hunters who pay $50,000 for a few days shooting wildlife, often from the back of a Land Rover, should try a real adventure, on foot and armed with only a spear. The animals have virtually no chance against a group of people with guns and telescopic sights, but against spears they are on a level playing field.

Here there were no mobile phones, no toothpaste, no T-shirts, no sign of anything modern. Boys as young as six are in charge of herds of goats a long way from any help, on the arid plains, and they would often run out to wave at us. Older teenage boys herd cattle. The Maasai do not believe in farming; their diet is free of fruit, vegetables or cereals, predominantly consisting of the cow blood and milk, with some meat and honey. Here, the ground is too arid to farm, and I was amazed that their cattle could

---

27 *Glacial floods that destroy everything in their path.*

survive on the dry grass. The cattle are always on the move, in long lines. Traditional medicines come from plants, bushes and trees.

The Maasai originally came from the north, a Nilotic people out of Sudan. They are tall, athletic and strong, and many have Caucasian features. One interesting theory suggests that on account of their swords, sandals, togas and warrior-like habits, they are descended in part from a Roman legion which had got lost in the southernmost fringes of the Roman Empire. But whenever I saw the Maasai, they were often smiling, now no longer killing rivals or intruders.

In spite of their starkly arid environment, they dress smartly. The men have long plaited hair, silver and beaded jewellery, and red cloaks. The red of the traditional Maasai *shuka* is visible for miles, in the expectation of its being a warning to wild animals to keep their distance. Even though lions – and indeed most other mammals except primates – are unable to detect red, seeing it as a greyish-blue/green, when most lions see a Maasai they flee, whereas they tend to give white people a bored and arrogant stare.

The Maasai men have a structured rites of passage regime: the first of these occurs at 15 years old, when they leave their parents to live for eight years in the wilderness, learning to survive as warriors; the second is when they return to the village to raise families; and the final one is when they become elders. Each transition is marked by elaborate ceremonies.

Many Maasai men travel into the cities to work, frequently as security guards. Then they regularly return to their Maasai homes with its unaltered, pure lifestyle, rigid structures, values and traditions. They play *bao*, a complex game rather like chess, on a board or with pebbles on the ground.

Women wear mostly blue cloaks and are shaved bald. They may be married at, or even before, puberty, and they have no say in the choice of husband. They do nearly all the work, collecting huge loads of firewood and carrying them on their heads, sometimes 30 miles. They build the houses: the walls out of sticks and grass cemented with cattle dung, and with thatched roofs. The *manyattas* (small groups of huts) are reserved for the warriors. The *enkangs* (larger villages for the families) are surrounded by a *boma* (dense, very thorny, hedge/fence) to keep their animals in and the predators out.

When a person dies, the corpse is left outside for scavengers; vultures are quick to strip a body to the bone, and hyenas crush the bones for the marrow. No one is allowed to mention the person's name again. A harsh end to a harsh life.

Evidence produced to date leads to general agreement that humans emerged from the Great Rift Valley, probably more than once. Before *Homo sapiens*, previous hominids had migrated to Europe and Asia 800,000 years ago but died out, possibly as a result of the colossal eruption of Toba in Indonesia 75,000 years ago, an eruption 100 times more powerful than that of Krakatoa in 1883. The current understanding is that modern humans derive from this area of East Africa from about 140,000 years ago, leaving Africa 80,000 years ago.

Should there be another cataclysm, the Maasai would survive well, needing nothing from outside their simple community structure. There are still over a million of them in Maasailand, which straddles the Kenya–Tanzania border. Maybe they've got it right and we've got it wrong.

Getting to an erupting volcano in an earthquake

Fabian and I drove on, bouncing along the dirt trail, leaving a mile of dust clouds behind us. We slowed as a herd of 1,000 donkeys plodded slowly by, evidently being raised for sale or barter. The terrain became gravelly grey desert, with the Rift Valley wall always on our left. A zebra lay dead on the track, inexplicably – we were miles from the nearest herd.

And then I saw the Mountain of God. It was even bigger and steeper than I'd expected, rising with precipitous sides to a white summit, and with long white streaks down its slopes. This was not snow or glacier but the sodium carbonate, bleached lava. This volcano is the height of two Ben Nevises, its summit over 9,700 feet. It is higher than Mount St Helens and over twice the height of Vesuvius. It looked majestic. And it looked dangerous.

We drove towards Lake Natron, found the campsite, near a pretty river in some woods underneath the Rift escarpment, and I checked into my tent. The Maasai village of Ngare Sero was close by.

The camp was managed by a German, Jens, who tried to dissuade me from the climb. 'It's very steep and very difficult. There are very slippery, exposed rock faces, and no fixed ropes. Many people don't make it. Some get to the top and can't get down, and have to be dragged off the mountain. You'll need 5 litres of water, and you must get down again before the sun heats the desert up. You'll need to leave here about 11 p.m. And there's another problem … the volcano's very active just now – there's lots of lava gushing out – and there's something we've never had before … earthquake: one a couple of days ago, one yesterday, and two today, getting stronger – signs that the volcano's ready to erupt.'

I looked at the volcano again. The route was up the steep north-west face. I asked why I couldn't go up the less steep southern flank.

'There's no more track – it's impassable now.'

I suggested to Jens that it might be better to do the dangerous bits in daylight.

'Maybe better at night because you won't see where you are. In daylight, people get scared and freeze up. It's just what I've been told – I've never been up. I'm not in good enough shape.'

I met several Spaniards who had tried it but been forced back by 'near-vertical' slopes, which they'd felt would be too difficult to descend safety.

I then met John, a strongly built Tanzanian, from Kilimanjaro, who offered to be my guide. I sorted and packed my gear into the backpack: for the night climb a headlight, altimeter, compass, GPS, gloves, ski hat, telescopic poles, jacket, carbohydrate drinks, water; for the return in daylight sunhat, glacier glasses, sun block, more water.

I rested in the tent. Suddenly, there was an earthquake – initially a vibration, then like a huge boiling cauldron, up and down underneath me. The tent shook and rattled. It was a different motion from the earthquakes I'd experienced in San Francisco, which had more of a rhythmic sideways motion. It was unnerving, not knowing for sure what the volcano would do next.

Climbing, and more earthquakes

I put on my boots and gaiters, and we left at midnight, driving along a dusty trail through long dry grass. When we had driven as far as possible, Fabian agreed to stay in the Land Cruiser in case there was an eruption and we had to get out in a hurry. We started under a starry night, with the Milky Way arching over us in the crisp, clear southern skies. It was very black as there was no moon, and I couldn't make out the shape of the volcano, only the absence of stars where it rose steeply above us. A meteor shot across and into the void behind the looming black shape.

It was 1 a.m. John led the way at a rapid pace. Our two headlamps danced their beams of light. Beyond them was an unknown, invisible blackness. There was a path through the long, white grass, straight up the ever-steepening slope with no zigzags. We were on a ridge between two steep gullies. The one on the right was a dangerous canyon. John told me not to veer right – not even a foot to the right – as there was a sheer cliff below.

Further over, a faint white outline indicated where a big lava flow had rushed down the mountain the previous year. There were no lights in the desert below. Soon the grass gave way to heather.

The terrain became very difficult, with steep slabs of tuff covered by loose ash. My boots would not grip this at all, and I relied totally on my shortened, sharp-pointed sticks, looking for cracks and hollows to push against – I was using the poles to actually climb with, rather than just balance. It was exhausting work, slipping backwards, and not seeing any sign of progress except the altimeter readings. After an hour I checked the GPS. We had only made 1,000 feet. A strong, cold wind was blowing around the mountain, kicking up dust, which choked my throat and gritted my eyes. Its sharp volcanic particles sparkled in our headlights.

Nearing the Oldoinyo Lengai summit at dawn

I slipped often, and was thankful for my gloves which, taking a hammering, protected my hands. I was often moving forwards on my hands and knees. No rest. There were no flat spots, no respite from the remorseless slope. My headlamp was essential, as I was using both hands to climb with.

Soon we were above the windy area, and could smell the sulphur spewing forth 3,000 feet above us. We reached halfway, at 6,600 feet. The hardest part was the next two hours, up even steeper, more slippery lava, tuff, ash and dust. I was exhausted and unable to continue: breathing, heart and legs all maxed out. I took a long rest and tried again. I could not accept that this medium-sized mountain would be the first to beat me. Then I took a bad fall and damaged my left leg. I tried to continue, stopping every 300 vertical feet for recovery, regaining my proper heartbeat and breathing, recovering my leg strength. But soon I could only manage 150 vertical feet between rests. I would never get up and down before the water ran out. The air was 30 per cent thinner at the top of this mountain. I had not trained enough. I was not as agile and energetic as my younger self, but my endurance was key. My goal was defined by the altimeter on my wristwatch. Every hour I calibrated this to the true altitude off the GPS. The altimeter was reading only the air pressure, which of course fluctuated with the weather, and the air temperature, hence its density; the instrument often showed a difference of 200–300 feet from the GPS altitude – sometimes higher, sometimes lower.

I drank my carbohydrate and minerals drink and got a miraculous burst of energy. And then, at around 3 a.m., there was another earthquake. We found this unnerving, knowing that there above us were millions of tons of molten lava contained only by fragile walls. And then a bigger earthquake, triggering a rock slide down the gully to our right. It was even more unnerving hearing the rocks crashing down yet not being able to see them.

'This is not normal,' John said. The fear was that a major eruption could take place, and as we were downwind of the summit the ash would blow on top of us. Lava flows had recently come down either side of us. It was still pitch-black, and now, if possible, even blacker, because cloud – or could it be ash? – had obscured the stars.

Climbing in the dark is different because you can't see more than a very little of the situation you are in – just the 10 feet immediately around you, lit by your headlight. I didn't know what was ahead of me or on either side of me – I could only make out my next ten or so footholds. Coming down in the dark would have been almost impossible, due to the inability to see over the sharp drop-offs, which were in black shadow below us. Should an eruption occur now there was no chance of getting off quickly.

We nearly decided to go back. But as there were no more rock falls or rumblings while we were deliberating, we continued. At 6 a.m. it began to get light and I could finally see what was ahead. My spirits soared. The top section was hard as concrete, 40–45 degrees, embedded with golf ball-sized black stones. They must have been ejected from the volcano, landing in molten lava. The black stones were a godsend, as the slope was too steep to get a stable foothold without them. It was much steeper than a flight of steep stairs, but with no steps – it was all incline.

This was the dangerous area. I had to avoid a fall. If I did, I would have to fall face down and try to self-arrest, as if on an ice slope with an ice axe. I would need to avoid a roll, which could take me hundreds of feet down, probably fatally. I knocked a rock loose and it bounced down in huge arcs, disappearing from view. The stakes were high. Now, there was a narrowing canyon above us. At the top was a gateway, which John called The Goal. Steam and smoke were ahead. John was wearing thick woollen gloves, but even with those he sat astride a fuming vent to gain extra warmth in this cold, windswept landscape.

At the caldera

We crested the crater rim at 9,167 feet, and there below us was a fantastic sight, like a grey moonscape but with special effects befitting *The Lord of the Rings*. Hornitos belched and blasted gas, smoke and steam, rumbling like huge steam locomotives. One was 200 feet high. It was clear that black lava had recently emerged from this steamy area; I could see where it had overflowed and tumbled down the mountain. I ventured onto the white crater crust, treading carefully as it was known to collapse – and collapse into a boiling pit of black lava, which glows red at night and is fast-flowing, with a viscosity more like water than basaltic lava. I did not venture too far in to this cauldron, lest a sudden increase in the mountain's activity should catch me. This was really primeval – the inner workings of the planet right before our eyes. I checked the GPS. We were at 2°45'31.6S, 35°34'42.2E.

Erupting hornitos on the summit

All too soon we had to head back down, anxious to beat the noon sun. Clouds scudded across below us. I lengthened my poles, leaning hard on them as my boots were slipping. John told me to keep the poles below me at all times, walking them wide apart to avoid any chance of tripping over them, and never letting them get behind or above me, as that could cause a catapult away from the rock face and a long way down the slope. This was a new technique, much more demanding than the usual one. I fell a dozen times. John also fell several times. I had one long fall of about 15 feet, only stopped by jamming my pole into rock and below my leg. I slid again when I removed the pole, and dropped until I hit a ledge. Without my gloves the abrasion would have skinned my hands.

John, PC and Fabian after our return

Then we were back in the steep tuff and ash. We went down in the middle of gullies, skiing on the loose volcanic sand; my gaiters did a good job of keeping the stones out. Then I saw the place where John had warned me in the dark about the cliff above the canyon. We had been right above it in the pitch-black night; it was an overhang. To our left was the long, violent lava flow from the previous year, running all the way to a Maasai hut, where it had reached the end of its headlong 3-mile rush. It was frozen in huge black and white waves, some 50 feet high, where it had stopped.

Ahead was the Rift wall, 3,000 feet high and thousands of miles long. There was no sign of life, and now the brutal African sun was beating down on us in full force. We were 150 miles south of the equator, and the sun was north of us. I covered up, using my gloves, hat and bandana to keep the radiation off me in the thin mountain air. I could see Lake Natron steaming in the distance, white and shimmering.

We got back at 1.30 p.m. I'd finished the 5 litres of water – a gallon in 12 hours. Fabian had been waiting for us in a howling hot wind. He gave me a huge hug of congratulations, and said, 'The volcano corrupted last night,' referring to the earthquakes.

Back at camp, there was another earthquake. The Maasai chief said this had never happened in living memory. A large boulder was knocked off the top of the Rift escarpment and crashed down 3,000 feet.

We drove back. A huge relief.

The zebra was now a skeleton with only its ribcage left, finished by the vultures. We passed where the bus had crashed – hundreds of Africans were there for a memorial service, most of them having arrived on farm trailers towed by tractors, standing room only. Back in Arusha, and then in Dar, the newspapers reported that the tremors had been felt as far as Nairobi and Arusha, causing panic in the streets. The USGS had identified the epicentres as within 10 miles of Ol Doinyo Lengai and 6 miles underneath. There was another earthquake the next day, at Richter 6.0, which I felt in Dar, 600 km away. More boulders had been reported crashing down the Rift Valley escarpment.

I'd got there and back just in time! Shortly afterwards the volcano erupted in a major way, and the Dar newspapers reported that 1,500 Maasai had fled the region. A Ngare Sero villager said, 'We heard roaring sounds before the volcano started discharging ashes and lava.' The Tanzanian Geological Survey was advising people to keep 100 km away.

I had made it to the summit of this violently active volcano, but I had not trained enough, and that had made the project much more difficult and risky. However, to have trained appropriately I would have had to spend eight hours a day wearing my pack and climbing boots, on a treadmill at a 45-degree incline and covered in loose sand, with thick dust blowing around the gym – not to mention snakes and leopards lurking about the place and rocks crashing down from a ready-to-blow furnace hissing and rumbling overhead. But nothing could beat the experience of the Mountain of God. It was an apt name.

| Big dunes at Sossusvlei, Namibia | Wreck on the foggy Skeleton Coast |

Namibia

In 2004 I took some time off work in Tanzania, went to Windhoek in Namibia, and rented a 4×4 pickup with two spare tyres. I had always been fascinated by the 1,500 km Namibian coast, mostly the Skeleton Coast, since reading Geoffrey Jenkins' 1959 novel *A Twist of Sand*. I covered 3,000 km in five days of driving on high-quality dirt roads. Namibia is the second most sparsely populated country in the world,[28] and at the time, although it was shortly after a long and violent war, it was very safe. First, I stopped at Sossusvlei in the Namib Desert to climb the beautiful red sand dunes, some of the biggest in the world. Then to the coast, where I was able to fulfil another lifelong dream: dune-boarding.

I then headed north, up hundreds of miles of deserted Skeleton Coast, which was often windy and foggy with the cold rough South Atlantic breaking to my left. It was truly unique because of its scale, its lack of vegetation and its remoteness. The occasional shipwreck broke up the monotony. The coast was dry, foggy, sandy, cold, windy, lifeless, remote and desolate all at once. Sometimes a pale sun broke through. This went on and on and on, for hundreds of miles. It exceeded my expectations. It was like nowhere else. I was in awe of it.

North Africa

In December 2011 Mike (then aged 18) and I went to Morocco on holiday. There were virtually no tourists or foreigners, as it was just after the Arab Spring revolutions that had swept across North Africa earlier that year. Morocco had handled the disruptions well, helped by the stability of its monarchy, and in fact it was a very safe place to be.

We spent our first night in a delightful riad[29] in Marrakech, and visited the Djemaa el-Fna, where we played with cobras around our necks – an amazing experience in a mystical smoke-filled atmosphere.

We then drove south, past ruined mud-brick castles nestled in river gorges, to the Sahara, where we rode a couple of camels across the dunes. This was quite different from riding a horse, as we were perched, about twice as high, up on the camel's hump. We capped off our stay with hiking in the snow-covered high Atlas Mountains. It had been a magical trip.

In 2014 work took me to the Sinai peninsula in Egypt. This was right after a series of huge riots which had resulted in in a military coup d'état removing President Morsi from power: Egypt's first democracy in

---

28 After Greenland (and Antarctica, which isn't counted).

29 A traditional-style town house, built around an internal courtyard.

Mike in Morocco on the edge of the Sahara

10,000 years had lasted less than two years. Again, foreigners and tourists were nowhere to be seen, so it was a fantastic time for me to visit the ancient sites, starting with the pyramids of Giza. I went with an Egyptian colleague from work, and was the only Westerner at the site. The pyramids were much bigger than I'd expected, and took my breath away. It is still a mystery how they were built, without iron tools and to a precision of a few millimetres. They were the tallest human-made structures for 3,800 years, and were probably built by up to 40,000 men.

We walked around the back, where the stone had been quarried, then climbed up a few stone courses and went inside. We were on our own, crawling up narrow passages, to the vault of King Khufu. The roof above contained granite blocks of 80 tonnes, which had come 500 miles down the Nile from Aswan, then hauled 13 miles overland to the site and up about 250 feet. This had all been done about 4,500 years ago, long before Stonehenge was built.[30] The engineering achievement was quite amazing.

I then sailed in a felucca up the Nile to the temples of Karnak, Hatshepsut and Philae. In many of these places I was the only person there, aside from the armed guards. Everything was in amazingly good condition, considering its age. Thankfully, these architectural treasures have not been destroyed by the vandals or armies that have descended on these lands over thousands of years. The obelisks here, carved from a single piece of solid granite, weighed up to 700 tonnes. Each bore immaculately chiselled and highly detailed hieroglyphs.

Ethiopia

In January 2013 work took me to Ethiopia, to negotiate a gas exploration project with the Ethiopian government. This is a country rich in culture and history, with an incredibly hard-working people eking out a living from crops,

---

30 By comparison, the bluestones at Stonehenge are 2–5 tonnes each, and were hauled 170 miles.

mostly grown in the mountains up to 12,000 feet. I travelled to the Simien mountains and hired a bodyguard with a Kalashnikov AK-47 so that I could go hiking safely.

Ethiopia is one of the most beautiful countries I have ever visited, much of it sitting on top of lava flows thousands of feet thick along the Great Rift Valley. There were vertical cliffs thousands of feet high,[31] and thousands of gelada baboons. This area is aptly called the Roof of Africa, and quite majestic I found it. It was also pristine, and spared the effects of mass tourism as a result of its decades of war.

On the "Roof of Africa" in Simien Mountains

My bodyguard

Threshing corn

---

31 In times gone by an accepted way of removing political opponents was to push them off those cliffs.

8 Climbing unclimbed peaks in Arctic Greenland

We were in Arctic Greenland, attempting to climb a hitherto unclimbed peak under the light of the midnight sun. Paul, Mike and I were on the lead rope, and we reached a rock buttress at the top of a long snow slog. Paul worked his way up a very steep ice pitch, hammering and screwing in ice screws along the way. Another rock outcrop on the right allowed him to install some more reliable protection , then we were onto a very steep 60–70-degree ice climb which felt almost vertical. At the top on the left was another rock outcrop. Paul had anchored onto this with a bombproof set of nuts and chocks, and once he'd belayed me up there I could see why; we were perched on a ledge with everything dropping away on the other side to a near-vertical cliff above the glacier below.

Above us was a steep snow slope. Paul chipped the crust off with his axe to reveal hard blue ice below. 'There's nothing to grab hold of for protection,' he said. This was a blow after all the hard work getting there.

'Can't we have a go?' I asked.

'I think the whole slope could slide off the ice, and then we'd all go over the edge.'

I looked down the cliff and imagined all three of us free-falling off the edge, still tied together. 'Sounds like it's off?'

'Afraid so; if we tried it we could have some unhappy families.'

In awe of Nansen

In 1968 I was helping my father throw a lifetime of my grandparents' possessions onto a huge bonfire we had built in their garden. Books, files, letters, pictures, paintings, furniture, ornaments, wartime relics, clocks no longer working, modern clothing, Victorian clothing – in short, almost anything that was not saleable or wanted by a relative. It was a sad and rather gruesome task, and at the age of 18 I dreaded the day when I'd have to do the same thing with my own parents' belongings.

My father called me over: 'I thought you might like this – it was my father's.'

I looked at an old brown leathery book: *Greenland* by Fridjof Nansen, printed in 1897. Inside it was an inscription saying that my grandfather, Lewis St John Rawlinson Clutterbuck, had won it as a school prize in 1898.

I had always been in awe of my grandfather. He had been an only child from a broken home, and had grown up as a very serious young man, judging from the photos, in the British Army artillery. As a gunner, he'd contributed to the design of the 25-pounder, one of Britain's best wartime weapons. I knew him as a broad-shouldered, quiet man with a steely focus. He was often called Colonel. He married Isabella Jessie Jocelyn, and within a century they had over 50 descendants. She was an aristocratic lady, descended from a military background: from the MacNeills of Barra in the Outer Hebrides, from the Norse nobles who had invaded with William the Conqueror, and from the Shah of Persia. The MacNeills' crest was (and is) inscribed with the motto 'Conquer or die'. The Persian and British ancestors had met while fighting the Second Afghan War of 1878–80.

I was intrigued as to why my grandfather had this book, and felt honoured to have been given the chance to inherit it. Inside, there were drawings of square-riggers in stormy high seas, crashing through icebergs and heaving pack ice; kayaks braving the surf; sledges on the Greenland ice cap; Norwegians on skis, falling into crevasses, being pushed along in front of sledges with the wind behind them, the sides of their tent rigged as sails. Between the drawings was woven a fascinating story not only of the research Nansen did to develop cutting-edge technology in sledges, skis, wooden glacier goggles, stove, tents and two giant fur sleeping bags that could each contain three men, but also of the Inuit lifestyle, with their wild nightlife inside steamy shelters in Arctic winters, and the way they hunted large whales by harpooning them from kayaks, then holding on, sometimes for days, till the whale tired out, then going in for the kill. Attached to each harpoon was an inflated bladder, whose buoyancy would exhaust the whale each time it dived, and without which it would have been a disaster to tie a whale to the tiny kayaks. It was in 1888 that Nansen's group was the first recorded expedition that crossed the ice cap.

I had since prep school followed the tales of Amundsen, Shackleton and Scott in Antarctica. As an adult I was still in awe of these explorers from a century ago, and longed for a chance to visit the ice caps of Greenland or Antarctica.

My chance came in 2005, when I was able to carve out a slot in between family commitments and my work in East Africa. Paul Walker had been in contact with me for several years, with plans for expeditions to previously unexplored regions of eastern Greenland. Paul was the most experienced Greenland explorer on the planet, and probably had more unclimbed peaks, or first ascents, under his belt than any person in history. He ran his Tangent Expeditions from a cottage in the Lake District; the business was primarily focused on organising logistics to get in and out of remote areas in Greenland. He'd been planning an expedition to an unnamed region on the edge of the ice cap: the Kangerdlugssuaq ranges, where there were thousands of unclimbed mountains. Two expeditions had approached the edge of the ranges we intended to climb, but no one had made it as far as the area he had earmarked. Access from the sea is very hard and sometimes impossible, as the pack ice extends dozens of miles off the east Greenland coast all year round. And along this 400-mile stretch of coast there is not a single settlement.

West Greenland is a more benign place, which is why the Vikings had settled there from the 10th to the 15th centuries. They navigated with a sunstone, a crystal of cordierite which polarises blue when pointed at the sun on even a cloudy day. Recent evidence indicates that as the climate cooled the settlers died of starvation, unable to sustain their Scandinavian agriculture, while the Inuit survived, as ever, off the icy seas. Apparently the Inuit believed that Europeans were a cross between Inuit and dogs. Erik the Red, a Viking fugitive from Iceland had, in giving Greenland its name indulged in a bit of spin in order to encourage Icelanders to emigrate there. It would have been better named Iceland instead – but then Erik would have lost out on his agricultural development in the two western valleys that were settled by the Vikings.

The development of ski-planes has given westerners access to the ice cap, which is up to 11,000 feet high in the middle. However, in 2005 there was only one ski-plane in Greenland, an area 17 times the size of England, but that plane was in west Greenland, and the Kangerdlugssuaq was out of its range.

Preparing for unclimbed Arctic mountains

However, we did manage to track down a plane capable of reaching Kangerdlugssuaq; it was based in Iceland. It was a 19-seat Twin Otter, but as it would be carrying drums of fuel for the return flight it would only be able to take four of us at a time. We would go, then, in two parties. There were no maps of the area, but Paul had an old aerial photo from 1981, which showed the nunataks sticking up, although we had little idea how high they were.

'When we get to Kangerdlugssuaq, the nearest people to us will be in Iceland,' Paul explained in his calm Yorkshire accent over the phone. As Iceland was hundreds of miles away from Kangerdlugssuaq, it seemed like a good place to get away from it all.

Paul described the area as follows:

> A vast group of ranges stretching right down the east coast of Greenland on huge glacier systems reminiscent of Antarctica. These ranges comprise the least explored region in Greenland. The peaks are surrounded by huge Arctic glacier systems on one side and the vast Greenland ice cap on the other. These ranges offer by far the single largest expanse of unclimbed alpine peaks in the Arctic. The ranges are the most difficult to get to in East Greenland. So we will fly direct from Iceland to the mountains, landing at a pre-determined glacier landing site. However, to do this the aircraft is at the limit of its range. This huge region is unnamed. We have simply called it the Kangerdlugssuaq ranges, after the large fjord of the same name.

We were headed to a region of over 10,000 square kilometres that no one had ever been to before; it was unmapped, unnamed, unexplored, unknown. This was magical – Antarctica is better mapped and better explored than that, as a result of the many scientific expeditions sent from various countries over decades. Just how steep would the mountains be? Where would there be steep ice, or soft snow, or rocky ridges? I felt much the same as a 19th-century explorer would have done.

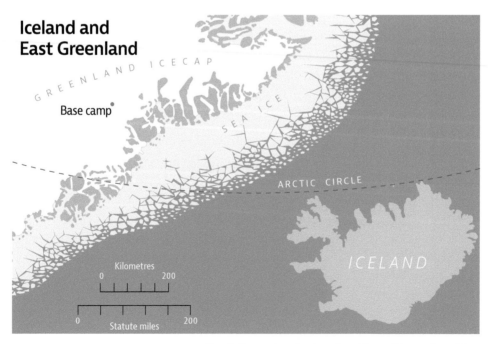

East Greenland, showing Base Camp location

I found out a bit about my fellow companions, all very experienced and passionate mountaineers.

Jon Dallimore, a Himalayan expedition leader with a lot of Karakorum experience, specialised in developing emergency mountaineering medical systems. Jon was one of those people who was always optimistic and positive, helping any of us in trouble.

Mike O'Boyle, an IT research scientist, was a passionate rock and ice technical climber with alpine and winter ascent focus. Mike's northern accent and practical, cool head were the rock climber's hallmark.

Tim Campbell-Smith, an alpinist and a surgeon, also had a Himalayan expedition background. His permanent good humour was uplifting when times were hard.

Dave Craven was a hardened mountaineer, just back from a crossing of the Iceland ice cap in a permanent blizzard, their pulk sledges being blown upside down by the wind and sastrugi. Dave was another northerner, a technical rock and ice man.

Geoff Bonney was a geologist and another Himalayan veteran, with Andean and Alpine ascents behind him, including the Matterhorn. He said it was an easy climb, although dozens of people are still being killed by this mountain, amounting to some 500 deaths to date. He had completed four previous Greenland expeditions and was just back from Milne Land, an uninhabited island in the Arctic. 'We were chest-deep in snow,' he told me, 'and the plane froze into the snow. We had to hammer its skis and dig it out – and then it was damaged when it caught a ski in a crevasse.'

Tina Nielsen was another surgeon, with mountaineering experience in Antarctica, the Andes and the Himalayas, climbing to 24,000 feet. Tina was one of those people who never complained of hardship and just seemed to love adventures.

Compared with this lot I was a relative rookie, and had the added disadvantage of being a 55-year-old veteran, having retired from mountaineering 23 years previously, on the basis that as it was a young man's sport I was already too old for it. However, I'd always been passionate about it, and had taken part in a handful of wonderful expeditions to Alaska, Patagonia, the Himalayas and several North American peaks.

However, in the coming weeks I had two problems to address.

First, my gear had been hanging up rusting in my garage. It was all obsolete: heavy, clumsy and much of it unreliable. I was able to justify to Bonnie the purchase in the US and the UK of new kit on the grounds of safety. I therefore ended up with four ice axes, three sets of crampons, several packs, ski boots, ice-climbing boots and much more to choose from. The new gear was fantastic: feather-light, easy to use, immensely strong. Crampons I could step into rather than strap up; short, light ice axes with razor-sharp teeth; warm, dry, windproof clothing. I was back in the world of nuts, ice screws, belay plates, abseiling rings, seat harnesses, and all manner of gloves and boots for every situation. Fortunately, having worked in Arctic Alaska and Russia over a 14-year period, I already had plenty of cold weather clothing.

The second problem was getting back into shape. Having given up climbing to focus mainly on offshore ocean racing, I had developed the wrong set of muscles. I'd been keeping fit by swimming and weight training, but needed to improve my cardiovascular strength. I decide to join my local gym, where the manager, Danny, had been trained in Arctic warfare in Norwegian winters when he had been a commando. 'Work out mainly on the stairs machine,' he said. 'Put on your heaviest boots, add some lead ankle weights, fill your pack with bricks and go for it. Get your heart rate up to the maximum for your age group and keep it there as long as you can. And please don't tear up the machines at the gym.' I was also hauling tyres while cross-country skiing on some of Surrey's finest turf runs.

Soon I was immersed in graphs, with heart monitor strapped to my chest, running up the equivalent of the Eiffel Tower in ski boots inside 13 minutes. I was pleased with my progress. Then with six weeks to go I blew a hamstring. I went to see Martin Dyer at the local physio. Martin specialises in sports injuries, and he was frequently tasked with getting professional sportspeople back on the field in the fastest possible time. I'd heard that hamstrings take longer than six weeks to heal. Martin got it repaired inside four, using a multipad electric shock machine and sonic devices to rebuild the muscle tissue. Nicola McCardle, at the same clinic, then dug deep to align everything in the right direction, so as to prevent permanent damage. They performed miracles.

Paul had organised several crevasse rescue practice sessions off a cliff in the Lake District, and there I met Dave, Mike, Jon and Tim for the first time. First we practised hauling each other up the cliff from the top, using prusik knots, pulleys and lots of carabiners to get up to 8:1 purchase on the victim's rope. This would be the rope by which we were supposed to be attached to each other while in crevasse areas on the ice – ideally in groups of three or four. Then we practised climbing up the rope from the bottom, using prusik knots, jumars, Tiblocs and other hardware. I was still handicapped by the injured hamstring, so a somewhat incapacitated participant. However, we began welding into a good team, and it was clear there would be no difficult personalities or relationship problems – these climbers were used to depending on each other, and most had climbed with one or more of the team before. There was a nice atmosphere of joviality, good humour and positive thinking.

I started reading up more about polar expeditions, and Greenland in particular. There was no information on the area we were going to, since no one we knew of had ever been there before. 'We'll find out when we get there,' Paul said. 'We can be sure that all the elevations of the mountains from the aerial photo are wrong at least.'

Gunnbjørn Fjeld, at over 12,000 feet the world's highest Arctic mountain, is in east Greenland, in the Watkins Mountains region, named after the first man to have explored the area. This was an extraordinary tale. In the 1930s, Gino Watkins had been assigned the task of gathering weather data through the Arctic winter for a new transatlantic route for the British Arctic Air Route Expedition. The party ran out of food, and left one man in camp on the ice cap while they went down to the coast to resupply. They returned but could not find the camp. Eventually, with the help of dogs, they found an air vent leading down through the deep wind-driven snow to the tent where the survivor had been buried for five weeks, unable to dig his way out.

West Greenland received more tourism and boasted the world's smallest capital city at Nuuk. Some of its towns had signs that read *Population: 3* and the even less densely inhabited *Population: 1*. The guidebook warned that inebriated Inuit sometimes shoot guns at aircraft as they come in to land, presumably as a sporting activity.

Greenland is the country with the world's lowest population density, at 0.02 people per square kilometre. Mongolia is sometimes regarded as having the world's lowest population density, but is in fact 50 times more densely populated than Greenland. Greenland is also the world's largest island, and the world's most northerly country. It is one of the few countries you can fly into, see no one (no customs officials, no immigration, no tourists, no local people even), and three weeks later fly out having been alone the entire time.

Where we were going there was no vegetation, no animals, no life. Even polar bears rarely visit the ice cap, as there's nothing for them to eat. They only come up the glaciers from the coast if the sea ice is difficult to cross, or sometimes they follow the scent of an expedition. I read that they are the world's largest land carnivore mammal, the only one to deliberately hunt humans for food. We were required by the Danish authorities to carry a rifle, just in case; the Greenlanders 'always welcome the bears with both barrels'. The guidebook advised against camping, as the bears had no mercy. 'They *normally* attack and kill people for food.' I read what to do if unarmed in the event I came across a bear: don't panic, move very slowly, don't walk, don't run, don't play dead – just keep eye contact and talk to it in a deep, confident, authoritative voice. How one could fool nature's most dangerous predator into believing that one was confident seemed a bit of a rose-tinted dream – this animal was known to eat the heads off frozen Arctic explorers. I could imagine the consequences of blinking or stuttering in such a standoff.

The ice cap covers the mountains of Greenland, and in the middle the sheer weight of the ice has pushed them down from their original 12,000 feet to below sea level. Round the edges, the mountaintops protrude as sharp peaks, or nunataks. Some of these rocks are the oldest on the planet. At the time, the ice and snow in the middle never melted – in summer it would just slowly evaporate in the dry Arctic air. At the coast, the ice cap tumbles 3,000 feet into the sea, often in near-vertical icefalls, sometimes in huge, long glaciers calving icebergs into a deep blue sea. One of them is the world's fastest, moving over 100 feet a day, with a volume large enough to supply water to 350 New Yorks every day. Other Greenland glaciers reach widths of 80 km.

At the time of writing the glaciers in west Greenland are reported to be melting more than before. However, east and central Greenland have also been reported as receiving more snowfall than before, so the net gain or loss of ice is not well understood, fuelling controversy in the climate change debate.

I read some tips on polar exploring that I found surprising, such as never cooking in the tent with a sleeping bag inside: the steam freezes onto the bag, so the advice is to keep it outside until just before you jump into it, keeping ice encrustation to a minimum. This is even the case for condensation generated by breathing; it freezes over everything inside the tent. Cooking also produces carbon monoxide, which if contained inside and inhaled can be deadly.

Ski-plane to the ice cap

A few weeks later we were on the plane to Iceland. As mentioned earlier, I'd been there with Bonnie 15 years before, and we'd discovered some majestic landscapes of lava and glacier, crossing the island on a dirt track that's impassable for 11 months of the year.

This time we overnighted at Reykjavik, then flew to Ísafjörður in the north-west – a bleak, windy, cold spot with a scattering of very fair-haired Viking-looking settlers, many of them blind drunk all day. It was 10 June 2005. Rusty trawlers in the harbour gave me an insight into the tough life the fishermen endured. Our Twin Otter was delayed while its skis were repaired following another rough landing in Greenland. When it arrived, we loaded it up for the advance party of Paul, Jon, Dave and Tim, including a huge fuel drum lashed down in the cabin. The pilot, Bjarki Hjaltason, packed a large mallet for knocking the skis loose if they froze in.

When the ski-plane got back to Ísafjörður, Geoff, Tina, Mike and I were off, again with the huge fuel drum lashed into the cabin, and our pulk sledges, packs, food boxes and so on. Halfway across the icy, stormy Denmark Strait, we crossed the edge of the pack ice – a mosaic of polygons on a black sea. Icebergs signalled the approach to the coast, and then we were flying up a broad glacier. We hit some turbulence and a window panel fell out. The ice got higher and was soon close below the skis, as nunataks flashed by my window, clothed in hard, green ice and

At Base Camp in Greenland

encircled by huge wind scoops where the winter storms had gouged out fantastic shapes. Crevasses yawned open in giant chasms. Icefalls tumbled down as hanging glaciers dropped millions of tons of ice from mountain plateaux.

On the ice cap

The landing on the sastrugi was bouncy. 'I'm not coming back here – it's too rough, and there's been too much ski and undercarriage damage,' said Bjarki, our heroic aviator. When we responded that it'd be very tough for us to move the camp to another location, he taxied the plane up and down eight times to flatten the snow, and we promised to level the strip. Then he pumped the fuel drum into the plane's tanks and roared off, going uphill so as to enable him to abort quickly if things got too rough. The problem was that he overshot the flattened bit. It all looked a bit bouncy again, and as the roar of the engines faded we wondered if he really would be back.

I was soon busy flattening an area for my tent with a snow shovel, ice axe and skis. My tent, a new TerraNova Quasar, was the best winter storm tent money could buy, but it was too low to even sit in. I put a neoprene liner inside, then three layers of foam mattress, to get good insulation from the 7,000 feet of ice below my sleeping bag, which would have been chilly on the bottom even though the bag was rated for −30°C (−22°F). While I was pitching the tent, a corner ripped off. Jon was able to sew it back on, as I was suffering from a migraine and unable to think, let alone sew.

The next job was to build an ice table for my cooker and footwell for my eating area. Inside, the tent was warmed by the high-altitude sun, and outside it the radiation was intense as it bounced off the ice. I covered up with glacier cream and dug out my glacier glasses. I got my skis on and headed off across the sastrugi to get a feel for the area. It was simply stunning. It was absolutely silent. We were surrounded by nunataks; to the north-west the ice cap looked like a blue-grey frozen ocean whereas in the other direction the ice dropped away into a broad glacier heading off down to the coast. I could see hundreds of mountains in the crystal-clear air, all unnamed, all unclimbed.

Nunataks follow a pattern; they are usually found near vertical cliffs on the side facing the strongest winds – so here they were on the west side – and they have a huge scoop around the windward side where hurricane-force winds scour out the snow and ice, and a long snow tail on the eastern lee side. These allowed us to climb up them. At the top of the snow slope was a bergschrund, and above that the snow and ice was steep, and stuck to the rock. It was hard, green, very steep ice; snow falling on it slides off. Above the steep ice there was a rock cliff protecting the summit.

There was lots to think about. Could I do the double ice-axe, front-point crampon technique in the night hours with a pack on my back? How much experience did the others have of this type of technical climbing? Would I hold them up? Would my new gear work? I examined the peaks around us. Some looked climbable, others did not.

I fired up the MSR petrol stove for a meal and it was soon roaring away. I hacked off some ice from Greenland's ice cap and dropped it into the pot. Our hot food was all freeze-dried, made in Norway, and all you had to do to cook it was pour water into a tinfoil bag – no plates, pans or dishes to wash up. I started to remember my camp rules, such as hanging up sunglasses and cameras inside the tent so as not to squash them, and brushing snow back out immediately.

The first night climb

At 2230 all eight of us left camp on skis, and I hooked up my pulk, getting a feel for how it slithered and pulled at me over the sastrugi. I was on my telemark boots, using cable bindings on broad skis. These were similar to the skis of 100 years ago, before skiing technology split into rigid downhill equipment and feather-light cross-country gear. My gear would, however, have to do everything: pull pulks fast across hard ice, climb uphill, turn on crusty snow, bounce over big sastrugi. The skis were strong, stable and light. As the slope steepened towards our first peak I put short kicker skins on. Some of the others had alpine touring bindings, which had the advantage of being suitable for ice-climbing boots, thereby avoiding a boot change.

At the foot of the peak, I changed into my climbing boots and donned my pack, crampons, climbing harness and helmet. We roped up into two groups of four, with Paul, Mike, me and Geoff in the lead group. The familiar sound of climbing hardware jangling off our harness loops filled the air. This is climbers' music, and status is enhanced by having a big array of weaponry jangling and clinking. In the past it had to look beat-up and battle-scarred, but now the trend is for gear to look new and shiny, with the highest-tech gadgetry on display. Ropes slung over shoulders, an ice axe in each hand, a helmet and black clothing complete the look. In my view Paul came out on top because his gear was so neatly racked in rows off his belt loops, or clipped neatly onto his pack. He looked the leader.

Pulks and skis were soon dots back down on the ice as we climbed steadily up a steep, crispy snow face. Snow turned to ice and we were soon front-pointing, plunging two ice axes into the hard-packed snow. We crossed a large bergschrund, and my right leg shot though the crust, leaving me suspended over the void by my crutch. Paul told me in his unflappable Yorkshire tones that this was to be expected, nothing to worry about. I peeked down and saw below me a translucent blue cavern, beautiful and breathtaking. No one else wanted to look inside it, though. Soon we were on top of the peak, awestruck by what we saw; it was hard to believe that no one before us had ever seen this stunning view.

Midnight cast long blue shadows across the mountains and ice fields. The sun circled around us every day; low in the north at midnight, then heading east, to a noon high in the south a bit higher above the horizon, then a long swoop down to the west and north – always going to the right, round and round incessantly, day after day. I shuddered at the thought of winter here – permanent black, screaming blizzards. Temperatures on the ice cap have been known to drop to −70°C (−94°F).

We climbed down across a col, and up to our next peak. Ahead was a rock chimney, which we dry-tooled. Seven of us made it to the top. Paul was a bit less unflappable on the summit ridge: 'If we go right, we'll make it to the top; if we go left, there'll be four dead climbers. If one falls off, we all go.'

In the morning, as we skied back in a crispy −10°C (14°F) across the sastrugi back to Base Camp, I was tiring. I slept until noon, then spent the day skiing and doing camp chores. My GPS told me we were at 68°11.521'N,

Under the midnight sun en route for Peaks 5 and 6

33°59.783'W, altitude 2,095 metres, and the compass variation was 28°W – we were close to the Magnetic North Pole. My watch told me the temperature, the barometric pressure, the compass bearing and the altitude. I was breathing steam in the warm sun. I also got acquainted with our toilet, a deep ditch built by Geoff in the ice, with a protective ice-block wall surround. Jon and Tim were busy building a restaurant with the ice saw and snow shovels.

Next night, we climbed a snow peak. It was hard work, and I was glad of my training, as I was huffing and puffing to the limit. We could see 50 miles in all directions, an area of around 8,000 square miles. We approached a second rock peak, but it was too exposed and dangerous, demanding multiple complex belayed pitches. We front-pointed up another ice slope to a rocky ridge. I refuelled with hot fruit juice from my thermos, and liquid carbohydrate. We were surrounded by rock walls and bergschrunds. Then we skied over to two huge wind scoops. Our return to Base Camp was into a blazing midnight sun and a light katabatic wind; the ice cap was −30°C (−22°F), and the wind was dropping under its own weight, accelerating down the ice slope to the sea.

During the day at Base Camp, Jon trained us in the use of some really amazing state-of-the-art mountain emergency medical equipment. Geoff was soon laid out with pneumatic splints and traction devices for broken legs, among a frightening array of needles and medical instruments arranged on the ice. Tim was eyeing an ice saw by one of the tents, no doubt thinking it would come in useful for an amputation.

Next night, we went for Peak 5, also named by us the Tooth, a rather forbidding-looking challenge shaped like the Matterhorn. It was a long haul with my pulk up a series of traverses on a big slope covered in large sastrugi. We changed to climbing gear at a pass, kicked steps up a 45-degree snow slope, then front-pointed up a 60-degree ice pitch. Paul wedged several nuts into cracks in a rock buttress, then hammered and screwed in ice screws for protection. When he belayed me, I knew it was going to be tough. The ice cracked and shattered as I plunged my axes into it. Below this crust was hard, sticky ice that looked bombproof, and the main problem was getting the axes out of it. While doing this, with all my weight on my front points, the ice around my foothold collapsed and I came loose. I put my weight on the axes as they ground into the ice in a slow-motion self-arrest. The others were watching from below, waiting their turn on this playground. It was no place for an accident; there were no medical facilities within air range, and to do a medevac we would have to get our Twin Otter back from Iceland. Then we were on top, with endless views over the ice cap, an awesome expanse of rolling, undulating, frozen waste – an ice desert reaching a thickness of 2 miles.

We traversed over to a second peak, and I repeated my trick of breaking through a snow bridge. Jon went in as well, but again only waist-deep. We kept our ropes tight between us in case of a crevasse fall. The peak had very loose, fractured gneiss, and Paul rolled some big rocks off so as not to risk a rock fall injuring one of us. As they rumbled down the ice gully and disappeared from view, the effect was to rub in our altitude and exposed location. It really was dramatic.

On the way back, one of the pulks failed, with an arm ripped out and beyond repair. Paul came up with an ingenious solution: lashing it to the back of another pulk. Geoff then hauled both of them, and took the next day off to recover.

After a long and deep sleep, I skied alone in the afternoon to a big, steep mountain, and enjoyed the solitude and the silence, which was absolute and total – something virtually impossible to find in normal life.

Beaten by the ice

That night, we attempted Peak 7. Paul, Mike and I were on the lead rope, and we reached a rock buttress at the top of a long snow slog. Paul worked his way up a very steep ice pitch, hammering and screwing in ice screws along the way. Another rock outcrop on the right allowed him to install some more reliable protection, then we were onto a very steep 60–70-degree ice climb, which felt almost vertical. At the top on the left was another rock outcrop. Paul had anchored onto this with a bombproof set of nuts and chocks, and once he'd belayed me up there I could see why; we were perched on a ledge with everything dropping away the other side to a near-vertical cliff above the glacier below.

Above us was a steep snow slope. Paul chipped the crust off with his axe to reveal hard blue ice below. 'There's nothing to grab hold of for protection,' he said. This was a blow, after all the hard work getting there.

'Can we have a go?' I asked.

'I think the whole slope could slide off the ice and then we'd all go over the edge.'

I looked down the cliff below and imagined all three of us free-falling off the edge, still tied together. 'Sounds like it's off?'

'Afraid so; if we tried it we could have some unhappy families. Trouble is, you never know what you're going to get until you get there.'

On the way down the ice pitches were even harder; it was difficult to see where to kick my front points in, and the ice was splintering and shattering everywhere. My crampons were not biting well, but my axes, an old battle-scarred 58 cm one and a new 65 cm one, were the opposite – after two hard plunges they grabbed so hard that I'd struggle to get them out. I had to work them loose and pull them upwards from the axe head, relying on my crampons to keep me stuck to the face. The others had newer, reverse-curved short axes, which were much better, but I'd chosen not to buy any, as Paul, in his usual optimistic manner, had assured me in England that all the peaks would be walkable. Maybe he meant 'Paul walkable'. Peak 7 had beaten all of us.

Peak 8 was a rock scramble to the top, and we did it unroped. I led the way, and named it Mount Michael, after my son. On the way, we were astounded to find a piece of lichen, about a millimetre thick and a centimetre across, growing on a rock. We all took turns looking at it. It was all on its own, seemingly 100 miles from any other life. We'd not seen any vegetation anywhere else. It was the only living thing we saw on the entire expedition.

The ski back was a nightmare. The sastrugi were hard and crusty at the surface but soft in the middle, so I kept digging my tips in and falling. Worse, the pulks had no brakes, and often pushed me into trouble. But my gear was great, the boots preventing injury, and my tough clothing survived the abrasive ice stoically. I found that the best technique down the sastrugi was telemarking: front knee bent, and back foot trailing and steering. The skies became overcast and the mood menacing as the midnight sun disappeared. My watch barometer showed the pressure falling. At Base Camp, I had a glass of port from my aluminium water bottle and then crashed until 1400.

When I awoke, the sun was burning me through the tent and was so bright I needed my glacier goggles on inside. This triggered another migraine, probably caused by a combination of rarefied air (775 mb, which is 25 per cent less than at sea level), dehydration (even though I'd been drinking loads of melted ice), and intense glare from the sun, doubled up by the ice reflecting. I'd been sunburned under my chin, inside my mouth and inside my nose from this reflected radiation. It had split Geoff's nose in two.

The sun was also evaporating the snow around my tent. I could never get the sun to melt any snow in my cooking pots, even in the middle of the day – the snow simply sublimated or evaporated into the dry air. We were all constantly busy shovelling snow around the tents to protect them in the event of a blizzard.

That night, we left at 2300, heading off on a bearing of 325 magnetic, at a punishing pace in a rising wind. A steep snow climb and a rock scramble brought us to the top of Peak 9. Paul led down a steep ice pitch in a gully, placing lots of nuts, chocks and ice screws. Tina could not continue, as the icy wind had chilled her to the point of being unable to operate the carabiners clipping onto the protection, so the second group headed back. Our group of four made it to the bottom of the ice gully and across to a steep snow ridge.

This was dangerous, with a rocky cliff below it to the left and a continuous bergschrund to the right, sometimes 20 feet wide across its jaws. 'We'll stay roped up,' Paul stated, 'but no one must slip, because if one of us goes, we all go. This is the most common form of death on a climb: being pulled off a traverse.'

'Then why rope up?' I asked.

'Good question,' was his answer. 'Pros and cons. You can't self-arrest on this crusty stuff, so if you're on your own you've had it. If we're roped up, one of us *might* be able to dig in, or jump off the other side of the ridge. If not, well … as I said, no one must slip.'

We stayed on the ridge to allow us to jump off the other side and manage this balancing act, but soon it was too sharp and crusty, and we had to drop down the right side. This was the dangerous bit – there was nowhere to

Mike, Paul, PC and Geoff on top of Peak 9

put in an anchor, except perhaps if we used a deadman or snow picket. After a kilometre on the ridge, we reached rock and hard ice, which allowed us to use proper protection.

At the top, it was blowing hard. I named it Mount Richard after my second son. Geoff was looking very cold from behind his black duvet hood, only his eyes showing in the icy blasts.

After an even worse ridge climb back to Peak 9 on account of the blustery wind, we got to the ice gully, which we climbed. I dropped a carabiner from numbed fingers inside my thick gloves, and it clattered down the ice gully onto the glacier below. I gave Paul one of mine to compensate him for the loss of his, but he didn't like it – 'Too old and beat up.' It had a 30-year history and looked it. Paul regarded it as a liability. After that I lost confidence in it, and when I returned to the UK I binned it.

The ski back was fast and downhill, with the pulks clattering across big sastrugi and the wind whipping our faces.

It was a cold day at Base Camp, and the tents flapped and shook with the wind, making sleep difficult. The toilet was also more of a challenge and best done quickly – hanging around too long could invite a nasty frostbite in a sensitive area. The view between the nunataks onto the ice cap made up, however, for its spartan nature. The cookers blew out. Everything was harder, including the ice.

Next night, Tina, Dave, Mike and I skied around the back of the big mountain north of us, past an extraordinary jumble of ice cubes the size of office blocks, presumably thrown up by the ice cap as it skirted the mountain and started funnelling into the glacier. In between these cubes were wide chasms. We kept our distance from them, as we were not roped up in this crevassed area. Then we were on the ice cap, which undulated gently to the horizon. On the far side of the mountain we found a huge wind scoop, with edges near-vertical, over 100 feet deep. Not a good place to fall into. We were skiing without pulks, as we didn't have to carry climbing gear, and covered the miles quickly all night. In the morning the temperature dropped, and we had a vigorous ski traverse, then a climb around a crevassed area back to Base Camp. My tent was iced up inside as I fell into a deep

On the edge of the icecap

sleep, but it didn't feel cold – my clothing was that good. I thought of Nansen and his colleagues inside their tent, which did not keep out the snow or wind, snuggled up together in their reindeer fur sleeping bags.

Flying out of Greenland

Next day, I tried to get out a week ahead of the rest so as to get back to work in Tanzania. Paul had arranged for the ski-plane to land and pick me up, then fly 150 miles north-east to the Watkins mountains, where England footballer Ian Wright and a Sky TV crew were filming an ascent of Gunnbjørn Fjeld. The bad weather had caused whiteouts over Greenland, and the pilots were out of hours. We spent two days flattening the ice airstrip with skis, shovels and pulks, thereby convincing Bjarki he wouldn't smash up his plane on landing.

That night, I enjoyed the Arctic peace and quiet in Base Camp. Dave and Mike were climbing a ridge a mile away, and I could hear them talking and relaying messages to each other. We'd been a great team. There were no difficult characters, there had been no raised voices. None of us was in this for fame or glory, but rather the sheer pleasure of climbing in a pristine area in a world where some of the best mountaineering areas are now crowded. Even Antarctica is teeming with adventure tourists. We wondered if anyone would ever come here again.

Next day, the plane could fly, having overnighted at Constable Point, but there was a whiteout. Bjarki radioed that he wanted our hand-built runway marked with skis. Paul lit an orange smoke flare. We heard the plane, and then suddenly it appeared, dropping steeply, and crabbing onto our airstrip in the crosswind: a brilliant landing. The props missed our vertical skis by inches, and then we were off, without time even for a farewell.

The flight to Gunnbørn Fjeld was magnificent: icefalls, huge crevasses, long wide glaciers, icebergs in sparkling fjords with patches of deep blue water, mountains of basaltic lava in huge horizontal black sheets stretched out below us.

We picked up the Wright team, exuberant from their conquest, and heard Ian saying how difficult it had been. 'It was so hard, and too cold. It was a hard trip.' Ian had a great footballing record: he was the top striker in Arsenal's history, England's most expensive player when he was transferred to Arsenal, and an England striker with 30 caps. The ascent had been filmed by Keith Partridge, the world's leading mountaineering cameraman (who had filmed the epic 2003 docudrama *Touching the Void*, based on Joe Simpson's true story of survival), and was broadcast on Sky TV.

We all flew back via Iceland, savouring the richness of the Greenland experience. Where else was there a better place to have an adventure?

Back at Kangerdlugssuaq, the others climbed for another week. The day they were due to fly out the plane couldn't make it due to more damage. Next day, a storm came down and lasted five days. Their tents were almost buried under a metre of snow. It was permanent whiteout. Tina's tent split down the middle. Geoff built an 'Icehenge', and posed in front of it with his ice axes crossed to honour his Welsh home and the Druids. Cookers were brought inside the tents, books read and re-read. The storm was set to stay, but a five-hour window allowed Bjarki to land in a spectacular cloud of powder and evacuate them all.

A few months later, Paul emailed me with news of the first-ever winter ascent of Gunnbjørn Fjeld, the world's highest Arctic mountain. Mountaineers had been trying to do this for years but had been driven back by the extreme conditions. Paul's team made it to the top in −40°C/F conditions, then were attacked by a polar bear on their last night at Base Camp. The bear severely damaged three tents and was driven off with flares and much noise and banging of pans, but then it returned, to be scared off again by the 'bear watch', which continued until daybreak. Another great first!

9 Mountaineering in unexplored Antarctica

We were attempting the first ascent of Rogers Peak in an unexplored region of Antarctica, and we were faced by an ice cliff of over 100 metres high, on top of a steep escarpment. We couldn't climb it. so we climbed a snow slope to the right of it, and then worked our way above a long thin bergschrund. This was the highest crevasse of the climb; above it the ice was attached to the rock and below it the ice was slowly sliding downhill.

As we gained elevation the surface steepened and became loose ice on top of iron-hard, solid ice. If I slipped I'd pull Simon off, and we'd both slide into the bergschrund, with the risk of breaking legs. Or if we bounced over it and couldn't self-arrest we'd then slide over the top of the cliff and fly through the air in a 200-metre free fall. I was acutely conscious of what another climber had told me: 'Antarctica is a place where an adventure can become a crisis and then a disaster in a matter of seconds.'

Antarctic legends

It was at prep school that I had first become fascinated by Antarctica. Outside a dormitory called The Cabin hung a picture that had mesmerised me. It was entitled 'A Very Gallant Gentleman': Captain Titus Oates, slowed by an old war wound and gangrene, stumbling in the dark to certain death into a fierce Antarctic blizzard, to allow his comrades in the tent (shown in the background) to move faster to their supply depot. It was 16 March 1912. Back in the tent were Captain Robert Scott, Dr Edward Wilson and Henry Bowers. Scott's diary recorded Oates' famous last words: 'I'm just going outside and may be some time.' Scott wrote that Oates' regiment would have been proud of him.

The men had been on their way back from the South Pole. The three survivors managed a few more miles, until they too died in another blizzard, only 11 miles from the supply depot, stocked with fuel and food that could have saved them. With no fuel, they couldn't melt snow to drink. Hypothermia and frostbite soon set in.

The weather that autumn has since been determined as a once-in-a-century anomaly, with temperatures reaching −40°C/F at sea level at the end of the Antarctic summer, some 20 degrees colder than normal in that area. At the Scott Polar Research Institute in Cambridge, UK, I read the original copies of the team's final letters home, written a few days before they died. They were full of praise and respect for each other, and encouraged their loved ones to forgive them and get on with their lives. They were written neatly, obviously the result of clear minds and charitable thoughts, and not a hint of blame. It is hard to imagine such sentiments in today's world.

The *Titanic* sank two weeks later, again in an extremely low temperature anomaly, related to abnormally low solar radiation – much lower than today. These two disasters meant that 1912 was a bad year for Britain; later, they were often blamed on the British arrogance of the time, following a century of global domination as the world's supreme superpower, ruling the largest empire in history, spanning a quarter of the world's population and land areas.

But then the two world wars destroyed Britain's economy and contributed to the brain drain. In addition, those wars, and the appallingly violent aftermath of the Second World War, set back all of Europe, allowing the USSR and USA to move in and take over after five centuries of European world domination.

Many years later, I went to the Oates Museum in Selborne, Hants, where some of Scott's possessions were displayed. The display was very moving: the letters to his mother; the light cotton clothing they wore, flimsy and ineffective compared with modern gear; a long heavy wooden sledge; canned rations (no vitamin C) and snow goggles; movie footage of them manhauling their sledge, sinking waist-deep in the snow; photos of them at the South Pole. This saga was set up as an example to troops in the trenches in the First World War, who were expected to sacrifice their lives for their colleagues and the nation.

In school debates I would often tell the Scott story. In the Britain of 1960, he was still seen as a hero, whereas other Antarctic explorers such as Amundsen and Shackleton were considered less so. Then in 1979 Roland Huntford published *Scott and Amundsen*, glorifying the latter and demolishing Scott; this coincided with an era in which British self-confidence was at an all-time low. However, attitudes were about to change; Margaret Thatcher became prime minister that year, then North Sea oil turned the British economy around, and a couple of wars were fought and won, so over the next three decades British self-esteem bounced back.

The British explorer Sir Ranulph Fiennes later broke a number of polar records including, with Dr Mike Stroud, the first unsupported crossing of the Antarctic continent in 1992–93. It was an amazing achievement, as they'd each hauled 485 lb, more than double the amount each man in Scott's teams had hauled. I met both of them after their return.

As usual, there was the media outcry: 'Why do it?' For Fiennes, it's because he makes his living as a travel writer; millions of people buy his books and find his stories inspirational – good enough reason in itself. For Dr Stroud, an expert on human health under extreme conditions, his medical discoveries from data gathered on the trip have been invaluable. A normal daily calorie intake for an adult is around 2,500 calories. Scott's expedition diet had allowed his team to take in around 4,500 calories/day – about half what it has turned out was actually needed for manhauling; on their expedition Fiennes' and Stroud's daily energy expenditure had exceeded 10,000 calories while over the expedition their fat and cholesterol levels dropped. The implications of these results for a normal person's health management are profound, as we now know that high fat and cholesterol can be burned off with rigorous exercise – which Stroud also believes slows down the ageing process.

In 2003 Fiennes and Stroud were also the first to complete seven marathons on seven continents in seven days. Mount Vinson in Antarctica is one of the seven summits of the seven continents. By 2007 the seven summits records for both men and women were held by British mountaineers Andrew Salter and Joanne Gambi. At the time of writing, most polar records are held by British, American or Norwegian expeditions, preserving the competitive nature of this sport over the last century. Many of the advances in outdoor gear for the average person come as a result of these expeditions. Plus, as always, the expedition sagas make great fireside reading.

The second inspiration for my fascination with Antarctica came from my second boarding school. It was another painting: Dr Edward Wilson, sketching with a glove off as his huskies relaxed around his sledge. When I went up to Cambridge I felt delighted to be following in his footsteps. Wilson had effectively been Scott's second in command on both his first expedition (1901–04) and his second expedition (1910–13). He was a doctor, artist and scientist, drawn to Antarctica by his fascination with new discoveries. He was the central, stable figure, welding the individuals into a team and affectionately known as Uncle Bill.

On the first expedition, Wilson, Scott and Ernest Shackleton got about halfway to the Pole from their base, the furthest south of any expedition. On the second, Wilson led a party of three to Cape Crozier to collect emperor penguin eggs for research into his theory that birds were descended from dinosaurs. The trip had to be done in the middle of winter due to the incubation pattern of the embryos, so it was probably the toughest polar expedition ever completed. It was pitch-black the entire time, and the men travelled by the light of candle lanterns. They relayed their two sledges in two batches, thus covering three times the apparent distance. Temperatures dropped to below −59°C (−75°F). A blizzard blew their tent away, leaving them huddled on top of their unfitted groundsheet. When they left base, their fur sleeping bags weighed 10 lb each. When they returned, they weighed 40 lb each, the extra 30 lb solid ice, which never melted and grew thicker every day. It's hard to imagine today's explorers being tough enough to survive that sort of hardship.

Wilson regarded getting to the Pole as only one of the expedition's objectives, rather than the main one, and was not troubled by Amundsen's arrival there a month earlier. He collected rock samples with plant fossils on the way back, which proved crucial in the understanding of both Antarctica's past and the planet's history, especially continental drift and plate tectonics. Sadly, much of the material brought back was neither analysed nor published for many decades; his theory wasn't accepted until the 1990s. Had Wilson survived that second expedition, it's possible that dinosaur-to-bird evolution and plate tectonic theory would have been advanced by half a century.

Their tent and their bodies are now buried under the Antarctic ice, moving slowly towards the sea. A memorial to them in Antarctica reads 'To strive, to seek, to find, and not to yield'.

Early expeditions

Antarctica has an amazing history; some of its rocks date to 3 billion years ago. It separated from South America 20 million years ago, and cooled. The Scott party brought back samples of coal, indicating its forested past. It only became its current high, icebound shape with the onset of the ice ages 3 million years ago. It is now the highest, driest, windiest and coldest continent. The ice sheet averages 1.6 miles thick. It is the world's largest desert, with precipitation at levels similar to that of the Sahara. Temperatures have been known to drop as low as −91°C (−132°F). Its largest land animal is the size of a flea, and is found in coastal areas only. The only animals larger than this are either marine creatures or birds, both of which can escape the freezing climate if needed and return to repopulate. In the interior, no creature lives.[32]

In the middle of the last ice age, from about 115,000 to 12,000 years ago, there was much more ice cover than now, causing the sea levels to be 100 metres lower. In between the ice ages (about every 100,000 years) the West Antarctic ice sheet melted, raising sea levels about 30 metres above today's levels. Humankind may have survived some 20 of these ice age cycles. The same will happen again as a result of natural causes related to the orbit of the earth and associated ice age cycles, probably within 50,000 years, irrespective of any human efforts to reduce global warming.

The ice sheet discharges through many glaciers, many of them gouging paths up to 40 miles wide through the Transantarctic Mountains. Icebergs can be up to 150 miles long and drift for six years, sometimes as far northwards as 26 degrees of latitude, almost to the tropics.

It was in 1773 that Captain Cook was the first person to cross the Antarctic Circle. Antarctica itself was first visited in around 1820. Over the next century, British ships dominated the ongoing quest: partly imperial, partly scientific and navigational, partly commercial, mostly whaling. Scott's 1901–04 expedition was the first to venture inland to any degree, using dogs on the first attempt at the Pole. His team was the first to get onto the polar plateau. In 2001 I went to Dundee to see his ship, the *Discovery*; it was much smaller than I'd expected, and he had relied mainly on sail power to reduce the need for coal on those long voyages.

In 1907–09 Ernest Shackleton got to within 97 miles of the Pole, discovering the huge Beardmore Glacier – the gateway through the Transantarctic Mountains to the polar ice sheet. He turned back in order to have enough

---

32 Other than the human researchers in their artificial environment.

provisions to make it home, thus avoiding certain death. As it was, the team only just made it, being unable to reach key depots; scouts were sent ahead to bring supplies back to the sledge party. Shackleton later said to his wife that he thought she'd rather have 'a live donkey than a dead lion'. His team also climbed Mount Erebus, the first significant Antarctic climb, to 3,800 metres, even though they lacked suitable gear and they hauled their sledges up steep slopes on hands and knees. Having no rucksacks, they then carried their equipment in their arms on a five-day climb to the erupting summit crater.

In 1910 Amundsen set off for Antarctica, having fooled his team and the media into believing that he was going to the North Pole. He reached the South Pole on 14 December 1911. He got there a month earlier than Scott due to an earlier start (12 days prior), a slightly shorter journey (by 80 miles / seven days), and faster speeds (about 10 per cent), using dogs – more effective than Scott's expedition, which employed dogs, ponies, mechanical sledges (at that time state-of-the-art, as military tanks would not be developed until 1915) and manpower in various proportions. With them he brought a vehicle mechanic, a horseman, a dog handler and a Norwegian ski instructor. Ponies worked best for the British, although eight were lost when sea ice broke up and killer whales harassed the party. Neither ponies nor dogs could be safely taken across the Beardmore Glacier crevasses (many dogs and ponies had been lost in crevasses), so for the bulk of the trip they relied on manhauling, which had proven fast and effective in previous Scott and Shackleton expeditions.

Scott knew that if Amundsen found a way across the Transantarctic Mountains he would get to the Pole first. And Scott, with fewer dogs in his team, knew he would not be able to match the Norwegian's speed. Had he expected a race, he would undoubtedly have secured more dogs, handlers and strong skiers before departing. He had planned a trip of 144 days, and by 139 days they had covered 95 per cent of the journey, but were then stopped by an extreme blizzard. Frostbite and hypothermia killed them.

Amundsen's planning had been meticulous, and his prior experiences with the Inuit in the Arctic had taught him crucial skills, especially in dog-handling. In 1905 he had been the first to navigate the length of the Northwest Passage, with a crew of seven in a small fishing vessel. Much larger expeditions had tried and failed for 400 years.

He had to get back from his South Pole expedition before 1912, as he'd forgotten to bring the 1912 nautical almanac for astronomical sight reduction calculations, and the 1911 copy had caught fire, miraculously with the last quarter saved. At that time, navigation was by theodolite, and the almanac's tables were essential.

A common thread among these early explorers was the financial challenge. Scott, Shackleton and Amundsen had all met with family setbacks when they were young, plunging the family into financial stress. The Victorian financial system was very unforgiving, with no welfare services, and the debtor's prison a likely outcome for unpaid debts. Raising the money for expeditions was as difficult then as it is now.

However, Scott's wife, Kathleen, insisted that he do the expedition; polar success would ensure glory and fame, and even in 1910 wealth through lecture tours, book rights and film rights. It would also inspire confidence in the next expedition. Money for expeditions came mostly from private investors, occasionally with some government funding, as in Scott's case. In the event, both Amundsen and Scott departed on their South Pole journeys in debt, with insufficient funds raised to cover the costs, hoping to raise the balance on a successful return. There is a myth surrounding an advertisement apparently placed by Shackleton in *The Times* prior to his 1907 *Nimrod* expedition to Antarctica:

> Men wanted for hazardous journey. Small wages, bitter cold, long months of complete darkness, constant danger, safe return doubtful. Honour and recognition in case of success.

Scott also saw these expeditions as a means to faster career growth in the Navy, along with the associated higher income.

Expedition failure could therefore cause serious financial disaster, and the leader would be held accountable for this. Scott's diary entries included a note relating to a request he'd made to the public to prevent the families being held accountable for investor repayments; the public had responded enthusiastically, raising more than enough funds (£75,000, or £3.4 million in today's money) to repay the investors. The surplus was then used to set up the Scott Polar Research Institute in Cambridge, still active today.

The Scott team was, however, the last to stand on the Pole itself for another 44 years.

In 1911 Australian Douglas Mawson landed on the other side of the continent, at Commonwealth Bay, where katabatic winds reach 200 miles per hour, nearly three times hurricane force 12, which is 74 mph on the Saffir–Simpson scale. This is indeed a windy area, with hurricane-force winds 20 per cent of the time (and 30 per cent in winter).

Mawson had planned to survey this unexplored side of the continent. He survived an amazing 600-mile saga, travelling with two companions and dog teams. One man was lost down a crevasse with his dog team, sledge, most of the food and their only tent. The second man died on the return to base, only 100 miles away. They had been surviving by eating the dogs. Mawson struggled on, sawing his sledge in half with a pocket knife to lighten the load, and desperately trying to get back before his ship, the *Aurora*, left for the winter. He made it back to base, only to find that the ship had left six hours before. But his planning had paid off; a few members of his original party had waited for him at base camp, and there they sat through the winter – their second on the continent – to be rescued the following spring.

In 1914 Shackleton returned to Antarctica, intending to cross the continent. The survival story is still an epic, and is used in management schools for lessons in motivating people in desperate situations. First, the *Endurance* was trapped and crushed by pack ice before she reached the shore. Ten months later she sank, having drifted 500 miles north. The men, having decamped, lived another five months on the ice, then manhauled, rowed and sailed three lifeboats to an icy Elephant Island. As they would have all died there unless rescued, Shackleton took an incredible gamble: he and five others sailed in one of their lifeboats, the *James Caird*, the 800 miles to South Georgia across the stormy Southern Ocean in winter. Leaks in the decking were so bad that the men were only saved when those leaks froze up in the huge seas. Rare glimpses of the sun allowed sextant shots. Eventually they made landfall – but on South Georgia's southern shore, so they had to cross the island to reach a whaling station at Grytviken. This had never been done before, due to glaciers, crevasses and 200-metre mountains. Three of the men crossed it in a 36-hour dash, at one point glissading thousands of metres down an icy snow slope as they'd expected to freeze to death if they stayed at altitude any longer than absolutely necessary. Finally they had to descend a 150-metre ice cliff, as steep as a church spire, cutting steps and using their ropes in stages.

Meanwhile, on the other side of Antarctica, *Aurora* had dropped her party off on the Ross Sea side, to lay depots for the *Endurance* party. The *Aurora* was anchored to the mainland with wire hawsers, but they snapped in a blizzard. She was then frozen in, and drifted north for 10 months. She eventually returned to New Zealand, but she had unloaded virtually no provisions or equipment for the shore party, so while they were able to use the huts from Scott's and Shackleton's previous expeditions, in the absence of adequate food they had to slaughter 500 seals a year, knifing them at their breathing holes. The men kept the huts warm by burning seal blubber, which covered everything in thick-black greasy soot. In this way they survived three years, with the loss of three men, and despite their privations laid all the depots for the *Endurance* party – which of course never arrived.

Shackleton, once at Grytviken, organised the relief expeditions to Elephant Island and the Ross Sea group, and got the rest of his men back safely; he has been internationally idolised as a leader of men ever since. In truth, all of these men – including Scott, Amundsen and Nansen – were outstanding leaders and explorers, and they all had their share of firsts: Nansen was first across Greenland; Scott had gone furthest south and was first to explore the Antarctic ice sheet; Shackleton was first within 100 miles of the South Pole; and Amundsen was first both through the Northwest Passage, and to the South Pole. Scott, Shackleton and Amundsen all died on polar expeditions. Each one benefited from the pioneering work and knowledge developed by their predecessors, each gruelling expedition leapfrogging an earlier one to take a step further.

More recent explorations

In November 1929 US naval officer Richard E. Byrd flew over the South Pole in a biplane; he had made it over the top of the glacier leading to the ice sheet by jettisoning hundreds of pounds of provisions, and his exploit gained him the rank of rear admiral. After the Second World War the US embarked on a massive military training and mapping exercise, partly to prepare for a potential Arctic war in the Cold War era. As a result, it is the USA that now has the biggest presence on the continent.

Until the 1970s Antarctica was still virtually unknown. In the 1950s most of the continent, an area bigger than the USA, had never been seen by anyone at all. Mount Vinson, at 4,900 metres (16,100 feet) its highest peak, and Lambert Glacier, the world's largest, were only discovered in that decade. In 1957, Sir Vivian Fuchs led the Commonwealth Transantarctic Expedition 2,158 miles across the continent, conducting seismic surveys along the way to determine the ice thickness and the topography of its buried mountains. For the reconnaissance parties they used tracked vehicles, which had many crevasse accidents, and dogsleds.

What has humanity gained from all these expeditions? Fascinating, inspiring stories read by millions, development of outdoor clothing, skiing equipment and snowmobiles, and, as mentioned above, scientific advances, which have led to understanding of plate tectonics and continental drift, climate change, data on global pollution and so on.

In 1961 the Antarctic Treaty came into effect, preserving the continent's status, without national ownership, for peaceful and scientific purposes only, with military and commercial use prohibited. In the 1990s non-indigenous animals, including dogs, were banned from Antarctica, and all current travel is either manhauled or mechanical (typically snowmobiles or planes).

By the new millennium, there were some 4,000 scientists stationed at various bases across the continent, mostly in the summer months along the coast. Few, if any, of these bases are ever accessible to visitors. The observations and experiments have been instrumental in researching climate change over the last 400,000 years, and in identifying the hole in the ozone layer.

Some 20,000 tourists visit the continent annually, almost all of them by cruise ship to the Antarctic Peninsula, south of Cape Horn. Only 200 visitors venture to the interior, and most of these go via Antarctic Logistics and Expeditions (ALE), the only non-government base on the continent. ALE was started up by three British and two Australian managers specialising in Antarctic logistics, mountaineering and environmental services. Access is only by air to ALE's summer camp at Patriot Hills, some 670 miles from the South Pole. From there, explorers can take a Twin Otter ski-plane to other locations. However, the cost of this trip is staggering. The fuel alone is amazingly expensive; Fiennes quoted in 1993 that a 45-gallon drum which sold for $120 in Punta Arenas would cost $6,000 in Patriot Hills and $24,000 at the Pole. In the interior of the continent the temporary population density is around one person per 5,000 square miles, and those that stay are never there for more than a couple of years, so the permanent population density is effectively zero. Greenland is normally held up as the least densely populated country on earth, at 14 square miles per person, yet it is 350 times more densely populated than Antarctica – which then in winter is about one-twentieth of the levels in the brief summer months, just a few scientists in pitch darkness and raging blizzards, taking measurements and having an unforgettable experience.

Preparing for the expedition

In 2007 I decided I'd go to Patriot Hills. But first, how to get to there? I read every account I could and found that ALE had a Russian cargo plane on charter, an Ilyushin 76. Written accounts, including that of Sir Ranulph Fiennes, emphasised the basic nature of this mode of travel and the terrifying landings on the blue ice. Ninety-five per cent of the time the weather was too bad to fly (usually too much wind, or whiteout), so you can be waiting up to 2–3 weeks for the flight; the problem was that the only reason the blue ice strip was ever clear of snow was because of the prevailing, and very strong, winds. I did some more research and found that of some 960 Ilyushin 76s built, 41 had crashed in the last 15 years. That meant that 1 in 20 had crashed – far from encouraging. Add to that the world's stormiest waters in the area south of Cape Horn, the windswept blue ice strip at the other end, severe downdrafts, crosswinds, risk of whiteouts, and a large mountain alongside the ice strip, and you have a pilot's nightmare.

Next on the list, I needed better gear. My Greenland kit was good for −20°C (−4°F), and revolved around a set of plastic ski boots with cable bindings, with another set of leather climbing boots, which required a changeover every time I went from pulk hauling with skis to climbing with crampons. This wouldn't be feasible in Antarctica, at −30°C (−22°C) and with the strong katabatic winds, storms and blizzards expected. I had to get a single set of boots for both duties. I plumped for La Sportiva Olympus Mons boots, which are triple-layered and good for Everest. I also bought Silvretta 500 bindings, to be mounted on my new Hagan Tour Expert ski-mountaineering skis. I would carry three jackets, six hats and six sets of gloves for layering. Add to that a Himalayan down jacket, and I was set for any wind chill.

By 2006 I was finally ready to book the plane through ALE. The waiver made for sobering reading:

> Risks to air travel: the general lack of air traffic, air traffic control facilities and meteorological prediction facilities in Antarctica and the Sub-Antarctic region all mean that information normally available to aircrews is often unavailable. Search and rescue infrastructure is, of course, similarly limited. Delays of days or weeks must be anticipated … they cross first the stormy Drake Passage, then the Antarctic Peninsula region, notorious for its adverse climate. Hazardous, little known terrain covered in ice and snow that may disguise or completely obscure dangers such as unstable slopes and crevasses; extreme weather conditions that can change rapidly and without warning; extreme low temperatures that, particularly when compounded by strong winds, can have rapid and adverse effects on the human body and its metabolism; storms frequently occur that can prevent local flights from departing and at times, even prohibit anyone from leaving their tent.

It was made clear that I would have to pay for any emergency evacuation. I didn't know how much it would cost to get an Ilyushin 76 emergency medevac back to Punta, but their Twin Otter was offered at a special discount price of $10,000 per hour. A round trip to Punta would be about 24 hours, or $240,000 – and that was the cheapest plane! Bonnie asked what I wanted done with my body in the event of accident. I said it should be flown home if practicable and if that made economic sense, but if it was at the bottom of a crevasse that would obviously be impracticable, and that would have to be my grave.

I got in contact with Nick Lewis, who was, like me, working in Africa in the oil industry, managing environmental work. He was a leading alpinist and mountaineer, and had survived a horrendous accident in the Ellsworth Mountains two years previously: falling when a snow slab came loose off hard ice in −45°C (−49°F) conditions, breaking his leg and ripping his pectoral muscle off his arm. He was now climbing again, thanks to carbon fibre and titanium repairs. He gave me some invaluable information and advice.

I also contacted Simon Garrod, who suggested climbing in a region east of the Driscoll Glacier, stating that this area, north of Union Glacier, 'had not seen too much traffic'. This, in Antarctic jargon, means that either no one had ever been there before or that 'traffic' referred to an expedition of two people that had passed close by a decade previously, with no one before or since. This area would, then, allow me to experience a true Antarctic wilderness, some first ascents, some first routes, and tens of thousands of first footprints or ski tracks. Simon had previously worked for the British Antarctic Survey as base commander, and I offered to collect rock samples so as to do something useful rather than be in this pristine wilderness as just a tourist.

Simon and I were going to the Ellsworth Mountains, to the southern Heritage Range, where Mount Vinson was located. The Ellsworths had first been visited only a few years before the moon landing, in 1969, and while the Heritage Range had first been seen from the air in 1959, no one had set foot on it until 1961. Patriot Hills is 670 miles from the nearest habitation at the South Pole, and is 1,800 miles from the nearest town, Ushuaia in Tierra del Fuego.

I'd been in touch with Sarah Moses of Cancerbackup (now Macmillan), an excellent charity that had previously given our family some wonderful care and help. I was funding the Antarctic trip 100 per cent myself, and she told me that Cancerbackup would like to support my adventure. They put together some web pages with interactive maps, photos, blogs and fundraising info, and as a result donations soon started pouring in. Then I travelled to Cambridge to get more information from the Scott Polar Research Institute and the British Antarctic Survey, including all the travel reports from the region, three of them to the west of where we intended to go.

In 2007 as D-Day approached I ramped up my fitness programme, again on the step machine in the gym, resuming my Eiffel Tower equivalent in 13 minutes, sometimes with climbing boots on, dragging tyres through loose gravel (a polar travel tradition), and going up and down the local Blackdown Hills with my pack full of water bottles.

I pored over 200 black and white low-resolution aerial photos from the USGS, taken by the US Navy in the 1960s. The aircrews on these flights had been the first people to see these ranges. The most useful of these images were the obliques, but the mountains – often 25 miles away from the plane, at 5 miles up – showed up as just a few millimetres high. It was possible to pick out what could not be crossed – steep cliffs, icefalls, large crevasses over 8 metres wide – but it was impossible to read the surface: blue ice, steepness, smaller crevasses. In the event it turned out that what had looked feasible from the photos was often impossible to cross safely.

Most of the region we intended to explore east of the glacier had never been visited before, and none of its peaks attempted. Further east we couldn't find any evidence of exploration, but to the west of our intended route three parties had been through, two of them geological expeditions. Simon had led one of them (for which I'd gathered the trip reports in Cambridge). The advantage of this was that if the terrain prevented us getting through to the east we could be sure of a route to the west.

Getting to Antarctica

The journey to the Heritage Range involved five planes: the first one Heathrow to Miami, the second to Santiago in Chile, the third to Punta Arenas near Cape Horn, the fourth the Ilyushin 76 cargo plane to Patriot Hills at the southern end of the Ellsworths, and finally a Twin Otter ski-plane to the glacier.

On the first three legs, the main worry was losing one of my checked bags: two waterproof bags full of 300 items of expedition gear, and a ski bag. Around 3 per cent of bags carried by commercial flights are mislaid, so that made it a 9 per cent probability that I would lose one. I could only carry on one small bag of essential gear, so, since much of my gear could not be replaced in South America I wore as much as possible in Heathrow and Miami airports. This heavy-duty kit attracted some interest from the Heathrow baggage scanner staff, especially the shoe-scanner section; even more so in hot, humid Miami. Once through security, I would go into the gents as a mountaineer and come out as a tourist, with the heavy gear packed into another soft carry-on bag.

To my horror, my skis never arrived in Santiago, and the Chilean airline was unable to track them. There were no skis in Punta Arenas, so I cancelled my flight there – a big decision, as the Ilyushin left on a fixed schedule and the ticket for that flight was over $20,000, with no chance of booking a later flight. Over the weekend I had a frantic time in Santiago finding suitable skis, but succeeded in the end. Thankfully I had brought with me a spare set of my specialist bindings, so I located a mechanic in a surf shop who had the right drills – accurate to one-tenth of a millimetre – and gave him a copy of the installation instructions in Spanish. I also bought ski poles, a snow shovel, an ice saw and ski climbing skins. When I arrived at the airport, I discovered to my amazement that my original skis had shown up; they had been sent to the USA and from there to Buenos Aires, then on again, so now I had two sets.

I arrived in Punta Arenas on another back-to-back overnight flight; I had now been on the go non-stop for 49 hours. I was near the bottom of the world's longest country, 4,300 km, stretching from the tropics all the way to Cape Horn. Chile also claims part of Antarctica, stretching from what they call O'Higgins Land (after Chile's

194

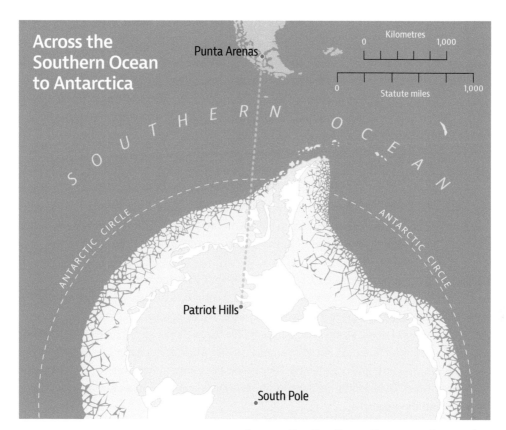

Across the Southern Ocean to Antarctica

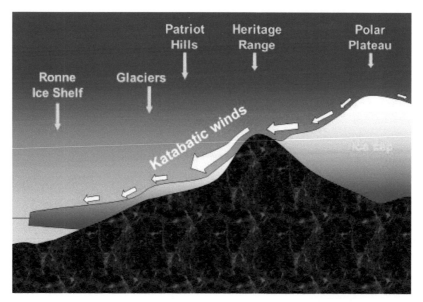

Katabatic winds

19th-century liberator from the Spanish) to the South Pole. It's impossible to drive the length of Chile, and the part where fjords and glaciers stretch from the ice cap to the coast is navigated by a weekly ferry full of cattle.

At Punta Arenas I met up with ALE staff members and Nick Lewis, who had helped me put the plans together. I met other adventurers due to fly out with me too, mostly Norwegians and Americans heading to Mount Vinson or the Pole. Two ALE staff checked all my gear: I wouldn't be allowed to fly on their plane unless I had everything on their list, in good condition. To get just this far I'd previously filled in a long medical and climbing experience questionnaire.

ALE informed me that the Ilyushin could not fly in the near future due to exceptional katabatic winds of up to 60 knots (70 mph) at Patriot Hills. However, all our gear was loaded so that the plane could get away at short notice. The temperature at Patriot Hills was −19°C (−2.2°F), or a wind chill of −44°C (−47°F). ALE warned us of severe frostbite, with 20 cases last year leading to amputations, skin grafts, loss of career, and even divorce due to loss of earnings capability. I learned of the deaths, broken bones, crevasse falls, storms and other sagas from previous years too. ALE advised us to wear full Antarctic clothing in transit on the plane in case it crash-landed in a remote area.

Then followed a nine-day wait in Punta Arenas for a weather window, with three daily 'skeds', at 0630, 1000 and 1800 hours, often putting us on a one-hour alert. During this time, I kept in shape by climbing the hotel stairs, and doing press-ups and step-ups on the bed. I also went jogging, mindful of the marauding packs of wild and stray dogs. Punta Arenas is very windy, and garbage flies through the air 50 metres up, sometimes landing on power cables and telephone lines. As it's such a cold city its inhabitants keep the heating on year round. I liked to get away and hike the hills and waterways. There were penguins, views over 100 miles to glaciated peaks, and some fascinating history in the fight for control of what had until 1914 been the main seaway for shipping between the Atlantic and the Pacific.

In 1581 the Spanish had sent 23 ships to this, the southernmost region of Chile, with 3,000 people aboard. Only five ships and 500 people made it. Then all the ships were swept away from the settlement, unable to return, and those ashore starved to death; today, the site is called Puerto Hambre (Port Hunger) in honour of the victims. In 1843 the Chilean military established a base at Fuerte Bulnes. The story goes that the French arrived shortly after with the same intention and on being told that they were too late sailed on and annexed Tahiti instead. My walks to these regions were along wild windswept shores, often beneath huge lenticular clouds.

Then all of a sudden a weather window opened, and we rushed off to the Ilyushin to throw our packs on top of a huge load of cargo, including ALE's Sno-Cats, lashed down in the middle of its long, high fuselage; as this plane had been designed to take Soviet tanks it was ideal for the job. We piled hundreds of loose items – packs, skis and so on – on top. Then, as this was a Soviet military plane with no frills, designed 40 years earlier,

Inside the Russian Ilyushin 76

Ilyushin unloading

we sat in a windowless space alongside the cargo on seats designed for paratroopers and which appeared to have been made as uncomfortable as possible, presumably to encourage a jump. Then the Big Beast, as the Ilyushin is affectionately known, thundered and roared into a force 9 gale and was off over Cape Horn, the Southern Ocean and the sea ice. There were two large cranes on rails overhead, swinging wildly. As it was far too noisy to speak and we were all using the earplugs we'd been issued, we communicated in sign language. I went to the bomb-aimer cockpit to check out the views below, but it was all cloud, and later the perspex got iced up.

We flew across Drake Passage, where the massive Southern Ocean storms sweep from the west, rotating clockwise in an incessant circle around Antarctica. These are the stormiest waters in the world, where gales blow for days on end.

As we descended, all of us, unable to see outside, looked anxious. A big bump and a roar as the engines went into reverse thrust told us we'd landed. As the brakes could not be touched on this blue ice, reverse thrust was the only way to stop. I'd heard stories of the Big Beast doing a 180-degree spin on the ice.

As we taxied to a group of Sno-Cats and Skidoos the tail ramp was lowered. Then we climbed down a ladder on the starboard side and stepped onto the blue ice, slippery as a skating rink. The blue ice is generated by katabatic winds roaring down the slope of the Antarctic ice cap and over the hills, blowing all the snow off and ablating the surface. Katabatic winds extend only 100 metres above the surface, but have been clocked at over 200 mph, stronger than any hurricane. The air was −17°C (1.4°F), and the views along the Independence Range were breathtaking. The mountains 300 metres above Patriot Hills were holding back the ice cap. Further north, however, the ice cap flowed down to the ice shelf in giant glaciers: the Union, the Splettstoesser and the Minnesota.

At Base Camp

At the camp I met Simon Garrod, who was leading the expedition and had been getting the gear together. I also met Rob Collister, who I'd not seen for 35 years; Rob had been at school and at Cambridge with me, and now he was here guiding a BBC cameraman who would be filming us prior to our departure. Next day Simon and I practised crevasse rescue drills, rigging up prusik knots to climb up the rope, and pulley systems to pull the victim out, using ice axes and snow stakes for anchoring. Not too hard in ideal circumstances – but in practice, and in extreme conditions, I knew it would be very difficult for me to pull Simon out.

The sledges were alarmingly heavy, about 75 kg each. In addition to the 45 kg of my personal gear there was, split between the two sledges, climbing hardware, two sets of crevasse rescue gear, two MSR cookers, two tents, two sat phones, and food and fuel for 22 days. We expected to use half a litre of fuel per day, so we had ten 1-litre containers (totalling about 2 gallons). Everything was organised around our being able to survive the loss of either sledge into a crevasse. When we were not roped up I was to carry the climbing rope, to cover the more likely situation of Simon falling into a 'slot' in front of me. I wasn't sure what we'd do if it was me that went, with sledge and climbing rope, into a crevasse.

The main hazards we faced on this trip were:

> Crevasses, mainly on steep mountain slopes – most crevasses were bridged, often by a thin cover of snow, and hidden.

> Falls off steep blue ice, with broken limbs a risk, and inability for the other person alone to rescue the injured one .

> Whiteouts, with inability to read the snow surface, and increased risk of falls, or loss of direction.

> Blizzards, and risk of tents being shredded.

As there were going to be just two of us we had to be especially careful, as it's very hard for a person on their own to rescue an injured colleague. We couldn't rely on air rescue, as the weather could delay flights by ten days or more. If we were in an exposed location and away from our camp, the survival time before frostbite and hypothermia kicked in could be a matter of hours. If there had been three or four of us, as on a Vinson Massif climb, we could have been more adventurous. I suggested to Simon that if I was unable to pull him out of a crevasse I could lower a sleeping bag to him, and a tent if he was on a ledge or the bottom. However, he said that as crevasses are −45°C (−49°F) inside it'd only extend the agony. 'Better that you chop some ice blocks and drop them onto me to finish me off,' he said, jokingly – I think …

Ski-plane to an unexplored mountain range

Then at 9 p.m. on 28 November 2007 it was time to go. We lifted the sledges into the Twin Otter and we were off, flying over pointed peaks, glaciers, icefalls and wind scoops. The plane lined up on the unnamed glacier we'd planned to land on and touched the surface, the pilot testing the sastrugi and checking for crevasses. We roared off again, banking hard left as a wall of rock and ice ahead blocked our way. A second pass flattened the tops of the sastrugi, and on the third pass we landed.

The plane dropped us off and departed in a cloud of powder, leaving us in a world of silence. We clipped our skis on and started hauling, but we found the going desperately slow and hard. It was too steep to climb with skis, and we would zigzag 6 km to climb only 2 km up the glacier, a gain of 200 vertical metres. But although it was backbreaking work it was exciting to think that we were the first people to go up this beautiful valley. When we decided to set Camp One, we looked across to the Drake Icefall, cascading down in icy blue, steep and wide. Many

The Twin Otter ready to leave

Mount Vinson 200 miles away

of the mountains were perfect pyramids, higher and steeper than the Egyptian ones, and more than 100,000 times older – Cambrian rocks, over 500 million years old. The mountains and glaciers surrounded us and seemed to be telling me: 'This is a harsh place, even on a sunny day. We've been here millions of years. You do not belong here. Be careful – the weather can turn bad very quickly.'

Setting camp involved digging the powder out so that our tents would be stable if the wind scoured out the snow around them. We anchored the guy lines with 2-foot poles and shovelled more blocks of snow onto the snow valances that encircled the bases of the tents. We also anchored the sledges with snow stakes or shovels to prevent them blowing away. If a blizzard was expected we'd build a wall around the tents, cutting blocks with ice saws. Simon warned me against storing my skis overnight by sticking them into the snow vertically, as the wind could easily break them in two. The GPS showed us to be at 1,036 metres (3,400 feet), 79°36.3'S, 83°22.6'W. I wanted to write my journal as the midnight sun radiated my tent, but it was too cold for a ballpoint pen to work. So I snuggled down into my –30°C (–22°F) sleeping bag, put my eye mask on, and dropped into a broken sleep on the hard foam mats, three layers deep – one for the whole tent, two for the sleeping bag.

Up an unexplored glacier

Next morning, we practised more crevasse rescue, then broke camp and hooked up the sledges. I backed up like a carthorse getting into the shafts. I leaned forward 20 degrees – but the sledge, now iced up, would not move. A sharp tug, a lean forward to 30 degrees, and it moved 6 inches. I was horrified. We had nearly 100 km to go, about 200,000 tugs and steps. After 15 minutes, I had used up my initial energy and slogged on, counting my steps to 100, then 200, and if possible 300 before a 10-second rest. I hoped that in any future life I'd not be a beast of burden. Simon opened up the gap, seemingly inexhaustible. My head was pounding, my heart hammering, my legs aching.

Initial route

The slope was relentless. After two hours, I was soaked in sweat and took off my hat, but within seconds my head was coated in a frozen layer, like a crash helmet made of ice. I swapped my gloves for some lighter ones, and rolled up the big ones to fit in my waist bag. The slope became flatter, but a steep rise loomed ahead, guarding the pass we intended to cross into untravelled regions beyond. I pulled out my thick gloves, but they had been frozen into a ball from the perspiration iced up inside, and would not unroll. Warming them inside my jacket enabled me to put them on.

It was incredibly gruelling work, but a good way to lose weight quickly – I was burning up calories for warmth, as well as exercise, about twice as fast as I could consume my food. During the trip I lost 12 lb in 11 days. The workout, together with abstinence from alcohol and coffee, was good for my health. However, cumulative wear and tear on muscles, ligaments and joints are a problem for polar sledge haulers. In addition, frost damage and sunburn (worsened by the ozone hole, the altitude and the reflection off the ice) cause cumulative deterioration to skin and limbs.

PC on pass near Mount Sporli

Peak 1   My MacMillan Cancerbackup charity banner

As we pulled the last stretch, Simon commented that hauling sledges across Antarctica would be an excellent punishment for the most hardened criminals; aviation fuel could thus be hauled thousands of miles efficiently at minimal cost and low environmental impact. It would be very efficient, with a low carbon footprint, since manhauling uses less energy and produces less waste than dog teams, ponies, skidoos or aeroplanes. However, human rights groups would most likely condemn our idea as a cruel and inhuman punishment.

Simon suggested we set Camp Two then ski ahead to recce the pass to the glacier on the far side. We put on our climbing harnesses and split the rope into thirds: Simon with the first third in 12 coils over his shoulder, the middle third stretched between us, and the remaining third coiled over my shoulder. I put on my gear sling with ice screws and carabiners, then clipped on to my waistband: two prusik loops, more locking carabiners, Tiblocs, jumar ascender, web slings and other hardware. We carried no rock-climbing gear, as Simon knew from previous trips

Simon Garrod on Peak 2

Simon on top of Peak 2

that the rock in this part of Antarctica was cracked and shattered – no good for putting in belay protection. Packs on, with two snow stakes each, ice hammer and axe clipped on, we skied off rapidly up the slope on half-length 'kicker' skins.

The terrain changed from soft powder, deposited in a windless environment, to a more forbidding icy slope carved up with hard sastrugi waves. As we climbed to the pass the wind strengthened and reached 20 knots, plunging us into a −35ºC wind chill; the surface soon became too rough to ski and we swapped to crampons, but we reached the pass within the hour. We were the first to climb this unnamed glacier and reach this pass, and ahead was unknown, untravelled, never before seen from the ground. If we went over with the sledges, we'd find it very hard to get back up what, judging by the aerial photos taken in the 1960s, we'd expected to be steep and crevassed. But, as mentioned earlier, the photos from 25 miles away were insufficient for us to assess the slope angles, blue ice, crevasses and sastrugi, so if we continued and went on down, we might find ourselves trapped, unable to get out to the north, west or east, and only able to get back up here again by doubling up to haul the sledges, one at a time, back up the steep sastrugi we could see below us.

We looked for ways out of the glacier to the left, in gaps between the line of peaks stretching ahead. All the slopes were split by wide crevasses filled by snow bridges. Above them were areas of blue ice, steep and impossible to cross. We examined a possible route up the east side of Mount Sporli, but it would be risky; were either of us to be injured in a fall or dropped into a slot, the other would have a serious challenge getting the injured person back up the slope and down to the camp. And there was nowhere here to land a plane – which would anyway be delayed by up to ten days waiting for a weather window.

The wind was stronger now, so an injured person would probably only last a few hours without a tent. If we'd been in a party of four there would have been better capability to deal with an emergency. But for two it was far too risky. So we checked each other for frostbite, then cramponed back down the sastrugi and skied the rest. I called the area Disappointment Pass.

PC crossing crevasse on Driscoll Glacier

Another attempt

Next morning we set out to climb a snowy peak we'd seen on the way up to Camp Two; it had a 65-degree icy slope with on its top a huge cornice overhanging by 20 metres. Simon thought there might be an easy route around the back, so we skied over and climbed up on crampons, shortening our rope to avoid snagging it on rocks.

At the top was a stupendous view, south to the ice cap and north to the Rutford Ice Stream, which collected all the glacier outflows and fed them into the Ronne Ice Shelf. At the top it was below −20°C (−4°F), but a slight wind made it seem much colder, and we needed facemasks. The GPS told us we were at 1,442 metres (4,730 feet). We took some photos holding the Cancerbackup banner. I told Simon that the peak should be named Garrod Peak in recognition of his years of Antarctic service – and he said the whole region could be named Garrodland.

Back at Camp Two, Simon cooked up another excellent meal, pre-cooked in Patriot Hills and quick-frozen in the Antarctic air. These meals were delicious but heavier than dehydrated food – they would have made excellent curling stones.[33] They all stayed solidly frozen until we cooked them.

In the morning, my water bottles in my tent were frozen solid. Ditto my toothpaste, my ballpoint pen and my sun cream, essential in this region of high radiation (the reflection from the ice had already burned underneath and inside my nose). We set off for Peak Two, up a ridge to the east of Disappointment Pass. We dodged crevasses on each side, their jaws concealed by snow bridges – Simon had a gift for spotting them. He cut steps with the axe up a steep snow gully, and we came over a col, only to be blocked by a large blue ice wall ahead. We backed off and found a snow ridge to the summit. The top was a rocky spike, and the other side a 300-metre cliff drop onto a glacier. Suddenly a rock crashed down the cliff and bounded across the glacier in huge leaps.

I tried snacking on a mountaineering energy bar, but it was as hard as concrete and threatened to break my teeth. So instead I refuelled with liquid carbohydrate from my insulated water bottle. We were at 1,575 metres, and we could clearly see the Vinson Massif nearly 100 miles to the north.

One of the better features of Antarctica is the very clear air and dark blue skies, with blue right to the horizon. Views of over 100 miles are the norm on a sunny day. In much of the civilised world you're lucky if you can see 5 miles. But there is nowhere on the planet with air clearer and cleaner than that of the Antarctic. The famous ozone hole is still there, but now recovering, thanks to successful environmental legislation worldwide.

The ski back down to Camp Two was pure bliss, effortless on the gentle powder slope.

Next day was a big day, as we would have to lose all our hard-won altitude then regain it. We fuelled up with porridge and jam, and refilled water bottles and steel thermos with hot water, taking care to keep the threads dry so as not to risk them freezing solid.

Down to Driscoll Glacier, the big sledge pushing me along, its aluminium traces preventing it from running me over. Simon had gone ahead without his sledge to check for crevasses as we turned the corner to go up the Driscoll. When I stopped in the soft powder, there was no noise at all. In the Antarctic interior, the only sound is the wind. If it's calm, it's totally silent. Sometimes, you hear the 'Antarctic hum', an unexplained phenomenon widely believed to be a figment of the imagination, but possibly created by the aurora, which is sometimes heard to hum in the polar night.

---

33 In the Scottish game of curling, players heave granite stones of around 20 kg (44 lb) across the ice towards a target about 150 feet away.

We dropped to 840 metres. Simon reported large crevasses on the Driscoll. We now had to climb around 500 vertical metres, nearly two Eiffel Towers, with 170 lb apiece to haul up. Bad news, except that I was becoming fitter and stronger.

The early part of the haul was soft powder, its ice crystals reflecting the sun in a starry collection of blues, reds, greens and whites – an effect that only happens in very cold air. We passed by several crevasses 5–10 metres wide, 200 metres long, straight as arrows, some open, some bridged. Beautiful icefalls and hanging glaciers flanked our way. The slog would have been monotonous without the majestic scenery, and I admired the South Pole adventurers for their tenacity in what was in so many parts a barren flat white desert. However, our slope was ten times steeper than the slope to the Pole. We were also hauling more weight than a 'supported' (i.e. resupplied, from depots or by air) South Pole sledge. Simon was intrigued by dust on the snow surface, which also collected in the snow melted for cooking, and we wondered if it was space dust, which has been collected in Antarctica; 40,000 tonnes of the stuff is estimated to fall to earth annually. Simon had previously led geologists to find meteorites in Antarctica, often on blue ice ablation areas.

By this time things were starting to fail. Simon's pack belt broke, as did his ski bindings. He had a rivet kit to effect repairs. His left knee was also playing up from a previous injury and operation, but heavy doses of ibuprofen and glucosamine allowed him to keep up the relentless haul. I had wrenched my left hand and it was swollen and ineffective. My right hand had multiple scratches that would not heal; they would not fully recover for over a month.

In addition, while all my equipment worked well, none of my gloves were able to deal with the low temperatures, and I was lucky that conditions weren't worse. Thin gloves for intricate work like setting camp up were next to useless and caused numb fingers, and if there was any significant wind the thick gloves failed to keep hands warm. My mitts were too clumsy, and also required taking the other gloves off before putting them on. Glove technology has not kept pace with boot improvements over the past decades, and while in Antarctica frostbite in feet is rare now, it is common in fingers (although usually only in inexperienced people), A century ago, it was the other way around: while huge fur mitts protected hands, feet got frozen in flimsy boots. Most mountaineering equipment is not rated for conditions below −20°C (−4°F), and even steel becomes brittle at low temperatures. When I'd worked in Arctic Russia, the Russians wouldn't work at below −40°C/F, as when steel was under load in those kinds of temperatures it would crack like glass.

High up the glaciers

Camp Three was in a beautiful setting, surrounded by ice formations. On 3 December we continued a hard slog to over 1,300 metres at the top of Driscoll, below Mount Sporli's sheer-rock west face. I was clocking off the altitude in 5-metre intervals, longing for the end of the climb. We turned left over a pass, looking forward to joining the Schneider Glacier going downhill to the north. But alas, the USGS map was wrong, and what we joined was the Schanz Glacier – going uphill. The existence of the map had implied that the area was explored, but it had mostly been drawn from aerial photos with some helicopter reconnaissance, and the mountains had been named after people who had never set foot on them, such as a helicopter mechanic from the 1960s aerial photo expedition.

We set Camp Four under Sporli at 1,350 metres, with fantastic views in all directions: the Vinson Massif to the north, ice cap to the south-west. The night was cold as the wind picked up, and next day we hauled another five hours, then decided on an early Camp Five to get some rest. As with all camps, we worked fast to set up the tents and get inside, as body temperature drops fast as soon as the manhauling furnace is switched off. The blocks of hard snow we'd put around the tents kept them well in place, but as ever going to the bathroom was a big event, as the wind would whistle between naked thighs, and time was of the essence to avoid frostbite in sensitive areas.

The sun was going around us incessantly in circles: 13 degrees above the horizon at midnight in the south, heading eastwards to a high of 34 degrees above the horizon at noon in the north, then swooping down to the west for the evening. This midnight sun was much higher and brighter than in Norway, Greenland, Russia and Alaska; and at the South Pole in midsummer it goes round at the same elevation of 23 degrees, day and night.

Climbing up Driscoll Glacier

PC heading down Schneider Glacier

Next morning I called my son Richard's school on the sat phone, to answer questions from the class about our expedition and Antarctica. Then, on a bitterly cold day, we cramponed up a 35-degree slope in 15 knots of wind. I love the feel of crampons on hard snow – they stick like glue and defy gravity. You tread slowly, carefully, very deliberately, careful not to trip.

The final leg of the climb to Peak Three was up a snow ridge, dropping off to the right to an icy crevassed area, with fantastic views over the unexplored Rennell Glacier to the left and the Anderson and Vinson Massifs looming over a grey horizon. A halo warned us of a deterioration in the weather. We were at 1,865 metres, about 6,150 feet. We stayed an hour on top, as due to the absolute calm it felt warm in the −25°C (−13°F) conditions. But the slightest breath of wind even the airflow caused by walking at 2 mph, made a huge difference. And getting my cameras and video equipment to work was a problem solved only by warming them inside my clothing.

Antarctica has curious weather, with the strongest winds in places where on other continents you might find them weakest. Some areas are usually windy, as evidenced by sastrugi and hard blue ice, yet other areas, perhaps just a few yards away, are usually windless. The tops of mountains can often be calm while a strong wind cuts through the glaciers below. The strongest winds are always on the lee side, downwind of hills, where katabatics fall like river rapids from their own weight.

We could see all of the named peaks I'd identified on the aerial photos: Vinson, Sporli, Hall, Robinson and Rogers. All these peaks had well-guarded defences of crevasses, blue ice and steep rocks.

We descended fast to the glacier, which was now windy and overcast. So the night was bitterly cold, with blowing snow and no night sun to warm the tent. In the morning I dug out my tent and sledge, then we broke

Storm coming in

Camp 5

PC on Peak 3

Simon on Peak 3

PC on Peak 3

camp and hauled 18 km to Camp Six on Rennell Glacier, where it joined the huge, wide Splettstoesser Glacier, down at 975 metres above sea level between Rogers Peak and Orheim Point. We followed the west flank of Inferno Ridge, which we had intended to cross with sledges, but as was becoming a regular occurrence, it turned out to be much steeper than we'd expected. The headwind froze the steam I was exhaling into a gnarly ice formation on my face, typical of polar adventurer photos. Simon, completely encased in black, including facemask, looked like Darth Vader.

Menacing weather

It clouded over more, becoming grey and menacing. Fog rolled up the Splettstoesser from the north and wide grey lenticular clouds spread 100 km across the sky. I could see a crevassed area to the left, and I remembered Nick Lewis's warning that crevasses in Antarctica can be anywhere, including where you'd least expect one.

The Splettstoesser was 30 km across, narrowing to 6 km where it funnelled between Rogers Peak and the Anderson Massif. In the evening snow fell as thick cloud and mist spread across the area. After dinner we sat in the tent, discussing Antarctic history, world affairs, military history and the British Antarctic Survey. Simon and his partner, Carolyn – who, like Simon, was ex-British Antarctic Survey, and who was also in Antarctica but on the other side of the Union Glacier – were sea kayakers in their free time, and recently back from a voyage in exposed North Atlantic waters among the Outer Hebrides. In the winter, Simon spent as much time as possible ice-climbing in Scotland, his lifestyle being one of taking on big challenges in hostile areas.

I woke to a strong katabatic wind. While we were packing the backpacks for an attempt on Rogers Peak, a vicious katabatic gust blasted over Inferno Ridge and across Rennell Glacier, lifting snow hundreds of metres into the air in a giant vortex. Simon took bearings on the peaks to be able to find the camp in a blizzard without depending on the two GPS receivers. He then stated cheerfully: 'But then again, we could get back and find the tents shredded, so if the wind gets up it's Mission Abort.'

Rogers was not as high as Peak Three, but proved to have formidable defences. We skied to a large wind scoop and cramponed up along its right flank. The scoop was 100 metres deep, with near-vertical sides and at the bottom a jumble of large loose rocks which had cracked off from the cliffs, with their sedimentary bands at the top and metamorphic veins at the bottom.

As we climbed higher, the slope became icy and so hard that our crampons would not bite, and we needed to stamp our boots several times to kick a grip in. This was not conducive to treading stealthily over the area, which was crisscrossed with bridged crevasses. While Simon had an excellent eye for them, there were some that we found only with ski pole or ice axe. Many of the bridges were alarmingly thin, made of brittle, fragile, icy snow, and while the crevasses were mostly narrow enough to leap across, this was not easy, as we were going up a steep slope. The technique was to plunge the ice axe pick into the far side and pull up and across. As Simon felt his way upwards and ahead I would keep a taut line, ready to drop to the ground if he fell in. Once he had reached a secure spot each time he would then belay me up, using the axe as an anchor.

Dangerous crevasses

But this was such a dangerous place that we decided to retreat. The crevasses were too numerous and too close together. The other risk was sliding off the hard, icy surface and over the lip of the wind scoop, to fall 100 metres down onto rocks at the bottom. So Simon belayed me as I picked my way down. At one point I punched a hole with my ski pole and looked into a wide, dark blue crevasse, about 3 metres across – I was on a snow bridge only a few inches thick. 'Don't look where you've been – keep moving!' Simon yelled.

Then I was back on the steep ice, and while I found it easier to walk on the edge of the crevasse where a ridge allowed my crampons to grip, this was covered by loose ice and snow so it was walking by Braille.

Simon then led the way to the right, to a flatter area away from the wind scoop, but it was carved up by crevasses 8 metres wide, covered with snow bridges. He probed the first one with the axe and said, 'No way!' The biggest danger with a wide crevasse is not so much falling into it as causing the whole bridge to crack and collapse, dropping tons of icy blocks on top of you.

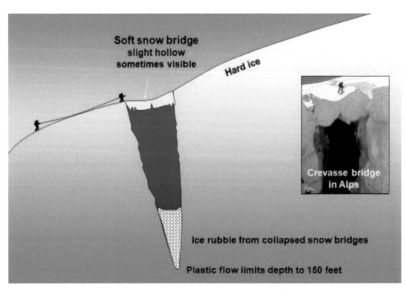

Crevasse schematic

Ice cliff on Rogers Peak

So there was no option but to go back down to our skis and look for another route to Rogers, our goal. We found a snow gully, steepening to what looked like an impassable rock cliff at the top, but when we got up there we discovered a narrow gully of loose rocks and snow, and scrambled up it, Simon belaying me.

On top was a fairyland of blue ice with a huge ice cliff full of seracs on our left and icefalls on our right. The top of the cliff was heavily crevassed. Ahead, the Splettstoesser and Minnesota Glaciers joined where they fed the Ronne Ice Shelf. This shelf is up to 600 metres thick and spawns icebergs as big as 5,000 square kilometres (55 times the size of Manhattan), which last for up to five years in the Southern Ocean.

The ice cliff was over 100 metres high, on top of an escarpment. This was a total surprise, not seen on the aerial photos. We couldn't climb it. Could we get around it? The ice under our feet was hard as steel, so our crampons often left no marks. We climbed a snow slope to the right of the cliff, and then along the top of it, working our way above a long, thin bergschrund, sometimes with its jaws open, sometimes covered over and concealed like a snake. This was the highest crevasse of this climb; above it the ice was attached to the rock and below it the ice was slowly sliding downhill.

As we gained elevation the surface steepened and became loose ice on top of iron-hard solid ice. My crampons weren't biting properly and I couldn't expect to self-arrest, as the loose ice provided no hold for my axe and the solid ice underneath didn't allow it to penetrate. If I slipped I'd pull Simon off, and we'd both slide over or into the bergschrund, with the risk of breaking legs. If we couldn't self-arrest after bouncing over the bergschrund, we'd then slide over the top of the cliff and fly through the air in a 200-metre free fall. I was conscious of what a climber had told me: 'Antarctica is a place where an adventure can become a crisis and then a disaster in a matter of seconds'. The edge of the cliff was below me, intimidating me, daring me.

Simon sounded agitated, saying: 'This is a very bad place to be. We should *not* be here. Everywhere we look there's a problem.'

We really needed to put protection in, and we carried four ice screws and four snow stakes. But the surface was too hard for snow stakes and too brittle for ice screws, as ice tends to shatter at low temperatures. The other problem was that it would have taken several hours to install and remove all that protection, and the weather

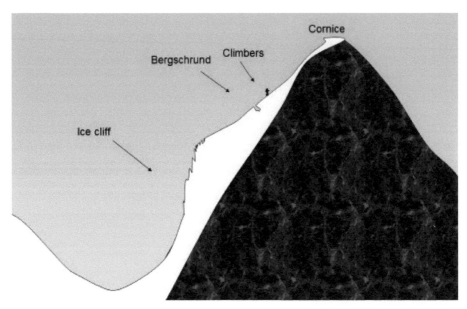

Rogers Peak schematic

was looking to break. Simon felt we needed to move quickly and get right off this peak before anything nasty happened.

Ahead and to the left was the ice cliff, hidden below a convex slope. Above us we could see the summit, 150 metres up, with cornices and wind slab. To our right and above us was loose, steep, fractured rock. To the left, the bergschrund. Retreat was dangerous too, as on going down the footing would be much more precarious.

We both agreed we were in a hazardous situation and should go back. I was reminded of Shackleton's quote after turning back 97 miles from the Pole: 'better to be a live donkey than a dead lion'. The best option was for me to cross the bergschrund, so that if I fell it would be from below it. The only hazard would then be the ice cliff. Simon was to belay me. The problem was how to set an anchor in the brittle ice. He found a thin crevasse and jammed his axe into it for a belay anchor. I probed the surface with my ski pole and ice axe and found the edge of the bergschrund, which I stepped across. As the bridge didn't collapse, it seemed that the bergschrund was narrow enough to be safe. Further down the slope I tripped on my crampons and somersaulted forward, but the snow was soft, and I was still roped to Simon behind me so I didn't slide far. If this had happened further up it would have been catastrophic.

We pushed hard to get back to Camp Six. We thought of trying another, easier route up the north side of Rogers Peak the next day, but there was an ominous-looking front coming in from the west, so we decided to call for the Twin Otter, which we'd seen before, ferrying climbers to Vinson. This was a wise move, as we found out later that if we'd stayed a few more hours we would then have been marooned for ten days in blizzard conditions. I'd brought a tiny New Testament with me, given to me by my mother-in-law for such a situation, expecting me to be able to take my time reading it. In ten days we'd covered over 100 km and climbed 2,500 vertical metres, more than the elevation gain on a Vinson climb.

Getting out before the storm

The Twin Otter arrived at 2100. When we flew back along our ski tracks it was interesting to see how many crevasses we'd skied past that I hadn't spotted from the ground.

Back in Patriot Hills, the weather, with an air temperature at −16°C (3°F), felt positively balmy. There were 35 people at the camp, including two who'd given up on a South Pole attempt, a research group led by Simon's partner, Carolyn, and 26 camp staff.

Over the next ten days our group of 35 got to know each other quite well, as in a polar version of Big Brother the weather closed in, preventing anyone from leaving. We were multinational; although the camp was British

PC kite skiing

managed it was staffed with folks from Chile, mainland Norway and Spitsbergen, the USA, Canada, Belgium, Greenland, New Zealand, Australia, Sweden and Latvia. I kept myself busy with camp chores, helping erect more tents and doing dishwashing in the warm cook tent. Tents were thoroughly dug in, with a tie-down rope anchored into drilled holes, snow blocks cut with a chain saw and piled up, then more snow packed around with the Sno-Cat. They could survive 70mph+ winds. A group of us went out on the Sno-Cat to see the remains of a crashed DC-6, now buried with only the rudder showing. The visibility closed in to 100 yards, preventing the Ilyushin coming in – it required at least 10 km visibility and good lighting contrast to land.

Ronny Finsås, one of the cooks, taught me to kite-ski. He was working the night shift in the cook tent, preparing 1 tonne of food for a big expedition. After cooking each batch, he would toss it out onto the ice to freeze it down hard. Ronny was also one of the world's top kite-skiers, having kited back from the Pole twice, and he was set on achieving a new record from the Pole to the coast. I'd seen him jumping 5 metres into the air off sastrugi, and I knew he'd clocked 100 km/h. In Greenland, kiters towing pulks had done over 400 km in a day, albeit on ice smoother than Antarctica's sastrugi. Ronny was Norwegian, and Norwegians still led the world in polar travel, as they'd done for so much of the last 100 years.

I started on my 2.6m² kite on long lines, and then on Ronny's 6m² sail on short lines. This proved much easier than expected, and I was soon clattering across the sastrugi on a wild and semi-out-of-control exhilarating ride. It felt similar to windsurfing or waterskiing, which I'd done a lot of. Simon too picked it up quickly, thanks to his solid off-piste steep-skiing experience and some kitesurfing. A month later, Ronny set the record for kite-skiing from the Pole to the coast in five days, solo and unsupported, including a record 502 km in 24 hours, while towing a pulk on a long line. Quite amazing. This had to put him right at the top of the world's kite-skiers.

Blizzard for 11 days

We were stuck for 11 days as the biggest Antarctic storm in over 20 years swept over, creating whiteouts and continuous snow, sometimes in blizzard conditions. Everyone in the camp was living in tents, the staff in the smallest mountain tents. All were getting buried and the light powder snow was getting inside. People were recording −12°C (10°F) in the top – warmest – area of their tents. The wind lifted the floor of my tent and froze everything inside, including water bottles. Many tents became so buried – some in drifts 2 metres high – that they had to be dug out and moved to a new location on top of the snow. Some laundry had been hung out earlier and was now, frozen stiff, thrashing around wildly in the blizzard.

In the whiteouts no one could leave the camp, even for 100 yards. The Twin Otters were tied down to three large anchors dug into the snow, their propellers lashed down, the engines protected from blowing snow with their own polar jackets. Our meteorologist, Marc De Keyser, gave gloomy weather forecasts every morning – a summary of information downloaded at agonisingly slow speed via his solar-powered laptop. His laconic comment would often be: 'Yesterday's bad situation has now got even worse.' He was practising for the Antarctic Marathon at Patriot Hills, which he later won, breaking the record in nasty conditions.

One day, as the snow drove across us, we played volleyball. It was a hard-fought six-a-side game for a trophy, and we collected some splendid bruises, partly because in the sub-zero conditions the ball was rock-hard. Then the Fuchs team organised a Polar Olympics, with events including blindfold sledge-hauling, tossing the mountaineering boot and so on.

Around 80 cm of snow landed in the camp, and was packed down to about 40 cm on the runway. This was very unusual in an essentially desert climate. We had 97 days of food stored in a labyrinth of underground tunnels cut

Volleyball at Base Camp

out with chainsaws. We often quoted the line from the TV sitcom *Dad's Army* – 'We're all *dooooomed!*' It was interesting to hear seasoned Antarctic professionals like Simon extol the virtues of 100-year-old designs – the Scott pyramid tent, and the Nansen sledge – which were simple and reliable, and had had all the bugs worked out. More recently designed equipment was often lighter, but more likely to fail in extreme conditions. Someone built a good igloo.

My camp life took on a routine: first thing, wipe down with a wet flannel in my sub-zero tent (using water from the cook tent if mine was frozen up), excellent meals in the cook tent, toilet functions in accordance with ALE's policy of air freighting out all waste in line with the Antarctic Treaty (human waste liquids into used aviation fuel drums, solids into tough plastic bags), evening lectures on Antarctic exploration in the cook tent. In the whiteout night and day were much the same, and we had to move from tent to tent by following orange flags.

Our communications equipment was powered by solar panels, installed vertically and in groups of three standing back to back like the Musketeers, to catch the sun 24 hours a day. ALE's environmental standards are outstanding, and set an example for the many government bases that violate the provisions of the Antarctic Treaty. Patriot Hills used very little fuel, prohibited any kind of waste being left behind, and was shut down for nine months of the year.

After nine days, the wind dropped, it stopped snowing, a watery sun appeared, visibility went beyond 100 yards and soon we could see the mountains again. I skied all over the place in the glorious new powder. Everyone in West Antarctica had been affected by this storm, which was notable because of its diameter and duration, dropping snow for a week or more. Some people were calling it the Storm of the Century, which was a bit of an exaggeration, especially since nobody had been there more than 50 years ago; perhaps they meant the 21st century. When I later, however, looked at the satellite photos I was astounded to see that the storm had been 2,500 miles across, about the same area as Antarctica itself.

The Vinson climbers flew in: some had summited, some had not, in temperatures up to −35°C (−31°F) and hurricane-force winds of up to 70 mph. There were injuries and broken bones, and 11 cases of frostbite; many hands and fingers were bandaged up. I spoke to some of the climbers, mostly Swiss, Austrian and American. Although the Swiss and Austrians were hardened, wiry men, many of them professional mountaineers and guides from the Alps, none of them had ever seen a storm as severe as that on Vinson. Fifteen tents had been shredded, sometimes with all contents lost. Ice walls two blocks thick had been blown away. Climbers had packed five into two-man tents and held them down. At times, it had been impossible to move between tents, at other times only by crawling along a fixed rope. The wind had sometimes picked climbers up and thrown them back down. They had taken off their crampons due to the risk of injury from them. Thanks to outstanding rescue work undertaken by the guides and ALE staff, no one had died, although there had been some close calls. Other South Pole adventurers had also had to give up, injured or delayed, due to the exceptional blizzard conditions, and be airlifted out.

Strong katabatics helped three snow blowers clear the landing strip, which needed to be nearly 3 km long and 50 metres wide. To clear over 5,000 tons of snow took two sunny days and a sunny night of non-stop work; meanwhile the mountains looked stunningly beautiful, with fresh powder being blown off the cliffs.

Then orange smoke flares were lit. Simon went to the start of the runway with a heliograph to guide the pilots, and the Ilyushin flew in a few feet over his head. We boarded, and were still finding our seats when the engines roared and we thundered down the blue ice, bumping a couple of times before getting airborne. Empty drums of aviation fuel were popping like a steel drum band as the pressure dropped. The end of a unique and fantastic experience, almost like being on another planet.

POSTSCRIPT

In this section I give credit to my wonderful family, who have been a foundation for me.

On 17 November 1989 Bonnie and I married in the Gun Room at Dalhousie Castle, a 13th-century fortress in Bonnyrigg, Scotland. Having decided to settle in England for a couple of years, we chose Surrey, in the south-east, and the couple of years turned out to be over 30 – in marked contrast to my childhood, when over a 20-year period my family had lived in 21 homes in a range of countries. Our odyssey had been full of adventure and excitement, but I'd always yearned for a permanent home, where I could have a range of long-standing friends.

1988 Bonnie, our wolf Jason
and my parents in Ireland)

1988 Our wolf Jason

Bonnie and I had two sons: Michael, born in 1992 and Richard in 1998. And now I've found that becoming a parent has been a voyage of discovery in itself. Very sadly, Bonnie died in 2021 after a 15-year struggle with cancer; she had originally been given only two weeks to live, but her main objective – in the event, fully realised – had been to see Mike and Rich graduate from university before she died, and she led a very full life throughout.

Many of my journeys were several decades ago, and written up 'back in the day'. Much has changed since then. Cultures have changed a lot, too. Most of these changes are positive: people are kinder, schools are more liberal, poverty has reduced, people live longer, and there seems to be little overt threat of nuclear war. But the environmental challenges grow as the population increases and consumption of energy rises. Waste is a serious issue.

The adventures I've related were my brief shining moments, and I hope you have enjoyed them as much as I did. And here's a thought. What further edges are there? The solar system, our galaxy, the universe, more universes? What was there before the Big Bang? We simply don't know. Is our universe finite or infinite? There's lots more to explore, and there are always edges to cross …

1988 Skiing in Zermatt

2006 Mike, Rich and Bonnie outside our home in Florida

2006 PC and Mike on Harley Davidson in Florida

2008 Mike and Rob Collister
on Ogwen climb in Wales

2009 PC in French Alps

2009 Rich in French Alps

2009 PC and Rich in California

2011 Rich climbing out of
crevasse in Switzerland

2011 PC climbing out of crevasse Switzerland

2012 Our family car

2014 Mike and Rich off Cornwall

GLOSSARY

½ oz, ¾ oz, 1½ oz Grading of spinnakers by weight of sailcloth in ounces per square yard, ½ oz the lightest, for light winds, and 1½ oz the heaviest and strongest, for stronger winds or closer reaching.

720 Racing penalty requiring boat to complete two 360-degree turns.

Abeam At right angles to the direction the boat is facing.

Abseil or **rappel** Controlled descent down a rope from a masthead or clifftop, using a descender brake such as a figure eight descender.

Aft The rear (stern) end of a boat, or a direction towards that end.

Ahead In a forward direction.

Almanac Reference book containing densely packed information about sea areas, ports, aids to navigation, tides and celestial navigation, usually updated annually.

America's Cup The cup was given its name only after it had been won by the *America*.

Anchorage An area suitable for anchoring, sheltered and with good bottom holding ground.

Apparent wind The wind's direction and speed measured relative to you when you're moving across the surface of the sea or land. Your movement affects the measurements; the faster your motion the more the apparent wind speeds up and comes from in front of you. C/f **true wind**.

Astern In a rear-facing direction, or backwards.

Astro-navigation The science of navigating by celestial bodies, usually the sun. Also called celestial navigation.

Autohelm Type of self-steering that can be set to be controlled by the apparent wind direction or a compass bearing. It is electrically powered. C/f **Windvane**.

Backing Wind direction changing against the direction of the sun (in the northern hemisphere that's usually from north-west to south), usually a sign of worsening weather. C/f **veering**.

Bar Shallow area of sand, typically across the entrance of a river where the two conflicting flows meet, and often rendering navigation extremely dangerous due to breaking seas.

Barber hauler Line attached to **headsail** or **spinnaker clew** to haul it downwards, getting a better shape for offwind sailing.

Batten Strip of stiff material (often thin wood or plastic) set into a sail at right angles to the **leech**, to improve its shape. A Wayfarer's mainsail has four battens.

Beam reach Sailing at right angles to the wind.

Bear away Turn away from the wind. C/f **luff up**.

Bearing The horizontal direction of an object relative to **grid north**, or **magnetic north** or a boat's direction.

Beating Sailing as close as possible (or close-hauled) towards the wind (usually about 45 degrees) in a zigzag course, by **tacking**.

Beaufort scale Wind force scale. Light winds are 1–3, moderate 4, fresh 5, strong (or half gale) 6, gale 7+. Ideal sailing winds are 3 upwind, and 4 downwind or on a broad **reach.**

Belay Technique for keeping a safety line tensioned by a climber to protect the lead climber from a fall.

Belay plate Device attached to the belayer or rock face that controls the payout of the safety rope to the lead climber.

Bergschrund A stationary crevasse that separates fixed ice above from moving glacier ice below.

Berth Location in a harbour used for mooring vessels, usually alongside a wall.

Bivvy sack Very small emergency tent for one person.

Block Pulley; or blocks, a set of pulleys.

Blooper An extra spinnaker, often flown without a pole and alongside a standard one.

Boat roller Inflatable roller to allow boat to be hauled up or down a beach.

BOC The British Oxygen Company singlehanded round-the-world race.

Boom Horizontal spar at the bottom of the mainsail.

Bow Forward part of boat.

Bowsprit Short pole extending forward off the bow to allow bigger headsails or asymmetric spinnakers to be set.

Broach When **running,** losing control with the boat making a sharp turn to windward, often heeling heavily and leading to capsize. Occurs when overpowered and/or in large following seas, or with an inexperienced / inattentive / fatigued **helm.**

Broad reach see **reach.**

Bulkhead Strong internal wall.

Buoy Floating aid to navigation, often with a light; or for mooring; or to mark a lobster/crab pot.

Burgee Flag at top of mast, mainly to indicate **apparent wind** direction, but can also indicate club membership.

Cable 1/10 nautical mile, about 600 feet.

Cap shrouds Side shrouds that extend to the masthead to prevent it leaning or even falling, often without **spreaders.**

Capsize Roll over until the mast is in the water, or to 180 degrees.

Carabiner Spring-loaded shackle to connect climbing hardware and ropes.

Catamaran Boat with two hulls. C/f **monohull, multihull, trimaran.**

Centreboard Board in the centre of the boat that can be pivoted downwards into the water as a temporary keel, preventing the boat drifting sideways. On running aground it can pivot back up again. C/f **daggerboard.**

Chimney Vertical crack in rock 1–3 feet wide, which can be climbable without equipment.

Chock Metal wedge for jamming into a crack in the rock. Also called **nut** or **wedge.**

Chord A wing mast's longest diameter.

Chute An asymmetrical spinnaker.

Cirrus High, wispy clouds, often signalling the approach of a depression and worsening weather.

Cleat Small metal fitting, traditionally with two arms, to hold ropes in use. A jamming cleat has a deep groove with ridges that can hold a rope firmly without the winding needed for conventional cleats. C/f **clutch.**

Clevis pin A patent fixing pin with a slender locking ring.

Clew The bottom corner of the sail that's furthest from the mast (or in a headsail/spinnaker, the free corner); c/f **tack.**

Clipper Fast, square-rigged sailing ship of the 19th century, with three or more masts.

Close-hauled Sailing as close to the wind direction as possible (generally about 45 degrees in a dinghy) while maintaining good **headway.**

Clutch Heavy-duty jamming **cleat,** manually opened and closed to lock or free lines.

Cockpit Area in which crew steer and sail the boat, below the deck level.

Col Lowest point on a mountain ridge between two peaks; similar to a pass but may be impassable.

Companionway Steep steps/fixed ladder from the **cockpit** down into the cabin.

Cordierite A blend of magnesium silicate and aluminium.

Course magnetic Direction of travel, in degrees magnetic.

Crampon Spiked plate attached to boot sole to grip on ice, whether it's horizontal, sloped or vertical.

Cumulonimbus Thundercloud.

Cunningham Line for tensioning the mainsail **luff.**

Daggerboard Vertical board that can be raised or lowered vertically within a housing, to reduce leeway. Unlike a **centreboard,** it cannot kick back up on running aground.

Deadman Snow anchor that lies flat.

Dead reckoning Estimated position based on the last known position, the course steered and the time elapsed. But it does not formally take currents into account, so it can be very inaccurate.

Depression (or **low**) Area of low pressure, usually with rain and strong winds around it, anticlockwise in the northern hemisphere. Wave low is a secondary low following the first one on its cold front.

Diamonds Inner stays often passing from mast base over a spreader in a diamond shape to the upper part of the mast to prevent mast bend; on a **wing mast** they rotate with the mast.

Dinghy Small open boat without a keel or a cabin. If it has an engine, that will only be a small outboard.

DNF Did not finish.

Doghouse Protected area above deck, over the **companionway** and forward of the **cockpit.** While it provides shelter from the elements, its location does not permit its occupants to control the boat.

Downwind Direction that the wind is blowing towards; away from the wind.

Drifter Lightweight loose-luffed large headsail for light airs.

DR see **Dead reckoning.**

Dry-tool Climbing technique using crampons on rock, so as to avoid removing and refitting crampons on mixed rock and ice.

Ebb tide Falling tide; refers to both the height and the direction. C/f **flood tide.**

EPIRB Emergency Position Indicating Radio Beacon.

Fair tide Tidal stream going in the direction of travel. C/f **foul tide.**

Farrier A trimaran class.

Feather To point slightly higher than **close-hauled,** mainly to reduce power and heeling.

Fender Soft bumper used to keep a moored boat from banging into a dock or another boat.

Foiling catamaran Fitted with hydrofoils.

Flood tide Rising tide; refers to both the height and the direction. C/f **ebb tide.**

Following sea Wave or waves going in the same direction as the boat.

Foot The lower edge of a sail. C/f **leech** and **luff.**

Fore triangle The area bounded by the forestay, the mast it's attached to and the deck.

Foredeck Deck area in front of the mast, usually a wetter and more dangerous location than the rest of the boat.

Foresail Sail in front of the mast. C/f **headsail, jib, genoa.**

Forestay Wire from the bows holding up the mast.

Foul tide Tidal stream going against the direction of travel. C/f **fair tide.**

Foul weather Strong winds, often with rain.

Front-point Climbing up steep ice slopes using the front forward-facing spikes on crampons.

Furler Device to roll up the **headsail.**

Genoa Large **jib** or **foresail.**

Geographical position Location on the Earth's surface directly below a celestial body, which would then be vertically overhead.

Gimbal Device to allow swinging, usually for a cooker, to help keep it horizontal at sea.

Gooseneck Fitting that attaches the boom to the mast.

GPS Global Positioning System. Satellite-based radio navigation system providing continuous worldwide position-fixing.

Gradient winds The winds that curve in towards the centre of a **low.** In the northern hemisphere apply Buys Ballot's law: 'Back to the wind: low left'.

Great Circle The shortest possible route from one point to another on the globe. C/f **rhumb line.**

Grid north The north per the gridlines on a map. C/f **magnetic north** and **true north.**

Growlers Chunks of sea ice, usually broken off an iceberg.

Gudgeon Attachment with hole for connecting to a **pintle.** Used in pairs, these secure the rudder to the hull.

Gunwale Upper edge of hull.

Guy The line that controls the spinnaker pole.

Gybe Change direction downwind with the stern of the vessel turning through the wind; unless the mainsail boom is controlled it will suddenly slam across the boat, destroying anything it hits.

Halyard Line used to raise a sail.

Head Has various meanings, including the toilet.

Headland Promontory, usually high, with cliffs, usually on a convex section of coastline.

Headsail Sail in front of the mast; also **foresail, jib** or **genoa.** But not a **spinnaker/chute/kite.**

Head to wind Pointing the bow directly towards the wind.

Headway Forward progress through the water. Also called **way.**

Heaving to Stopping a boat by lashing the helm to leeward with a headsail hauled to windward and the mainsail freed off to leeward. This setup allows a slow drifting to leeward.

Heavy weather Force 5–6 or more.

Heeling (of a boat) tipping sideways in response to the force of the wind.

Helm Device for steering a boat (in a dinghy, a tiller). Also the member of the crew who is steering.

High Area of high pressure; has light winds, if any. C/f **low.**

Horizontal sextant angle Measured between two objects in a horizontal direction; the measurement of the angle combined with the known distance between the two objects enables calculation of the object's distance away. C/f **vertical sextant angle.**

Hornito Tall column of lava.

Hounds The point where the stays/shrouds meet the mast.

Ice axe Tool for climbing ice or self-arrest, with spikes and/or blades.

Icefall Very steep glacier, heavily crevassed, often with chaotic blocks and **seracs.**

Ice screw Threaded tubular screw for use as an anchor in ice.

Ice shelf Floating sheet of thick ice fed by glaciers.

IOR International Offshore Rules.

Jib Relatively small headsail, smaller than a **genoa.**

Jumar Braking device used for sliding up a rope, usually for very steep climbing.

Jury rig Emergency rig, usually put together from whatever materials are available after a dismasting.

Katabatic wind Descending wind caused by cold, dense air flowing downhill by gravity, often at high speed.

Keel Bottom of a vessel; or heavy weight on the bottom of a boat, or below the hull, often lead, to keep a boat upright and help prevent sideways drift.

Keelboat Boat with a keel, usually a yacht.

Ketch Two-masted yacht, with the smaller **mizzen** sail on a mast aft of the mainsail and forward of the **rudder.** C/f **yawl.**

Kevlar Strong, synthetic material used in items such as sailcloth and bulletproof vests.

Kicking strap (or **vang**) Adjustable wire to prevent the boom rising.

Kite see **spinnaker.**

Knot Unit of speed: 1 nautical mile (approximately 1.15 statute miles) per hour.

Landfall Arrival at land after a sea passage.

Latitude Distance north or south of the equator (0°), measured in degrees, then either decimal points or minutes and seconds. The poles are at 90°N and 90°S.

Lazy guy Spare spinnaker **sheet,** after a **gybe** it's usually used as the new guy.

Lazy sheet Spare spinnaker **guy,** after a gybe it's used as the new sheet.

Lee Direction away from the wind.

Leaded monohull A monohull boat with a lead keel.

Leech The aft edge of a sail. C/f **foot** and **luff.**

Lee shore A shore downwind of, ie to the lee of, the vessel, which may then run the risk of being blown onto it. Opposite of **weather shore.**

Lee side (of, e.g., an island or peninsula); the side of the island/peninsula that's sheltered from the wind by the height of the land. *Not to be confused with a* **lee shore!** C/f **weather shore.**

Leeward In a downwind direction, the direction towards which the wind is blowing. C/f **windward.**

Leeway The amount that a boat is blown sideways by the wind.

Lifelines Lines to help prevent crew members falling overboard.

Longitude Distance east or west of the Greenwich Meridian (0°), measured in degrees, then in either decimal points or minutes and seconds. Most of the International Date Line runs along the 180th meridian, but diverts to avoid splitting island groups.

LORAN Type of radio navigation in use before satellite GPS. Did not cover all areas, often not accurate.

Low The centre of an area of low atmospheric pressure. C/f **high.**

Luff Leading edge of sail. C/f **Foot** and **leech.**

Luff up To steer a sailing boat more and more towards the direction of the wind until the pressure on the sails is eased. C/f **bear away.**

Magnetic north The north shown by a magnetic compass. C/f **grid north** and **true north.**

Mainsail Large sail with its **foot** along a **boom** and its **luff** along the mast.

Mizzen A secondary, smaller sail, aft of the mainsail. C/f **ketch** and **yawl.**

MOCRA Multihull Offshore Cruising & Racing Association.

Monitor A type of windvane.

Monohull Boat with one hull. C/f **catamaran, multihull, trimaran.**

Mooring Attaching a boat to a mooring buoy; or the buoy plus its cable and holdfast; or the area where boats are moored.

Mouse line Thin rope used to lead the way for a thicker one.

MSR A brand respected for its products' ability to function in extreme conditions.

Multihull Boat with more than one hull. C/f **catamaran, monohull, trimaran.**

Nautical mile Unit of distance at sea, about 1.15 **statute miles** (1,852 metres / about 6,076 feet).

Navigation Process of fixing a boat's position and direction, and calculating how to reach the intended destination.

Navigation lights A system of lights that a boat must display at night to indicate its position and direction of travel. For a sailing boat, this is a white light aft, a green light to starboard and a red light to port; sailing vessels less than 7 metres must have ready at hand an electric torch or lighted lantern showing a white light that shall be exhibited in sufficient time to prevent collision.

Neap tides Occur when sun and moon are at right angles to each other relative to the Earth. The tidal range and flow are minimised. C/f **spring tides.**

Nets Trampoline-style netting strung between the hulls of a multihull boat.

Number 1, 2, 3 or 4 Size of headsail, No 1 the largest, its area about 150 per cent of the **fore triangle,** No 3 about same as the fore triangle.

Nunatak Glacial islands.

Nut Device for jamming into cracks in rocks. Also called a **chock** or **wedge.**

Off watch Off duty but on standby. C/f **on watch.**

Offshore Out to sea; or the wind direction when it's blowing away from the land. C/f **onshore.**

Offwind Downwind.

Oilskins Foul weather gear, named after clothing used in the 19th century made of canvas soaked in oil for waterproofing.

Onshore Wind direction when it's blowing towards the shore. C/f **offshore.**

On watch On duty, usually in a fixed rota. C/f **off watch.**

ORC Then Offshore Racing Council, now Offshore Racing Congress.

OSTAR Observer Single-Handed Trans-Atlantic Race.

Outhaul Line to tension the foot of a sail.

Overfalls Dangerously steep and breaking seas generated by strong currents over a shallow, rocky bottom.

Pacific High An area of high pressure normally found in a specific position; has light winds, if any.

Pahoehoe The type of lava typical of the Hawaiian islands: it has a high basalt content, so is very thin, flows fast, and sets into rope-style formations.

Para-anchor Heavy-duty water parachute that can stop a boat almost dead. Typically 10–20 feet in diameter.

Phosphorescence Blue-green light emitted by phytoplankton.

Pilot Navigation book containing details of passages, weather statistics, ports and navigation aids. Not in annual form.

Pin end A buoy marking the far end of the start line from the committee boat.

Pingos Hillocks with ice cores, formed by permafrost.

Pintle Pin or bolt on which a boat's **rudder** pivots. Each pintle rests in a **gudgeon.**

Pipe cot Bunks made of a framework of pipes connected by webbing or similar.

Pitch Climbing section between two **belays.**

Pitchpole When the bows dig in and the boat capsizes 180 degrees stern over bow.

Plane To accelerate such that the boat rises above its own bow wave and rides it.

Pooped Swamped by a high following sea over the stern.

Port The left side of a boat when you're facing forward. Shows a red light at night. The word comes from the ships that had a steering oar on the starboard side, so it was the other side that was parked up against the wharf when in port. C/f **starboard.**

Position fixes Visual, radio or satellite measurements that enable the fixing of a boat's position independently of its **dead-reckoned** (estimated) position.

Preventer A line that controls the main boom.

Prusik knot Used as a friction hitch around a rope to climb up it, often used in crevasse rescue.

Pulk Small, lightweight sled. Usually with two aluminium tubes extending forwards for better control downhill.

Pulpit A protrusion from the bow, with a safety rail around it, enabling a crew member to handle the foresails.

Putty, on the Has run aground.

Radar reflector Passive device in the form of an octahedral corner reflector made of small aluminium sheets slotted together, that when hauled up a yacht's mast reflects a ship's radar transmission, creating a much brighter echo on its radar screen than that produced by the yacht alone.

Radio beacon Radio transmission beacon that allows homing or approximate direction plotting, up to 200 miles off.

Rappel see **abseil.**

RDF Radio direction finder, to take bearings of radio beacons.

Reach Sailing direction with the true wind from 60 degrees to 160 degrees: fine reach with wind slightly before the beam; beam reach with wind abeam; broad reach with wind aft of the beam, but not dead downwind.

Reacher A sail tacked to the bow, fuller than a normal headsail and designed specifically for reaching.

Reefing Reducing mainsail area, either by rolling the sail around the boom or by tying down slabs of sail to the boom.

Reefing claw Device to allow attachment of kicking strap to a boom with a rolled reef.

Rhumb line A course that maintains a constant bearing to true north; on a Mercator map it's a straight line, but in real life it's longer than a **Great Circle** between the same start and end points.

RIB Rigid inflatable boats.

Rigging Wires and ropes usually attached to the mast: standing rigging does not move and generally supports the mast; running rigging moves and is usually for hoisting and dropping sails.

RORC Royal Ocean Racing Club.

Round the Island race A one-day race around the Isle of Wight.

Rudder Steering device located aft. For the rudder to be effective the boat needs to be making enough **headway.**

Running Sailing with the wind from astern, or aft.

Runners Running back stays, which are tight only on the weather side, loose on the lee side, therefore have to be swapped over while tacking or gybing. Main purpose is to keep the forestay tensioned, but also help keep the mast up in a fore-and-aft direction.

Safety harness Clips onto the lifelines, to help prevent a crew member falling overboard.

Sastrugi Ridges and grooves in hard snow caused by wind erosion. Can be hard to cross.

Screacher Specialised heavy-weather reaching spinnaker.

Sea anchor Parachute-shaped device deployed into the water to reduce speed and hold bows head to wind in severe weather. Also **para-anchor,** a larger version which stops a boat dead when deployed from the bows; and a smaller drogue, which slows the boat, deployed off the stern.

Sea breeze Thermally induced onshore breeze, generally on sunny days with light offshore **gradient winds.** Usually from midday until evening, its range extending up to 20 miles out from the shore.

Sector light A light with directional information, usually a white sector indicating the correct angle of approach, and red or green sectors to indicate being off course and likely to be in dangerous waters.

Self-bailer Device for sucking water out of the bottom of the boat at speed.

Serac Block or tower of ice, often in an icefall.

Sextant Navigational instrument for measuring angles very accurately (often to better than 1 minute or 1/60 of a degree), usually of a celestial body to the horizon.

Sheet A rope running to the **clew** of a sail. It's used to control the setting of a sail in relation to the direction of the wind.

Shipping forecast Marine weather forecast, mainly used for wind force and direction in specific named sea areas.

Shroud Standing rigging from each side of the boat to hold the mast up.

Sight reduction tables Marine navigation tables to enable calculation of celestial body position and comparison with measured positions, so as to be able to plot lines of position.

Skins Strips of fur-like material attached to the bottom of skis to stop them sliding backwards but allow them to slide forwards; originally sealskin, now synthetic.

Slack water Period of no tidal currents at high or low water, between ebb and flood tides.

Slip face The downwind side of a dune.

Snatch block A block that can be clipped quickly using a snap shackle.

Snow stake Anchor for use in softer snow.

Snuffer A funnel-shaped device that when pulled down douses the sail; quicker than a furler.

Sock A tube of fabric that contains the spinnaker making it easier to hoist and drop.

Spectra Strong, synthetic material often used in ropes, for strength and low stretch.

Spinnaker Large parachute-shaped sail for sailing downwind on a broad reach or run. Also **chute** or **kite.**

Spinnaker flying Stunt where a member of the crew can fly high by attaching the tack and the clew to their harness.

Spinnaker pole Connects the tack of a spinnaker to the mast. Controlled by a **guy.**

Spreaders Short spars that stick out sideways from the mast; the increased angle of the **shrouds** running over them stiffens the mast more effectively than shrouds running direct from mast to hull.

Spring tides Strongest tides with the greatest range, occurring when the sun and moon are in line with each other and the Earth. C/f **neap tides.**

Squall Large, dark cloud, usually with strong, gusty winds and lashing rain, sometimes with thunder and lightning.

SSB Single Sideband Radio. Long range radio with a range up to some 700 miles.

Starboard The right side of the boat when you're facing forward. Shows a green light at night. The word is derived from the old steering oar or 'steer board', which preceded the invention of the rudder. C/f **port.**

Statute mile (sometimes called the land mile) Measures 5,280 feet, about 0.87 **nautical miles.**

Stay Wire that helps hold the mast erect.

Staysail Small inner headsail.

St Elmo's fire A natural electrical discharge.

Stern The aft end of the boat.

Stowage The amount of room for storing materials on board a vessel.

Stranded (of a rope/cable) Unravelled into separate strands.

Tack The bottom front corner of a sail. Also a leg of the route of a sailing vessel, with wind on the port side (port tack) or starboard side (starboard tack).

Tacking The process of steering through the eye of the wind to go from port to starboard tack and back while **beating** into the wind.

Telemark turn Type of ski turn for loose-heeled bindings, whereby the front knee is bent, taking most of the weight, and the uphill rear foot is trailing for stability, ready to become the downhill ski after the turn. Used for ski touring and mountaineering.

Tell-tale Small strip of cloth that, tied to a **stay,** shows the apparent wind direction.

Tibloc Patent ascender device.

Tidal race Area where there are strong and powerful tidal streams, often with eddies and **overfalls.**

Tidal stream The horizontal flow generated by the tides.

Tide rip Area where tidal streams are strong and violent.

Tiller In smaller boats, a long wooden handle for controlling the rudder.

Transom A panel running across the back of the boat, shaped to close its rear or aft end.

Trapeze Wire and harness for the crew to enable standing in a near-horizontal position outboard of the **gunwale,** to add extra stability to the boat.

Trimaran Boat with three hulls. C/f **catamaran, monohull, multihull.**

Tri-radial Specially cut spinnaker construction, stronger than earlier designs.

True north The direction of the celestial north pole; it's very close to **Grid north.** C/f **magnetic north.**

True wind The wind's direction and speed as measured at a fixed point on the Earth's surface. C/f **apparent wind.**

Trysail Small storm sail for use instead of the mainsail, attached to the mast.

Tuff Solidified ash.

TWOSTAR Twohanded Transatlantic Race.

Upwind Direction the wind is coming from, or passage into the wind.

Ute Pickup truck/utility vehicle.

Vanged out When going downwind, a vang, or kicking strap, holds the boom firmly to one side.

Veering refers to the wind changing direction with the sun (in the northern hemisphere that's usually south to north-west). C/f **backing.**

Vertical sextant angle Between the top and bottom of an object such as a lighthouse or cliff; the measurement of the angle combined with the known height of the object enables calculation of the object's distance away. C/f **horizontal sextant angle.**

VHF Very high frequency radio, for voice communications at short range, typically line of sight or up to 20 miles.

VMG Velocity made good. A calculation of the corrected speed and direction to a target that's directly upwind or downwind of the yacht.

Warp Line for attaching a boat to the dock, an anchor or a mooring.

Water, call for Demand to be given space to manoeuvre, according to the right of way rules.

Way Progress through the water. Also called **headway** when it's forward.

(To) weather To the windward side.

Weather shore A shore upwind from the vessel, hence a coastal land form that provides shelter from the wind. C/f **lee shore, lee side.**

Weatherfax Weather maps and forecasts by radio, either printed out or displayed on a screen.

Wedge see **chock/nut.**

Westing, had some in Able to sail westwards.

Winch Rotating drum, powered by winch handles, which haul in or pay out lines under tension.

Wind scoop Hollow in snow usually on the upwind and sides of a steep rock or mountain, caused by strong wind erosion from a constant direction.

Windvane A simple self-steering device driven by a small rudder and controlled by a vane in the wind. C/f **Autohelm.**

Windward Towards the wind. C/f **leeward.**

Wing mast Rotating mast with an oval section such that the mast-mainsail cross-section resembles an aircraft wing, providing increased power.

Yawl Two-masted yacht, with the small **mizzen** sail on a mast aft of the **rudder.** C/f **ketch.**